DATE DUE

THE EMERGENCE OF
CIVIL SOCIETY IN THE
EIGHTEENTH CENTURY

THE EMERGENCE OF CIVIL SOCIETY IN THE EIGHTEENTH CENTURY

A Privileged Moment in the History of England, Scotland, and France

MARVIN B. BECKER

INDIANA UNIVERSITY PRESS

Bloomington and Indianapolis

The paper used in this publication meets the minimum requirements of American National Standard for Information Sciences—Permanence of Paper for Printed Library Materials, ANSI Z39.48-1984.

Manufactured in the United States of America

Library of Congress Cataloging-in-Publication Data

Becker, Marvin B.
    The emergence of civil society in the eighteenth century : a
privileged moment in the history of England, Scotland, and France /
Marvin B. Becker.
        p.   cm.
    Continues: Civility and society in western Europe, 1300–1600.
    Includes bibliographical references and index.
    ISBN 0-253-31129-2 (cloth)
    1. England—Civilization—18th century.   2. Europe—Social
conditions—18th century.   3. Scotland—Civilization—18th century.
4. France—Civilization—18th century.   I. Title.
DA485.B38   1994
941.07—dc20   93-46327

1   2   3   4   5   00   99   98   97   96   95   94

To my wife, Betty, and daughters, Wendy and Dana—
the three joys of my life

CONTENTS

ACKNOWLEDGMENTS

The conversation, writings, and criticism of Frederic L. van Holthoon of the University of Groningen have been both a corrective and a spur; his happy combination of philosophical rigor and historical imagination has benefited me greatly. Thomas Green, my colleague and friend, read this manuscript and offered constructive and informed criticism. Of the authors cited in the notes, particular credit should be given to Stephen Buckle, Peter Borsay, Iain Pears, Nannerl Keohane, and Shlomo Avineri. Their writings were indispensable for my understanding of many a special topic. Most of all, the debt to my wife Betty for her generous and capable assistance is beyond measure.

Finally, a tribute to Sir Walter Scott, whose novels and poetry, so neglected in our times, were a never-failing inspiration to this historian in his quest for a balanced understanding of the benefits and costs of the genesis of civil society.

M. B. B.

INTRODUCTION

Adam Ferguson was the first writer in the English language employing the term "civil society" to proffer a systematic account of its genesis. He published his *An Essay on the History of Civil Society* in 1767 and was well-positioned in the Edinburgh literary world, having served as David Hume's successor at the Advocates Library. Later he held chairs (first in Natural Philosophy and later in Moral Philosophy) at the University. He was also a founding member of the Poker Club and Select Society of which Hume and Adam Smith were proud members. The triumph of an advanced commercial civilization evoked from him a response not so distant from that of many a literary contemporary:

> We may, with good reason, congratulate our species on their having escaped from a state of barbarous disorder and violence, into a state of domestic peace and regular policy; when they have sheathed the dagger, and disarmed the animosities of civil contention; when the weapons with which they contend are the reasonings of the wise, and the tongue of the eloquent. But we cannot, mean-time, help to regret, that they should ever proceed, in search of perfection, to place every branch of administration behind the counter, and come to employ, instead of the statesman and warrior, the mere clerk and accountant.[1]

It was Adam Ferguson who provided the most ambitious definition and explication of the onset of civil society:

> The commercial and lucrative arts may continue to prosper, but they gain an ascendant at the expense of other pursuits. The desire of profit stifles the love of perfection. Interest cools the imagination, and hardens the heart; and, recommending employments in proportion as they are lucrative, and certain in their gains, it drives ingenuity, and ambition itself, to the counter and the workshop.
>
> But apart from these considerations, the separation of professions, while it seems to promise improvement of skill, and is actually the cause why the production of every art become more perfect as commerce advances, yet in its termination, and ultimate effects, serves, in some measure, to break the bands of society, to substitute form in place of ingenuity, and to withdraw individuals from the common scene of occupation, on which the sentiments of the heart, and the mind, are most happily employed.
>
> Under the *distinction* of callings, by which the members of polished society are separated from each other, every individual is supposed to possess his species of tal-

ent, or his peculiar skill, in which the others are confessedly ignorant; *and society is made to consist of parts, of which none is animated with the spirit of society itself.*[2]

Ferguson remained deeply concerned about the effects of economic advance on the level of domestic intellectual life:

> Many mechanical arts require no capacity; they succeed best under a total suppression of sentiment and reason; and ignorance is the mother of industry. . . . Manufactures, accordingly, prosper most where the mind is least consulted and where the workshop may be considered as an engine, the parts of which are men. . . . In manufacture the genius of the master is cultivated, while that of the inferior workman lies waste. The statesman may have a wide comprehension of human affairs, while the tools he employs are ignorant of the system in which they are themselves combined. . . . The former may have gained what the latter has lost . . . and thinking itself, in this age of separations, may become a peculiar craft.[3]

Many other Scottish literati (Adam Smith was the most prominent example) were perturbed by the onset of specialization and the consequent anomie of civil society. The decline of martial spirit and the attendant rise of a standing army posed a severe threat to civilian liberty. Furthermore, the numbing and even stunting impact of the radical division of labor might serve to divest the plebeians of any hint of imagination or curiosity. The stultifying effects of mechanization and routinization of tasks, from diplomacy to shoemaking to soldiering, drained the mind and heart of initiative. If the process continued, no one person could have a generalized view of complex activities involved in governing a nation. Also, the decline of the martial spirit brought a depletion of the heroic sensibility, and this proved especially vexatious to the proud English and Scots. Remedies were sought for citizen anomie: these ranged from the multiplication of voluntary societies and religious sects designed to confer some identity on laborers in the city, to expansion of leisure-time educational opportunities for the plebes.

Adam Smith presented with force a most influential argument: the present time was a distinct phase in human development and therefore had its own moral character. The three preceding stages were those of hunting, shepherding, and agriculture; each had its norms and ethical precepts. Smith's *Theory of Moral Sentiments* was dedicated to an exploration and explication of the morality appropriate to his own times—a new age—that of a commercial society. What was disvalued in this world were the exaggerated conceptions of "gentlemanly honor." In its stead commercial development, which breeds civil society, rewards more modest and less heroic virtues. Of the aristocracy of inherited position, Smith wrote:

> By what important accomplishments is the young nobleman instructed to support the dignity of his rank, and to render himself worthy of that superiority over his fellow-citizens, to which the virtue of his ancestors had raised them? Is it by knowledge, by industry, by patience, by self-denial, or by virtue of any kind? . . . As he is conscious how much he is observed, and how much mankind are disposed to favour all his inclinations, he acts, upon the most indifferent occasions, with that freedom and elevation which the thought of this naturally inspires. His air, his manner, his

deportment, all mark that elegant and grateful sense of his own superiority, which those who are born to inferior stations can hardly ever arrive at. These are the arts by which he proposes to make mankind more easily submit to his authority, and to govern their inclinations according to his own pleasure: and in this he is seldom disappointed.

How different was the moral odyssey of the man of commerce:

> Politeness is so much the virtue of the great, that it will do little honour to any body but themselves. If ever [the private man] hopes to distinguish himself, it must be by more important virtues. He must acquire dependents to balance the dependents of the great, and he has no other fund to pay them from, but the labour of his body, and the activity of his mind. He must cultivate these therefore: he must acquire superior knowledge of his profession, and superior industry in the exercise of it. He must be patient in labour, resolute in danger, and firm in distress. These talents he must bring to public view, by the difficulty, importance, and, at the same time, good judgment of his undertakings, and by the severe and unrelenting application with which he pursues them.

Middling virtues of fortitude, patience, self-denial, industry, and the cautious application of thought to matters practical had advantaged middling and lesser ranks in a commercial society founded on an elaborate division of labor:

> In all governments accordingly, even in monarchies, the highest offices are generally possessed, and the whole detail of the administration conducted, by men who were educated in the middle and inferior ranks of life, who have been carried forward by their own industry and abilities, though loaded with the jealousy, and opposed by the resentment, of all those who were born their superiors, and to whom the great, after having regarded them first with contempt, and afterwards with envy, are at last contented to truckle with the same abject meanness with which they desire that the rest of mankind should behave to themselves.

The talents of the lesser folk, Smith argued, are essential for the civil security and economic health of a commercial society. He would soon analyze the economic reasons for the displacement of an idle nobility by an energetic commercial people in his masterpiece *An Inquiry into the Nature and Causes of the Wealth of Nations*. The pitch of commercial life was such that manners, courtesy, gallantry, and politeness might grace or disgrace private life, but these were "virtues" that little advantaged the public domain. Would this not lead, in Smith's apt phrase, to a self-serving "society of strangers"?

Nevertheless, and with the single exception of the eccentric Earl of Buchan, Scottish moral philosophers and economists acknowledged the necessity for agricultural and commercial improvement. The advent of civil society and consumerism was perceived as inevitable. David Hume was among the very first to recognize that a new type of society was in place which was neither a refuge from terror nor a realm for extended conviviality, but a type of market for the more efficient satisfaction of human wants and needs. The first expression of this effort to "think" society as an entity transcending its individual parts can be discerned in the writings of the French moralists of the seventeenth and early eighteenth centuries. It was from figures such as Nicolas de Malebranche, that gentle disciple of Descartes and other thinkers, that the English and Scots took cues. That men and women were motivated by contradictions between benevolence and self-interest became a staple of moral inquiry. That human vanity and the quest for attention and approbation were ineradicable and were the bricks and straw of human personality also became a sturdy conclusion of psychological investigation. To ground social action it would be necessary to posit a more problematic conception of the new moral order. It would not be possible to ground human relations in a shared vision of a cosmic order or in finely-spun networks of gift exchange, reciprocity, courtesy, or myriad forms of interdependence. The new idea of civil society projected a very different arena of exchange. The individual was now linked to the whole by vanity and self-interest, as well as by the less dependable but still very attractive ties of benevolence and sympathy. The problematics of social existence were both psychologized and defined in more modest and less demanding codes of moral obligation. Adam Ferguson was to point out that there was the risk of a decline in concern for society as a whole. In fact, society and the economy were now more frequently perceived as having a life of and even laws of their own. Civil society would be more genial and pleasant if sympathy and altruism were steady fare, but neither was essential for its continuity. David Hume, in his *A Treatise of Human Nature* (1739–40), commented on this vital concern:

'Tis certain, that no affection of the human mind has both a sufficient force, and a proper direction to counter-balance, the love of gain and render men fit members of society, by making them abstain from the possessions of others. Benevolence to strangers is too weak for this purpose; and as to the other passions, they rather inflame this avidity, when we observe, that the larger our possessions are, the more ability we have of gratifying our appetites. There is no passion, therefore, capable of controlling the interested affection, but the very affection itself, by an alteration of its direction. Now this alteration must necessarily take place upon the least reflection; since 'tis evident, that the passion is much better satisfy'd by its restraint, than by its liberty, and that in preserving society, we make much greater advances in the acquiring possessions, than in the solitary and forlorn condition, which must follow upon violence and universal license. The question, therefore, concerning the wickedness or goodness of human nature, enters not in the least into the other question concerning the origin of society; nor is there any thing to be consider'd but the degrees of men's sagacity or folly. For whether the passion of self-interest be esteemed vicious or virtuous, 'tis all a case; since itself alone restrains it: So that if it be virtuous, men become social by their virtue, if vicious, their vice has the same effect.

I

At a recent conference sponsored by the State University of New Jersey at Rutgers (April 9–11, 1992), it was noted that the failure of Communism had "left the

United States, and the West generally, as the sole positive examples of what the newly freed societies might become." The title of the conference was "Intellectuals and Social Change in Central and Eastern Europe." In the many discussions it was evident that the English and Scottish experiences were essential for political developments in the United States. When author Saul Bellow (winner of the Nobel prize for Literature) spoke about the ideas basic to the American experience, distinguishing them from those traditionally advanced by Eastern European literati, he was bracketing England and the States. His comparison fixed the central preoccupation of East Europeans on the higher and grander values and the attendant "struggle for fullness of life." For Britain, the United States, and much of the West no such heroic ambitions were manifest. Instead, they were devoted to "overcoming scarcity, conquering nature, forging a social contract founded on reason, pursuing justice and order, avoiding the *summum malum* (war, famine, poverty), while leaving questions of the *summum bonum* (art, metaphysics) outside the social contract, as private concerns." Perhaps Bellow was a little too glossy in his historical précis, but basically he may have had it right. He concluded his comments by averring that the American "utopian goal" was "relief from oppressive needs; to the degree that it succeeded, the question raised by its success was: 'Is prosperity a threat to the higher life of mankind?' " We might take a cue from Saul Bellow's observations concerning the limited nature of certain central political ideals. Granted that to do so we must follow only a single theme, though not a minor one in the score of European moral philosophy. At the outset we might identify it by what Bellow noted as the scaling down of heroic ambitions. I would refer to it as a minimalist composition endorsing a minimalist ethic.[4]

Already anticipated in antiquity and explicated on occasion in the Italian Renaissance (by Machiavelli and Guicciardini), this ethic was never realized in its full-blown form as a theory of human behavior and civil society until the eighteenth century. Ironically, the key formulation was achieved by moral thinkers raised in a backwater of European culture—that is, Scotland. But then these Scots would have been delighted to have this contradiction called to their attention because for them history itself was a study in ironies and therefore replete with unintended consequences. For this model of civil society was to prove normative and continues to serve as a guide for social and economic policy. Differing radically from Aristotelian and Thomist conceptions of government and social arrangement, it repudiated the idea that man was a political animal (*zoon politikon*)—that is, intended literally for political life. In no other context could his purpose (*telos*) be realized.

What is meant when we speak about the decline of "heroic ambitions" and the emergence of a "minimalist ethic"? First, a different anthropology as well as a different theory of *socialitas* (sociability) is projected. Neither the Aristotelian nor Thomistic versions of politics and human nature were to be endorsed. Not only was the conception of man as social animal judged inappropriate for explaining the mechanism of human involvement with community, but also that array of virtues once considered essential for good citizenship and a healthy public life was seen as anachronistic. Grand moral potentialities implicit in human nature were judged at best problematic. The Christianized version of Aristotelian moral virtues fundamental to systematic, scholastic thought came under review and was deemed insufficient to sustain moral order. Nor was the virtuous order likely to be restored by a statesman in a "Machiavellian moment." Politics was not so certain to be viewed as a stage for displaying one's virtue and vindicating one's claim to honor.[5]

To travel through history in seven-league boots from the sixteenth to the eighteenth century is to notice how the rigorous and exacting study of political theory changed. Instead of searching for grounding in subtle dialectics, the debate turned to investigation of human psychology. The main principles were derived from a study of human nature without reference to the disputed evidence of revelation. The forays of Adam Smith and David Hume incorporated many of these insights into the human psyche, but their researches into political philosophy yielded only unheroic and modest maxims of good sense. To their voices might be added an entire chorus of Scottish and English contemporaries whose devotion to the study of human nature prompted a shunning of high expectation.

An archaic or traditional tripartite division of society reaches far back into European and even Indo-European civilizations. This model, so satisfying to medieval thinkers, came to be rivaled over the centuries by a series of different configurations. Emphasis should be placed on the word *rivaled,* since the tripartite model was adaptable and durable, only gradually marginalized. To return to the early sixteenth century, we might take one example and have it stand for a legion of others: the Englishman Edmund Dudley in his *Tree of Commonwealth* (ca. 1509), divided the population of his nation into "clergy, chivalry, and community." He was of course introducing one of the many variations of the ancient strategy of dividing society into social groups (orders or estates), each having a particular function to perform. By fulfilling traditional roles (praying, warring, and feeding), each order or estate contributed to the well-being and harmony of the body entire. Not by accident was the metaphor for portraying this tripartite society drawn from the body (head, arms, and stomach). Similarly, imagery was readily taken from the solar system with its implicit concord. Were any social group derelict in fulfilling its role, the health of the body or its harmony would be under threat and descent into anarchy would be sure, certain, and swift. Society, then, was a by-product of the correct performance of duties and obligations incumbent upon each order or estate. These responsibilities were activated by devotion to a sense of honor; not to obey the code was to see the sacred cords of society severed. There was enough honor to go around, and within the honor community one discovers merchants and guildsmen as well as nobles. Wealth and power were perceived as following status, with social opportunities determined by public perception of lifestyles. Each order had a style of life deemed appropriate for it, just as each had its particular variation on an honor code. Archaic lifestyles were judged essential for forging the bonds of community; in essence, the community was sustained by a complex exchange system involving gifts, favors, offices, honors, and even women. Largess and good lordship were necessary for those who aspired to influence; these were celebrated as forms of social behavior vital for capturing public esteem.[6]

The tripartite model was of course normative rather than an accurate description of social grouping. But when reform of society was called for, the remedies advanced often included the founding of new orders of chivalry or enforcement of sumptuary legislation aimed at segregating the estates on the basis of dress. Defense of the estate paradigm and its ascription of honor to the various cadres continued to inform European social thought over the centuries. The usual political and moral arguments were propounded despite the fact that Protestants denied the clergy a separate estate and the nobility shrank as a warrior class. There was, however, a significant change in the import of this social theory: for example, in the eighteenth century Montesquieu and certain of his avant-garde contemporaries perceived the orders in a rather different way; they were regarded as intermediaries positioned between the ruler and people. This conception was enhanced by the German reformer Freiherr von Stein at the beginning of the nineteenth century and by Tocqueville soon after. To escape the double perils of harsh despotism and leveling democracy it would be necessary to look to the privileges of the orders, for they alone could serve as effective barriers between the power of the sovereign and his subjects. Parenthetically, it was in the Dutch republic of the seventeenth century and Scotland of the eighteenth century that the theory of separate estates gave way before a sustained effort to provide a novel system of social classification and definition of society. In both regions the nobles emigrated and the Calvinist clergy was not regarded as a separate order.[7]

II

The seventeenth century was the scene for the bearing of first fruits of moral skepticism—some bitter, some sweet. When eighteenth-century historians of philosophy looked back, they located the origins of the new philosophy, science, and natural law in the contest with French skepticism from Montaigne to Pierre Charron. It was in response to the anti-dogmatism of these skeptics that leading legal thinkers such as Hugo Grotius and Samuel Pufendorf worked to systematize and ultimately transcend the penetrating arguments of the French proponents of moral relativism. Of course the many forebears and allies of Pufendorf and Grotius included the English Francis Bacon, John Selden, Richard Cumberland, and Thomas Hobbes. Their contributions toward the displacement of classical ethics as well as of the scholastic idiom for discoursing on moral questions cannot be underestimated. Together, and with important variations and additions, these thinkers acknowledged the multiplicity and divergence of human beliefs and customs, thus taking seriously the French skeptics. The uncertainty of moral knowledge was a *donnée*. The work of the new moral science was not to offer crude rebuttals to skeptical arguments but to employ skeptical judgments as a foundation for an anti-skeptical science. Unsureness of moral knowledge rendered the Aristotle of the *Politics* vulnerable. So too was the "master of those who know" rebuffed for his moral theory as explicated in the *Ethics*. Pufendorf's argument was telling: Aristotle's conclusions were predicated on too narrow a ground—the experience of Greek city-states. Too high an intellectual premium was placed on liberty "which is a grave defect in a study intended to serve the interests of the human race."

Seventeenth-century moral philosophers and natural lawyers, then, took the challenge of the moral skeptics to heart. Descartes could begin to philosophize only after diving deep into the dark waters of doubt. So deep would he dive that he could doubt no more, and finally would confirm the absolute truth of the very process of doubting. Grotius responded to the skeptics only after careful consideration of the implications of their argument that the most primary desire of humans was self-preservation. He announced proudly in his *Prolegomena* to *The Rights of War and Peace* that it was vital for him to explicate in detail the skeptics' position:

> . . . since it would be a vain Undertaking to treat of Right, if there is really no such thing; it will be necessary, in order to shew the Usefulness of the Work, and to establish it on solid Foundations, to confute here in a few Words so dangerous an Error. And that we may not engage with a Multitude at once, let us assign them an Advocate. And who more proper for this purpose than *Carneades*. . . ? This Man having undertaken to dispute against Justice, that kind of it, especially, which is the Subject of this Treatise, fouîld no Argument stronger than this. Laws (says he) were instituted by Men for the sake of Interest; and hence it is that they are different, not only in different Countries, according to the Diversity of their Manners; but often in the same Country, according to the Times. As to that which is called NATURAL RIGHT, it is a mere Chimera.[8]

Patient consideration of ethical skepticism (both classical and Renaissance) was not designed by a Descartes, a Hobbes, Grotius, or Pufendorf to refute evidence of cultural relativism. Nor was it calculated to second conclusions offered by skeptics concerning man's irrationality. Taking these arguments seriously was not grounds for pessimism or cultural despair; rather, this concern proved to be an impetus for formulating theories of society and human sociability. These were rooted in doctrines of self-preservation and the force of self-interest—ideas close to the heart of the skeptics. The foundation of natural law was the human desire to preserve oneself. Exposed to wants and unable to secure his own safety, the individual required the assistance of his fellows. It was necessary that he be social in order to secure his own interests and promote his own rights. A more limited conception of sociability therefore obtained, far distant from the Aristotelian idea of man as a social and political animal. Natural law and moral law were simplified; both were deduced from the right of self-preservation. Finally, what was right (*honestum*) was useful (*utile*).[9]

Moral philosophy was simplified, with morality scaled down by a Descartes to magnanimity and by a Hobbes to a question of justice. The latter would reduce social virtue to peaceableness, whereas others would translate it into benevolence or kindness. In seventeenth- and early-eighteenth-century France, *gens de lettres,* from Corneille, Racine, and La Rochefoucauld to La Bruyère, reformed the language and science of ethics. The virtues of self-restraint lost their high standing and such vices as dissoluteness were no longer so readily judged weaknesses of the human soul. Often a battery of vices were grouped under the euphemism of vanity or pride and these were considered to have beneficial, if not unintended consequences.

So much less was expected of the individual and the very definition of sociability diminished the charge of obligation and duty. It was as if seventeenth- and early-eighteenth-century moral philosophers recognized that the ethical raiments in which upper-class Europeans clothed themselves were many sizes too large and in need of extensive tailoring. The following monograph is a description of some of the alterations involved in the downsizing.[10]

The present work follows my *Civility and Society in Western Europe, 1300–1600* and endeavors to map the transition from civility to civil society. In this odyssey we are confronted with many new landmarks. Perhaps the psychological one cast into boldest relief was the growing need for approbation. In an earlier time civility had invested heavily in the winning of civil distinction, the repudiation of reckless gallantry, and an honor code. With the onset of civil society, the very word "sensibility" lost something of its traditional definition as a mental faculty. In civil society sensibility became a designation for a style of life. This mode of feeling prompted people to be deeply preoccupied with the question of how they ought to feel about themselves as well as others. Civil society in the eighteenth century bred a strain of socialized dependence. Sensibilities were stretched so that approbation (public approval fostered by public opinion) became the cement of community. Greater responsiveness to general opinion was evidenced in the avid desire of individuals to express good taste in all things, from art to music to table to furnishings. The very science of esthetics was systematized at this time.[11]

A greater responsiveness to public opinion led to a more robust and positive definition of what had once been generally characterized as fickle and unreliable. This change was itself only one aspect of the extension of the semantic range of the meaning of the word "society." This is a point I shall be dealing with in the first part of this monograph when explicating the gradual displacement of older notions of society as mere fellowship and companionship in favor of a more abstract definition of a distant and more powerful entity.

Why select England and Scotland as venues for this study? The answer is simple: civil society, as we have come to know and understand it in the modern world, had its origins in Britain. Here I am tempted to repeat what the novelist Henry James said about Venice: "It is a great pleasure to write the word, but I'm not sure there is not a certain impudence in pretending to add something to it." In my case, it is not one word, "Venice," but two words, "civil society." What can I add from the historical experiences of England and Scotland that will illuminate a debate raging from the time of Jean-Jacques Rousseau to Jürgen Habermas and then back again to Kant, Hegel and Marx? That civil society had its modern beginnings in eighteenth-century England and Scotland itself underscores a crucial, if perhaps obvious point: this was a world far distanced from that of liberal democracy. In so many respects it was, as we shall see, a privileged society existing at a privileged historical moment. As I hope to suggest in the epilogue, this may be a heartening message for exponents of civil society in our own times. Numerous models of civil society can and do exist and flourish under a variety of regimes distinct from liberal democracy.[12]

III

Those who embraced the notion of civil society did not have an idea of social progress as an end; in fact, they were conservative (not authoritarian), and what they valued was social stability and the reduction of misery. But the price was not to be paid through the entailing of estates, restriction of trade, or promotion of monopolies. I have mentioned the decline of archaic values, practices, and customs, but the note struck must be muted. The same literati who championed the blessings of civil or commercial society sponsored good lordship and advocated paternalistic government. They favored benevolent landlords, kindly tenants, and hierarchy. Quite properly they were concerned that commercial or civil society would create instability. Although they spoke robustly for improvement in agriculture, favoring rational market-oriented projects to benefit rural life, these undertakings often failed. The best and bravest enterprisers went bankrupt and clear evidence was not at hand to endorse the superiority of modern methods. It was rather like the astronomical world between the time of Copernicus and Galileo, when it made equal sense to back the Ptolemaic universe or the Copernican one. Only with hindsight was the choice of the improvers always clear. Furthermore, there were powerful ethical and moral imperatives against rationalizing agriculture: the plight of tenants and the destruction of an intermediate cadre between landlord and tenant brought much suffering and cruel deprivation. Finally, there was the persistence of archaic customs and economic practices. These made eighteenth-century definitions of property somewhat ambiguous. Monetary wages had not established themselves as the sole form of remuneration; there were many archaic methods of appropriation.

Returning to the definition of "society," we notice that the old and new jostle one another. For example, David Hume and Adam Smith employed the word to designate fellowship as well as to indicate the more impersonal form. If this is confusing, so be it, for civil society was no simple construct. The question of how moral philosophers such as Hume and Smith thought on the ability of their commercial or civil society to reproduce itself is perplexing. How was it to endure through troubled future times? What gave it its force allowing it to be nourished and sustained? A careful reading of the Scottish moral philosophers in particular suggests that civil society was conceived of as emerging under the secure canopy of the *ancien régime*. Hume believed that civil society would be as secure in France as it was in Britain, but in this he was mistaken. Not only were its champions frequently aristocrats, but its very stability depended upon deference, hierarchy, and patronage. Hume and his literary contemporaries had the highest regard for custom and convention. We must put aside our modern, self-righteous views and acknowledge that the very order of this world depended not only on the market and play of interests but also upon the psychic pleasure which the less affluent took in the successes of their wealthier and mightier countrymen. The pleasure which the lowly took in triumphs of the well-born created a viable social psychology. Only under the cover of the *ancien régime* could this civil society thrive. Literati from Hume to Smith required just such aristocratic and princely protection: this was as essential to the successful writer as talent. More was at stake than just property rights and market forces.[13]

This was a privileged age and I would locate it in that hundred years before the American and French revolutions. Recent scholarship marks out that century as one in which the Marxists and E. P. Thompson simply got it wrong: class consciousness and economic struggle were not present in anything like the degree to which Thompson and his followers imagined. The situation of course changes in the 1780s, and I would be willing to speculate that between the American Revolution and the French Revolution there was a boundary. In fact it can be argued that civil society, developing roughly between the English Civil War and the American Revolution, would have taken an entirely different turn had it coalesced after the 1770s. This leads to a particular observation: civil society is not capable of satisfying manifold claims for social and economic justice, and before the 1770s, such claims were not so extensive. Scotland, for example, was managed politically and the dissident Jacobites were never able to gain widespread popular support. Indeed, the very menace of Catholicism served to strengthen loyalties to the establishment.

When Jürgan Habermas writes about civil society, he does so as a sociologist and political philosopher. Like so many other scholars attracted to this burgeoning field (many because of the events in Eastern Europe of 1989), he has no interest in the way in which the past plays upon the present. For example, my account would be entirely incomplete if I did not mention the importance of human memory. In the case of the British in particular, the seventeenth century was a dreadful time and, having passed through, they were not like passengers in a train going from one place to another; they recalled all too well where they had been and carried the baggage of their anxieties with them. The Scots held blighted memories of civil war and religious persecution and so did the English. The casualties were staggering. Religious wars on the Continent had brought European civilization almost to the abyss. What was learned was a monumental distrust of heroism, religious fanaticism, and reckless gallantry. This contributed to that downsizing of heroic virtue which I have already cited as a mark of civil society. These lessons were particularly absorbed by the Dutch, from whom the Scots learned much. David Hume's *History of England,* a widely popular and well-received work, subscribed to his own maxim, ''Reason is and ought only to be the slave of the passions.'' This aperçu provided him with the opportunity to demonstrate how Englishmen of the seventeenth century were betrayed by their violent and uncontrollable passions. Still, the historical outcome, although unforeseen, was benevolent: a system of balance emerged between king and parliament with the so-called *regnum mixtum,* if ''not the best system of government, at least the most entire system of liberty.''[14]

Civil society or commercial society was perceived by literary contemporaries as an ineluctible development. A stadial theory of civilization was subscribed to, whereby societies moved from hunter/gatherer to settled agriculture to civil society. The charting of human development through common stages lent change the cloak of inevitability. Different modes of production as well as institutions, manners, and styles were ineradicable marks of the civilization of hunters, shepherds, settled farmers, and commercial people. The movement was from crude to polished and the tide was moving in the direction of a full-scale civil society. How movement occurred from one stage to the next was unclear, but the chief mechanism for change was the advantage gained through the reduction of traditional obligations, responsibilities, and liabilities. This, coupled with the downsizing of the claims of an honor culture, released certain energies, as well as freeing capital. Intellectually we observe an infusion of epistemological modesty and deterrence of more ambitious and utopian social and political schemes. In Scotland civil society spawned a civil culture allowing for public space in which merchants, landlords, gentry, agricultural improvers, lawyers, doctors, and clergy met in the numerous voluntary associations proliferating throughout leading cities. Free of government tutelage, the discourse shifted from that of the Aristotelian world of the university and the theological domain of the Church into new venues. The universities themselves became very different places, with teaching in English instead of Latin and special lectures well-attended by literate artisans and tradesmen. The cruel wit of the court and the embattled dialectics of the older university were not so apparent. Over the eighteenth century debates in the Scottish and English clubs and societies were informed by a historical and even sociological spirit which distanced issues from older partisan, political, and religious controversies. Debates and exchanges focused not so much on what was right or even what was moral, but rather on what was likely, probable, ineluctible, and beneficial for society as a whole. It might be useful to compare topics selected for debate in 1754 with those of an imaginary construct of a hundred years earlier. We shall deal with these debates in detail in the second chapter, but for now a brief summary might suffice. Adam Smith, lecturer in moral philosophy, is sitting in the chair of the Select Society of Edinburgh, and these are a few of the topics proposed: Whether the numbers of banks now in Scotland, be useful to the trade of that country? And whether paper credit be advantageous to a nation?; Whether the bounty should be continued on the exportation of low-priced linen made in Scotland?; Whether the common practice in Scotland of distributing money to the poor in their own houses, or the receiving of the poor into workhouses and hospitals be most advantageous?; Whether in the present circumstances of this country it be most advantageous to increase tillage or grain?; Whether Brutus did well in killing Caesar?

A topic for a prize essay was set as follows: "Account of the rise and progress of commerce, arts, and manufactures in North Britain and the causes which promoted or retarded them."

A review of the questions set for debate or essay competition indicates something of the limits and restraints placed on discourse and inquiry. By historicizing or sociologizing issues, there was a turn away from metaphysical, theological, and factious political preoccupations. History and sociology provided a less charged and more neutral ground on which interested parties could meet. This is the very bone and marrow of civil society. The recognition of limits tends to support Habermas's views that this was an age in which "critical reason" triumphed. However, Habermas's incautious view is flawed: it is not the triumph of critical reason itself, but the victory of limited issues and historical analysis. The seventeenth century was as critically reasonable, but about vaster issues. The minutes of the Select Society (the discourse held there was replicated throughout Britain) suggests a turn away from grander matters and overarching themes. Perhaps, all in all, this privileged moment in world history—although a very modest one—is best epitomized by the observations already cited of Saul Bellow. We could also add the voice of Richard Pipes with his critique of Solzhenitsyn and the Russian's quest for an absolute:

> Society is not an association for the joint pursuit of virtue, since one man's virtue is another man's inequity such a conception inevitably leads to despotism. Rather, society is an environment for mutual tolerance and restraint of human weakness. How paradoxical it is that Western culture which is alleged to rest in the notion of human perfectibility, makes the broadest provision for sin, whereas the kind of ideology that Solzhenitsyn espouses, that deems men incorrigibly evil, insists on his never straying!'5

British literati and moral philosophers might have understood Bellow and Pipes quite well. Civil society would banish the "higher life" and single-minded pursuit of virtue to the outer rim of privacy. At the core was something more limited—rather like the agenda of the Select Society. The wonder is that despite its inability to satisfy the myriad claims for social and economic justice pressed upon it from the late eighteenth century on, and accelerated by massification and the Industrial Revolution, it still undergirds our political values and resists the utopian energy of our overheated contemporaries. Very unheroic, but very durable. Not responsive to romantic yearnings and messianic dreams, it understands well what Hume spoke of as the "artificial virtue of justice." We can't have justice; we can only counterfeit it. (But in that act we may be at our best.) It is a society for "mediocre" men and women, not for Solzhenitsyn's saints and devils. However, a melancholy note might be sounded: it is also, as Adam Smith averred, "a society of strangers."

THE EMERGENCE OF
CIVIL SOCIETY IN THE
EIGHTEENTH CENTURY

I

TOWARD AN UNDERSTANDING OF CIVIL SOCIETY

The theme of the emergence of civil society in the West in the seventeenth and eighteenth centuries, so eloquently (but abstractly) delineated by Jürgen Habermas in his justly celebrated *Strukturwandel der Offentlichkeit* (Neuwied, 1962), has re-cently become a subject of vital interest to historians, political theorists, sociologists, and economists. Habermas's writings caught on slowly in the world of Anglo-American scholarship. It was only a short time ago that his *Strukturwandel* was translated into English. Some reasons for this intense historical concern are not difficult to surmise. Events in Eastern Europe over the last five years or so have served as a catalyst. The failure of Communism and the recognition that the rudiments of a civil society were essential for economic development and social cohesion prompted Eastern European commentators, as well as Westerners, to explore the subject in depth.

In discussing the revolutionary events leading to the overthrow of totalitarian regimes, stern judgments were entered against the use of state power to thwart human rights, crush local initiative, and marshal the primitive force to community against the individual. Students of other societies in other continents—Latin America, for example—have recorded the bleak history of civil societies too weak to contain threats from generals and their military or the Church. Africa, China, and numerous other regions have been studied from a comparative point of view—that is, from the perspective of the experience of Western development of civil society. The explanations for their failure to develop institutions and forms of associative life that might have contributed to the foundation of a civil order have multiplied exponentially.

Recent historical literature on this theme has become something of a growth industry. The totalitarian system espoused by the Stalinists and their intellectual and political allies championed the power of state as the agency for obliterating competing forms of economic and associative life. These had been the very engines and motive forces of civil society: without them it was impossible to develop a much-needed market economy, as well as a set of intervening bodies between the individual and the state. Public space was cleared of that host of economic and voluntary organizations essential for the survival and health of industrial society in our century. Daily events in Eastern Europe testify to the heightened consciousness

I

of both political leaders and the general population as to how essential it will be to restore mediating institutions between the state and society.[1]

I

When exploring the question of the distancing between state and society, it might be well to go back to the seventeenth and eighteenth centuries. It was then that the term "society" was undergoing changes in definition. A secondary meaning was added to the traditional one of fellowship, companionship, and company—both social and business. It was then that it also came to mean something much less immediate and concrete. For the first time in the history of the West the word *society* defined an entity both distant and abstract. In English, French, Italian, and later German, this entity was characterized as impersonal and possessed of a life of its own. How to explain this change, not only in definition but also in the structure of social and economic relations over these centuries, involves an investigation into the decline of traditional types of social, economic, and political bonding. Any explanation of the many ramifications of this transformation should emphasize that new and old definitions jostled one another but sometimes lived harmoniously side by side. Key writers of the eighteenth century, not always consistently, tended to employ them where suitable: the older designating fellowship and the new denoting a more abstract entity. There was a heightened consciousness of the disjunction between private and public life, the result being the creation of a more ample social space. Gradually, the area between these two poles was colonized by new forms of voluntary association and associative life. Modern-day scholars have appropriately singled out these developments as a leading feature of eighteenth-century political and economic history. The formation of these robust associative forms worked to mediate between the respective domains of family and state. It was in this middling territory that civil society took root. Traditionally, the term "civil society" had been linked to the state and was generally treated under the broad rubric of *societas civilis*. Originally, *societas civilis* was employed as a synonym for "state." Beginning in the late seventeenth century and gaining momentum in the eighteenth, this awareness of the disjunction between state and society intensified. Increasingly, civil society was delineated by references to elementary property rights, intermediate institutions, a market economy, and the free play of interests protected from state intervention.[2]

Explanations of the nature and ramifications of this transformation should feature the decline of traditional types of social, economic, and political bonding. At the outset we should acknowledge that society continued to be bound by informal sanctions and claims (neighbor to neighbor, host and guest, kindly forms of tenancy, master and apprentice). Proliferating, however, were less immediate ties, and in general we witness an acceleration of the tendency toward the displacement of social relations from a Christian and archaic framework. It is this vector we must follow in order to appreciate the filling out of the lineaments of civil society. This displacement, though gradual, prompted particular changes which we shall discuss in some detail. These will include the relaxation of the heroic standards of virtue, communal obligation, civic duty, good lordship, hospitality and open entertainment, Christian benevolence, and a raft of others. Furthermore, we will observe that the need for ritual, ceremony, and the play of extravagant political language will be in declension. The political realm itself becomes much less fragile, and therefore less in need of the many forms of baroque elaboration. The sense of a generalized order existing beyond the common texture of dependency, alliance, and competitiveness gained ground. Confidence in public institutions, such as insurance and banking, reduced reliance on kinship. (Parenthetically, the old-fashioned ideas of trust, which had once proved to be a centerpiece for the political philosophy of John Locke, were shortly to become marginal in advanced philosophical discourse). The structural need that society had for opulence, conspicuous consumption, and the maintenance of batteries of servants and armies of "idle men" was in decline, and this was regularly commented upon by moral philosophers from David Hume to Adam Smith. Obligation, once ubiquitous as a tactic for gaining social credit, was being moderated; so too was the practice of indiscriminate charity. Still older forms, practices, and customs were far from fragile: social-wages were often paid instead of cash, and social credit was earned through an endless exchange of courtesies. Archaic practices persisted in government and politics, with venality of office, fee-taking, and gift-giving still in vogue. Yet in British government, as well as private life, more impersonal norms had secured a purchase they were not to lose. Still, the line was wavy and hard to trace. Only with the 1620s was the definition of corruption in government expanded to include gifts as well as bribes. Paying fees to have a court case expedited was seen as legitimate but bribing a courtier to secure a government contract was certainly not. In the case of Charles I's favorite, Buckingham, royal patronage was bitterly attacked as corruption. The purchase of state office from a prior holder was accepted usage but legally suspect, and those purchasing a title or honor were castigated as having committed "temporal simony."[3]

Recently, social historians have suggested that in England class formation was forged not only by individuals acting on the basis of economic interest but also as a result of the withdrawal of aristocrats and gentry from village communities. Like other sectors of English society, they retreated into the private domain of family life. While still controlling the economic fate of villages, they embarked at a distance from its boundaries. Ties between country gentry, the market, and country towns were of course centuries old, involving trade and the administration of justice. However, it was only in the late seventeenth century that social bonds garnered appreciable strength. Within half a century many a country town evolved into a cultural center with a fixed round of social sessions and entertainments. Country gentry were also attracted to the burgeoning provincial town by the lure of low-cost living. Affluent farmers—at least those of the "improving" variety—were likewise distancing themselves from the agricultural laborer. They removed their children from village schools and dismissed servants from their household, withdrawing into isolated farm houses securely fenced about. Indeed, this withdrawal of country gentry and lesser nobility in order to take up residence in the provincial town for part of the year made its mark upon urban architecture. The Georgian townhouse, often located on a square, was the centerpiece for the segregated neighborhood. It displaced the vernacular tradition, with its strongly local character, by favoring classical architecture, with its outward-looking international style. Within the household of the well-to-do and well-educated, servants were relegated to the servants' hall or kitchen. The Great Hall and huge dining table laden with food was modified as the norms of hospitality and largess lost pride of place. Meals were more delicate; refinement rather than abundance was valued. Eighteenth-century commentators observed that the exchanging of too numerous toasts was entirely unfashionable, belonging as it did to an earlier time. Pleasure gardens and public meetings allowed for the informality of card playing and tea drinking. Smaller, warmer rooms, well-furnished, were now the stage for a more intimate upper-class family life. Among wealthy merchants, lawyers, bankers, and others of that ilk (those composing an urban gentry), we observe the celebration of the joys and consolation of the family. Marital companionship and the pleasures of parenthood were held as ideals intended to strengthen affective ties. An end to swaddling clothes and wet-nursing was advocated and campaigns begun by publicists for breast-feeding by the mother. Family life at the upper levels no longer overflowed into the streets now that the well-endowed and well-educated retreated into their realm of domesticity. The consequences of this increased privatization of social life could be paradoxical: an autonomous sphere was generated where public issues might be vigorously debated and the power of the state resisted.[4]

The integrative force of traditional culture (herein not idealized as timeless, however) was placed under strain. Beliefs, recreation, and customs contributing to social cohesion were called into question by quality folk. There had always been a separate and clearly defined elite culture—extravagant and courtly as well as private in character—but these quality folk had joined in the more broadly based rituals, ceremonies, and plebeian pastimes. By the late seventeenth century, however, English polite society had become freer from the need to patronize local customs and the recreation of ordinary folk. Possibly for the first time there was a sustained effort by the literary laity, not the clerics, to demonstrate to gentry the errors of plebeian superstition and magical beliefs. Intellectual skepticism concerning popular belief proved highly fashionable, since these beliefs were associated with social inferiority rather than "ungodliness"; in the end this transference proved most damaging to popular culture. But perhaps most telling of all was the attempt to impose linguistic uniformity. Quality people were to shun the local speech world of dialect and variability in favor of standardized pronunciation: this was one of the avowed and esteemed purposes of Samuel Johnson's monumental triumph—his *A Dictionary of the English Language* (1755). Traditional culture was oral and local in character, encouraging rich diversity of speech and vocabulary. The development of a code of polite learning and culture favored the rule-making of the *Dictionary*.[5]

This tendency toward a withdrawal of the "best people" from common residential, linguistic, and cultural context shaped more than the townscape. It offered a "polite and commercial people" the prospect of a relaxation from a demanding public life in which liberality and local patronage were not so essential. This relief from the tiring parade of display, hospitality, exchange of gifts, favors, and services was now deemed beneficial for the health and wealth of society. In fact, as we shall observe, a sustained argument was advanced dismissing the reduction of the concept of society to kindness, courtesy, or gallantry. Formalities and the *punctilio* of former days were challenged by an easygoing indifference in English manners much commented upon by eighteenth-century foreign visitors. Traditional obligations and heroic virtues were no longer so taxing. In the instance of the Anglican clergy, they were aspiring to the status of gentleman. Many entered the priesthood with private livings, and since theology was no longer taught at the universities, the clergy did not study it. Their duties were not heavy and an easy moralism featured Jesus as the best and happiest man that ever was.

Hiving off of communal and corporate bodies were numerous new voluntary forms of associative life. The thrust was toward extending human solidarity and these bodies increased exponentially over the eighteenth century, colonizing a middling zone between government and society. Representing a world of varied interests and goals, these clubs, reading societies, and coffee houses with their newspapers and journals were to be the building blocks of civil society. The gradual separation of state and society allowed for organizing forms of political association, groups concerned with mutual improvement, and the dissemination of practical knowledge for agriculture and industry. These new forms of voluntary association opened the public sphere to expressions of public opinion. It was possible to communicate and test views and ideas in a more open forum. Indeed, the very term "opinion" was subject to new definition in the eighteenth century when it was paired with the word "public." Its semantic range was extended far beyond the traditional usage of denoting fickleness or unsteadiness. Public opinion had tended to be regarded as little more than narrow prejudice when contrasted with the timeless universality of truth. By the close of the eighteenth century, however, opinion in its public dimension was often construed as the collective expression of "rational objectivity." This favorable appraisal stood in opposition to the unreflective, blinkered, mindless loyalty exacted by traditional authority.[6]

In eighteenth-century France, freemasonry wove "networks of solidarity and hierarchy" through the recruitment of membership on the basis of opinion. The modern historian François Furet, in his splendid essay "Interpreting the French Revolution," revives the insights of Augustin Cochin, who had argued that an *esprit de société*, rather than an *esprit de corps*, had lent shape to emerging and embryonic structures surfacing in the century of the French Enlightenment. *Esprit de corps* was Cochin's shorthand for a traditional society based on special interests— that is, the masters guild, Parlement, the corporation, the church, and the nobility. Society was broken up into groups and founded on inequality. This conception was rivaled by notions of a different society predicated on an ideological sense of community. Such an idea of community was to be projected by many an enlightened *philosophe*. Traditional academic forms of learned society were to give birth to embryonic types of democratic organization which represented civil society's quest for autonomy. The many masonic lodges, ideally, were to serve as refuge from the formalities and intricate play of deference and status deemed too pervasive in the older society. Furthermore, confessional disputes, as well as private piques and quarrels, were to be banished from the fraternal order.[7]

In England and Scotland, as we shall observe, the demands of civil society prompted a literary and moral revision of traditional ethics. First, Francis Hutcheson, then David Hume, and finally Adam Smith introduced novel adjustments in moral philosophy which served to modify time-honored conceptions of virtue. Ultimately, virtue was to be defined in negative terms no longer anchored in the classical foursome of prudence, justice, temperance, and fortitude. Nor was it to bear the burden of that Christian virtue, *benevolence*. So defined, the claims of virtue could be satisfied most often by doing nothing. Further, the pursuit of self-interest was now not only condoned but presupposed. Civil society had little need for heroics, gallantry, or courtesy; morality was more a matter of common sense. Men and women possessed the capacity for decency, and in the generation after Hume and Smith, writers like Sir Walter Scott, who had been weaned on this order of moral philosophy, were capable of dramatizing an ethic challenging older prescriptions for bravery and daring. The patient lawyer who determined the facts and perused documents year after year in order to see that justice was done was now credited with displaying that most heroic quality, "civil courage."

The message of Scott's immediate literary forebear and fellow countryman, Tobias Smollett, runs toward celebrating the same middling virtues. At the moral center of the ending of the novel *Humphrey Clinker* (1771), we have Mr. Dennison's modest recipe for a life of health and prosperity imparted to Matthew Bramble (possibly the author's portrait of himself as a young Scot):

> I drained bogs, burned heath, grubbed up furze and fern; I planted copse and willows where nothing else would grow; I gradually enclosed all my farms, and made such improvements that my estate now yields me clear twelve hundred pounds a year—All this time my wife and I have enjoyed uninterrupted health, and a regular flow of spirits, except on a few occasions, when our cheerfulness was invaded by such accidents as are inseparable from the condition of life.[8]

Classical definitions of civil society as being coterminous with the state were now rivaled by political theory arguing for a disjunction, and therefore an opening for independent forms of associative life to be legitimated against state power. Furthermore, a sphere of economic relations (what the physiocrats of the eighteenth century termed *société naturelle*") was contrasted with political society (*société politique*). Whereas much political discourse remained fixed in the tradition going back to Aristotle and Cicero, allowing for little space between state and society, the new coinage gained currency. Moreover, the term "civil society" now assumed the meaning of *civilized* society. Adam Ferguson, the Scottish Highlander and Edinburgh savant, was perhaps the first to write an elaborate tract in English on the genesis of civil society. Published in 1767, his *An Essay on Civil Society* narrates a history of the human species in its transition from "rude" forms of life to a "polished or civilized" condition in parts of contemporary Europe. This transformation was, in Ferguson's view, not achieved without substantial social and psychological cost. Indeed, he viewed with alarm the decline of traditional forms of sociability: ancient bonds and ties of social obligation had been severed by this "advance" from rude to polished. Radical specialization in trades and professions, and the division of labor imposed in the interest of increased productivity, had led to the fragmentation of society. Similar conclusions had been drawn by his more celebrated contemporary, Adam Smith, who wrote movingly of "a society of strangers." It might be well to quote Ferguson on this sensitive topic:

> The commercial arts gain an ascendant at the expense of other pursuits. The desire for profit stifles the love of perfection. Interest cools the imagination and hardens the heart. But apart from these considerations, the separation of professions, while it seems to promise improvement in skill, yet in its ultimate effects serves, in some measure, to break the bonds of society and to withdraw individuals from the common scene. . . . Under the distinction of callings by which members of polished society are separated from each other, society is made to consist of parts of which none is animated with the spirit of society itself . . . members can no longer apprehend the common ties of society. The members of a community may, in this manner, like the inhabitants of a conquered province, be made to lose the sense of every connection, and have no common affairs to transact but those of trade.[9]

Ferguson's prescient observations of the decline of sociability provide a very different analysis of causes from those of his socially conscious forebears of centuries past. The Scotsman's eye was on those social and economic changes accompanying a radical increase in commercial activity. His intellectual forebears were certainly cognizant of economic and social change, but in general were not persuaded that relationships had been displaced from the traditional field of the chivalrous world of courtesy, the Christian domain of brotherhood, and the realm of the archaic. Even when they recognized displacements and social breaches there were useful remedies at hand. The notion of civility itself offered one possible solution; another was the implementation of the ideals of civic humanism. It had been a commonplace earlier to decry the decline of the duties of good lordship and of the obligations of hospitality and courtesy. Innate gregariousness was certain under the right conditions to generate the requisite levels of sociability required for sustaining the harmony of interpersonal relations. Charity, alms-giving, and chivalrous generosity were seen as most essential for weaving the bonds of community. The exhortation to demonstrate talent for friendship and companionship was omnipresent, as were urgings to shoulder lordly and communal responsibilities. These directives were a staple in the manuals of conduct, sermons, and even royal proclamations. By following these hallowed paths it would be possible to repair wrongs and thus knit the ravelled sleeve of the body social. Society was often understood as little more than the family writ large—as a direct by-product, that is, of the thousand social practices displaying human proclivities for benevolence.[10]

Ferguson's writings, as well as those of his Edinburgh literary contemporaries, clearly reckoned that society was not a by-product of acts of benevolence, charity, or kindness. These were not what wove its fabric, and furthermore, any such conception was based on a misreading of human nature. Pessimism about human nature was as old as biblical times. In the seventeenth century the influential legist Samuel Pufendorf had singled out what struck him as the central difficulty in creating a viable social order: the inconstant nature of the human condition. Man, it was specified, so often proved an "inconstant friend." The typical relationship between one man and another was, then, in the view of Pufendorf and certain of his theoretically minded contemporaries, not characterized by any sure sociability. The very fragility of abstract social bonds required that interdependence be mandated by the coercive power of politeness. Familial models of mutuality were replicated in a myriad of ties such as prince/subject, master/apprentice, tenant/landlord, and countless others. Strategies of supplication were omnipresent in rhetorical handbooks and letters in the England and France of the sixteenth and seventeenth centuries.[11]

Distinctions between public and private institutions were drawn in sand. Families, guilds, urban communities, and their rural counterparts each performed functions later connected with private agents and government. Fathers, guild masters, and landlords had special authority which latter-day German historians aptly term *Herrenschaft*. Guild and town ceremonials were elaborated to assert the primacy of the corporation at every stage in the member's life. Rituals surrounding birth and death rendered them social events by endorsing human interdependency. A fundamental element of community was the recollection of the dead. The use of organic metaphors to portray society and the state prevailed in the sixteenth and seventeenth centuries; they were not yet rivaled by the imagery of the eighteenth century and its fascination with mechanisms and the machine.[12]

Ties were mandated and trust engendered by munificence and bounty. Profits were to be received from acts of largess in a future time when the servitor made beneficent restitution. There were of course difficulties when responding to favors; courtesy required a delay in making the countergift. One must not be impatient to quit oneself of another. The rules of courtesy and rhetoric called for a suppliant to make no mention of his merit. Trust engendered by the exchange of favors and courtesies was, in the view of Marcel Mauss (premier anthropologist of gift culture), not inimical to narrow commercial bargains, nor was it innocent of the forces of the market. Further, those who pledged mutual fidelity were not unmindful of their own interests. An honor culture with its concern for reputation and display was more than a manifestation of subterranean archaism: the paternalistic obligation of landowners was part and parcel of their possession of wealth. Out of the practices of liberality and conspicuous consumption stemmed a thousand forms of social wages and credit. From this matrix was generated a complex world of claims, counterclaims, and responsibilities. This cycle of giving, receiving, and making restitution had far more content than symbolic form. It might be well to remember that despite the authority of the contemporary medievalist Georges Duby's graceful recent effort to pinpoint the demise of medieval reward culture (*faits du bien*) in the late fifteenth century, it was to have one of the longest third acts in European history. Similarly, it should be noted that Norbert Elias's attempt to locate the origins of civility in the northern Europe of Erasmus is neglectful of three hundred years of *la vita civile* in the Renaissance city-states of Italy.[13]

II

Jean-Marie Constant, in *La Vie Quotidienne de la Noblesse Française aux XVIe et XVIIe Siècles* (Paris, 1985), 296, makes the observation that "In fact, the sole desire of the *gentilhommerie* was the service of the king, or of a prince powerful enough so that their lineage could obtain authority and gifts. . . . the Capetian centralizing tradition was more strongly anchored in the mentality of *gentilshommes* than was the idea of noble power." Dispensing of favors, honors, titles, pensions, and rewards was not confined to France. One does not have to agree with Hugh Trevor-Roper's theory concerning the sixteenth-century crisis brought on by a backlash of country against courtly extravagance to appreciate the value of his assessment of the proliferation of royal *grâces*. He and Lawrence Stone have demonstrated how essential were *faits du bien* (rewards) for securing the monarchy. If we turn to the political culture of French nobility in the late sixteenth and early seventeenth centuries, we notice that personal bonds were vital for the cohesion of society and that they were frequently generated from gift-giving and reciprocation. Writing at the beginning of the seventeenth century, Eustache Du Refuge, in his *Traité de la Cour* (Paris, 1616), exhorted his readers to study carefully the high art of giving and receiving gifts (*bienfaits*) and compliments in order to "induce into our confidence" figures of influence at court. This was to be achieved, in the author's view, "by a declaration or demonstration of honor and obligation." Gifts were the cement of human society—"the prisoner's chains . . . with which one can bind and enslave others." The word *bienfait* is rendered in two late seventeenth-century French dictionaries as "kindness," "benefit," and "service," as well as "gift." The art of recognizing and fulfilling an obligation had a most elaborate and subtle psychology. The Sieur de Ceriziers made a neat distinction in his *Le héros françaic, ou l'idée du grand capitaine* (Paris, 1645) between gifts and salaries. The former "wins the entire affection of a man," predisposing him in one's favor, whereas one who receives a salary has no need to think of recompense. Gifts were not only tools for sealing personal relations; they also demonstrated greater sympathy for the worth of another individual. The recipient had the opportunity to display his own liberality in return and enhance his own dignity. We have noted the intricate protocol to be observed in making the countergift: never must obligation appear too heavy a burden. Claude Pelletier, in his *La nourriture de la noblesse* (Paris, 1604), advised the *donnée* in these words: "Allow his gift therefore to remain in deposit within your hands for a time, so that when you do the same for him, he will believe that your gift is offered more as a mutual exchange of friendship than to acquit yourself of what he has given you." As we have noted, the public and private realms commingled so that liberality and its attendant round of rituals generated social solidarity at every level of society, from lord to vassal to peasant and town guildsman. The nobility of the robe were very like the nobility of the sword in the conviction that generosity and fidelity were valuable qualities of character entirely appropriate to all professions and not just to soldiering. The memoirs, family histories, and genealogies of the nobility of more recent origin were eager to persuade the reader that largess and trustworthiness were not incompatible with the "civil" vocations they followed. Particular attention was called to the bravery and valor of this new nobility.[14]

Gift-giving was an essential of the French monarch's fiscal program, and this observation can be made also for the early Stuarts in England: service was exchanged for office; positions of honor were the currency of a culture of obligation. The definition of "merit" extended its meaning to include an assemblage of good qualities. The entry in the *Dictionnaire de l'Académie Française* (1640) also featured "prior obligations individuals had achieved for past service and affection." Merit signified, then, "to draw glory or advantage over someone for doing something." Genealogies of noble families sought to show that great damage might befall the crown if new families were elevated to positions of dignity and responsibility. Tirelessly they indicated that these *nouveau* folk were without any merit: they devoured the gifts of our kings, "served them little and were often ungrateful for them." Biographies, family histories, and memoirs were replete with references to the forging of bonds of affection and ties of trust between monarchs and their high-born subjects tracing back into the dim past. The language of service and fidelity laced these accounts. For the crown it was vital that it should bestow its favors on those who had demonstrated "proof of person," in their willingness to sacrifice themselves for the king. Secretaries in letters patent reviewed instances in which the noble recipient or his forebears had demonstrated exceptional bravery or fidelity even unto risking bodily harm or death. In fact, posts and distinctions were to be distributed only to individuals whose families had a history of honorable acts. Courage was perceived as the ability to suffer damage and privation; this in turn was synonymous with generosity. At the French court in the sixteenth and seventeenth centuries, deeds of honor were widely advertised with couriers regularly reporting the heroics of individuals on the battlefields of Europe. Especially important was the response of women in the crowd who rhapsodized over the martial bravery of those valorous ones so deserving of royal recognition. Well into the seventeenth century, *faits d'armes* and *combats singuleurs* were literary favorites in chronicle and fiction.[15]

Honor served to mandate relations between individual rather than simply to enhance the reputation of an individual. Therefore, when conditions of warfare changed in the seventeenth century and the opportunities for heroism and single combat declined, the duel emerged as one of the few theaters of virtue—despite its prohibition—in which an individual could display his valor. Richelieu forbade the duel in 1626 but he and Louis XIII were to prove indulgent: the Indian Summer of the duel had too long a lease. It was this field of honor that permitted individuals to give "proof of person," therefore demonstrating they could be trusted to risk life and limb to uphold pledges. French kings from Henry IV to Louis XIV had attempted to ban the duel, but the difficulties were daunting. In a tract against the practice (1650), a particular governor in a dialogue with the monarch tried to persuade the king to do away with dueling gradually. But the king understood only too well how difficult this policy would be to pursue: "What you say is all well and good; but if we ban duels, how will the nobility display its courage?" The governor replied that they would have to be satisfied to demonstrate their prowess "in your armies." However, dueling continued to thrive through the 1640s and 1650s. When it did decline, in the second half of the seventeenth century, this was more a matter of *"changement de moeurs"* than of government intervention.

By the late seventeenth century the language of fidelity, magnanimity, and the varied shades of affection betokening loyalty and good lordship was being rivaled by a new lexicon. Regularly, heroic ideas and ideals were being tested in the French theater from Corneille (1606–1684) to Racine (1639–1699), and often they were found to exact great psychological cost. Were one to study the trajectory of the vocabulary of the prolific playwright Alexandre Hardy (1579–1632) and compare his oeuvre with that of the next generation of dramatists, one would discern that Hardy's language was rooted in the archaic and grandiloquent. An absence of concern for *bienséance* (propriety) and *vraisemblance* (verisimilitude) was evident; instead his verse had a picturesque and extravagant quality not to be found in the latter-day theater. Tragedians were turning away from medieval themes of the downfall of the mythic and overmighty, whose doom was regularly proclaimed in the first act. Also, they were distancing themselves from the elegiac tragedies of the Renaissance. Playwrights dramatized the humanity of their heroic characters by portraying the enervating conflict between "liberté de l'âme" and "obligation envers une maison."[16]

Corneille's tragedies often treated the contest, smouldering in the breasts of characters, between private passion and the honoring of solemn obligation. Principal figures reached different solutions as to how to reconcile conflicting claims of *devoirs* (duties) on the one side and the lure of personal affection on the other. Corneille's tragedies, as well as the works of other leading seventeenth-century French playwrights, dealt with public questions such as the demands of *raison d'état* over and against the requirements of magnanimity and mercy. More than internal conflict was involved as characters vacillated and equivocated as to the morality of championing the public good at the expense of one's personal integrity. In Corneille's generation a type of Machiavellianism introduced the stark confrontation between *ragione dello stato* and the noble virtue of princely clemency. Suspense was certain and protracted as gloomy figures were caught in the dilemma between the demands of state with its harsh requirements on the one side, and the need to show mercy and generosity to the royal enemy on the other. Heroic drama in the France of Racine influenced the English Restoration theater in the time of Dryden with its contests between passion and intelligence, as well as between being and destiny. Always tinged with a note of sadness prompted by unattainable ideals, these heroic tragedies caught and held the attention of large audiences. The need to be released from ideal images of self may have been as great as the need to create them, and this may in part account for the success of this type of dramaturgy. Great souls were assailed with melancholy when confronting "les fureurs d'une guerre civile." So deep is the emperor's anguish in Corneille's *Cinna* that he, Augustus Caesar, is sorely tempted to renounce the throne. Was absolute dominion evil but necessary? Is this the message taken by Corneille in a time of fratricidal religious wars and political rebellion? The weight of costly choice in politics and religion contributed to the image of *l'homme tragique*. At the level of elite social life was it possible to ease the burdens of (in La Bruyère's words) the "esprits forts"? Could *l'homme tragique* be converted into that model of civility, moderate and tolerant in matters political and religious? Leading moralists were soon to be defining those very qualities as the essence of *l'homme honnête*. We shall observe that the new apostles of civility were intent upon scaling down the demands of aristocratic virtue and its exacting code of honor.[17]

III

Roland Mousnier is the premier contemporary historian of the culture of obligation for seventeenth-century France. He distinguishes clearly between the fidelity ties of the seventeenth century and the legal bonds of feudalism:

> These fealties did not involve any act of 'faith and homage.' The commitment did not require any oath, any ritual, any agreement in writing. The remuneration never took the form of a fief, any more than it was a fief or a censive that imposed the rendering of reciprocal services. These ties were of a different order: that of the gift of oneself that one person makes to another, the order of love.

Recent scholarship has registered numerous dissents from Mousnier's somewhat idealized version of a "society of fidelity." "An order of love," secured by pledge, appears to deny the play of self-interest in the calculations of the nobility of the seventeenth century. But, in fact, the force of self-interest would not surprise the crown or nobility during that era or, for that matter, a century before or a century before that. Indeed, one could speak of an order of love as a more generalized manifestation of interests. Under this dispensation one might be persuaded of another's allegiance. The fragile nature of society encouraged public and extravagant expression of a culture of obligation. The more uncertain the generalized cohesion of society, the greater the reliance on largess, the honoring of pledges, and fulfillment of the claims of chivalry. In the sixteenth century noble culture in France was markedly oral. Social rituals sanctioned charity and generosity "hors de l'orde commun." The very frailty of society and government prompted those customs and practices one associates with an archaic civilization: one was the *homme de mérite* by giving proof of a talent for valor, generosity, and fidelity.[18]

Profound social reasons, then, obtained for upholding the code of good lordship and benevolence. These would be gradually displaced only when society assumed a life of its own and social ties were less dependent on social wages and social credit. The institutions and forces serving to strengthen more impersonal notions of community did not themselves come into being at a specific moment in the seventeenth century; they had a long and honorable history. Likewise, *amour propre* and the play of self-interest long antedated the seventeenth century. But it was also in the seventeenth century that the problem of exploring and dramatizing the contest between "an order of love" and "love of self" became a regnant cultural concern. Whether Mousnier is too visionary and idealistic or his critics too materialistic and insensitive is not for us to say. Parenthetically, it should be noted that Machiavelli and Machiavellianism had challenged, even scoffed at, the efficacy of spiritual ties or moral bonds. There was a healthy medieval Augustinian-Christian tradition that resolutely argued for the sinful origins of state and society; however, neither the Machiavellians nor the Augustinians of the sixteenth century offered a positive version of enduring social relations in the City of Man. Indeed, Machiavelli had no conception of the history of civil society.

As we shall note, however, history being a study in ironics, it was the movement of Catholic Augustinians known as Jansenists who, in seventeenth-century France, while insisting on the ineradicable mark of Adam's Fall on all subsequent generations, were compelled to acknowledge, albeit reluctantly, the almost miraculous order and civility prevailing in contemporary society. It was from the Jansenist movement that the term "enlightened self-interest" was disseminated, if not originated. Self-love, no matter how horrendous a hindrance to the felicitous transit of the Christian soul to the next world, proved essential for the proper operation of society in this world. Furthermore, self-love (the sin of pride) counterfeited love of God (true Christian charity). Inspired by vanity and a desire to win the love of one's fellows, the individual, by dint of unintended consequences, gained human decency (*l'honnêteté humaine*) from mimicking Christian charity. From the philosopher Blaise Pascal to the moralist Pierre Nicole to the jurist Jean Domat (all Jansenists) to the Calvinist Pierre Bayle, we shall observe that the argument assumed the same shape. The most literary of them all—Pascal—was to marvel in his *Pensées* at "the grandeur of man amidst concupiscence itself, in knowing how to derive from it such an admirable order and in having made of it an image of charity."[19]

IV

One might observe that the "culture of obligation" and an "order of love" were to find few champions or few detractors in the following century. Much that was so vivid and morally compelling in the literature and drama of the seventeenth century would, a hundred years later, be considered old-fashioned—even obsolete. As we shall see, heroic tragedy became melodrama, losing that equilibrium between "horror and pathos" characteristic of an earlier theatricality. The playwright Crébillon achieved great success with his tragedies [*Idoménée* (1705); *Eléctre* (1708); *Xerxès* (1714) and, above all, with his *Atrée et Thyeste* (1707)] by dramatizing not the psychic cost of heroic choices but the delicious horrors of the melodrama. Despite the efforts of Voltaire to prolong the life of heroic tragedy (he wrote 27 of them), the genre was in an inexorable decline. Exotic settings and surface emotion turned the plays into sentimental exercises rather than tragedy.[20]

Recent interpretations of the seventeenth-century theater of Corneille by Paul Benichou and Octave Nadal suggest that even at his finest moment, the heroic personage sought to disguise or suppress his aristocratic agitation: hesitation, doubt, and even despair troubled his conscience as he was called upon to sacrifice personal satisfaction for the public good. The female heroine, likewise, found the choices almost unendurable when summoned to fulfill the demands of ancestral, personal, and filial honor over and against the promptings of the heart. The psychology of hero and heroine stemmed from the agonizing recognition that claims of loyalty were themselves irreconcilable. How complex were the wellsprings of family piety, friendship, and one's pledge of honor. How difficult to achieve a just sense of pride (*juste orgueil*). How easily the élan so necessary for attaining glory (*gloire*) could be undermined by self-doubt. How strong the defenses must be against any seizure of ''inner-doubt and despair.'' How vulnerable was the hero's spiritual and physical dignity. In Corneille's *Cinna* the specter of bloody civil strife haunts the dark corridors and lurks behind each tapestry. Not even Caesar Augustus's evocation of the grandeur of his rule can dispatch the ghosts of old murders:

> This absolute rule over land and sea,
> This sovereign power I exert over the world entire,
> This unlimited grandeur and illustrious rank
> That have cost me so much suffering and blood.[21]

To be released from the stern demands of the code calling for vengeance of family honor was nothing short of a miracle. The tangle of vengeance is the web of an honor community. In *Cinna,* Emilia, the daughter of a father slain by Augustus, upon being pardoned for her treason by the emperor, voices her astonishment:

> My hatred, which I thought was immortal, shall die;
> It has died and this heart becomes a loyal subject.

This literature was to undergo profound changes. No longer was it so certain to continue to posit a society requiring so much from its rulers and its hero subjects. Soon it would be easier for characters in drama and in novels to abdicate from earlier lofty ideals and exaggerated demands into a condition that might be described as ''mere humanity.'' Euripides' *Iphigenia in Aulis,* a favorite source for eighteenth-century drama and opera, underwent radical revision. No longer was it possible to justify the father's crime against his daughter as the fulfillment of the commander's duty toward his fellow countrymen. The stern ethic of many an ancient myth was tempered, even sentimentalized.[22]

The seventeenth-century literary evocation of the contest between ancestral piety, filial duty, and honor on the one side, and personal satisfaction (happiness) on the other, offered evidence of a heightened awareness of contradiction. The drama allowed for the psychologizing of the dilemma but not necessarily its resolution. A century later drama, opera, and the fine arts were less reluctant to draw moral lessons, avoiding the stern dichotomies, in favor of portraying the many shadings of sentimental attachment. Furthermore, these art forms were prone to generate a plethora of ideas concerning the need for tenderness, mercy, and reconciliation. In tragedy a new space was opening up between *amour propre* and *devoirs.* The word *devoir,* so common in the plays of the age of Corneille, had been a prime mark of civility and politeness. A hundred years later the burden of duty was lightened and the definitions of civility and politeness were charged with an easier and more agreeable current. So too the definitions of virtue, esteem, merit, and generosity. The semantic field of this vocabulary was being extended to embrace less heroic constructs. At first characters of the drama were held in the stern culture of obligation, but the playwright allowed them to display flaws and yet hold the sympathy of the audience. In both France and England we observe the thrust toward a refined moral psychology as well as a revision of the vocabulary of passions. We shall soon consider England. In France traditional genres were losing pride of place and new literary forms were becoming fashionable. Quests for perfection in love were rivaled by less exacting searches. Stern classical catalogues of morality were challenged and even displaced by a new literature of manners. In the salon of the seventeenth century, subtle analysis of the passions was endlessly pursued as a favorite literary pastime: a special topic was the presumed antithesis between love and jealousy. Ultimately, each would shade into the other. We shall encounter this duo again in the course of our inquiry.[23]

Observations on the passions took the form of maxims or *sentences* and were beyond counting in the plays and *mémoires* of seventeenth-century France. Fine distinctions were now drawn between love and friendship; the plays of Racine often detailed the transformation of love into hate. Similarly, the boundaries between desire and love, jealousy, emulation, envy, and finally, hatred and antipathy were repeatedly investigated. Again fine distinctions were made; in addition, the semantic range of key words such as *amour propre*, and most particularly, *intérêt*, were patiently probed. The psychology of the virtues and virtuous action uncovered by Montaigne a century before was now systematically analyzed by La Rochefoucauld, La Fontaine, Pascal, and La Bruyère. Interpretation tended to feature human limitations so that extravagant claims of friendship or the duty of revenge were somewhat miniaturized. Polemics were directed against the *Precieux* and their fascination with reckless gallantry and radical sentimentality. Already Molière's earliest comedies, Boileau's criticism, and Racine's prefaces to such plays as *Britannicus, Bérénice,* and *Andromache* challenged the grandiose and improbable.[24]

V

Descartes's *Traité des Passions,* published in 1649 and translated into English the following year, resembled other contemporary analyses of the state of the human mind. Fine distinctions were made between the passions and, in Descartes's case, he investigated with subtlety the differences between *amour* and *désir,* or admiration and atonement, or affection, *amitié,* and devotion. This analysis of the passions was to set the stage for grand investigations and refutations, as were those of Hobbes and Spinoza. Descartes was eager to validate the passions as useful and necessary for a happy life; however, they were not to be uncritically obeyed or easily capitulated to. Instead they were to be controlled and, ideally, the way to this achievement of self-mastery was through the exercise of that lofty virtue—generosity. Generosity was the key and general remedy for the irregularity of the passions. For Descartes *générosité* was not mere liberality, nor was it dependent upon *belle naissance, race* or illustrious pedigree; he would substitute the discipline of this virtue for Aristotelian magnanimity or the scholastic's conception of prudence. Generosity consorted with humility and, if exercising it appropriately, the generous individual would refrain from denigrating others or esteeming himself beyond measure. Further, this generosity inspired in others love and heroism. Descartes conferred prestige on this noble passion, perceiving a reciprocal relationship between this lofty virtue and gratitude—a principal bond of society.[25]

The passions were not to be subjugated or stifled, and for Descartes it was the active hero, not the stoic sage, who was most attractive. The passions of *gloire* and *honté* were essential and the generously minded were naturally meant to do *"grandes choses."* Descartes would reconcile the ideal of humility with that of humanity. Self-esteem was distinguished from aristocratic pridefulness. Good will was especially valued and, unlike wealth or birth or talent, is common to all: therefore, the generous individual will never be contemptuous and is himself humble. The prestige gained through love was reconciled with the claims of society. The idea of glory became more humane and benevolent, thus the need for self-assertiveness less compelling. But the idea of generosity, while considerably scaled down from its pretensions to grandiosity, munificence or extravagant display, did not altogether lose something of its archaic grandeur. In this Descartes's notions were not far distant from those of Corneille and Racine.[26]

Across the Channel the same brew was steaming, even boiling. A series of sharp disagreements centering upon the role of noble virtues in the life of society was to contribute significantly to the development of English moral and political thought. Here we note disputation as to whether gratitude, generosity, and fortitude could serve as more than ideals for the select few. Venality of office clouded the glossy picture of service and recompense between two "selfish" individuals. Did gifts, benevolences, exchanges of courtesy, and those many benefits flowing from reciprocity act to create a durable sense of social solidarity? Thomas Hobbes, like Machiavelli, was to dissent wickedly on these matters, maintaining that rivalry was commonplace between the obliged and the obliger. As in France, the heroic drama of the period was clouded with a melancholy occasioned by a recognition that such ideals are beyond human reach. Hobbes himself will write for those who would prosper, but he understood full well those human beings more properly concerned with matters of honor than of "mere" survival and prosperity. Yet these grander ethical ideals cannot be reckoned as essential parts of the workings of a political structure. There certainly was a context in which principles of generosity were not an aberration. Hobbes's political philosophy was, however, a deliberate departure from this context. He wrote for "tame men" and was not alone in asserting that in a civil state "fortitude is a royal virtue and though it be necessary in such private men as shall be soldiers, yet for other men the less they dare the better it is for the commonwealth and themselves." Between Hobbes and such intelligent opponents as Clarendon stood the disagreement concerning the place of generosity in the Leviathan. For Hobbes it was too rare to be presumed upon—an ideal to which "only a select minority can aspire." In the next generation, John Locke (1632–1704) was to speak loftily about the "generous Temper and Courage of the English Nation." But to read Locke is to discover that generosity was a virtue not to be presumed upon outside the limits of the family. Locke's pupil, Shaftesbury, at the onset of the eighteenth century, was eager to restore the concept of virtue from the strictures of Hobbes. He would do so, as we shall see, by discovering the source and origin of moral values not in reason but in sentiment.[27]

The prospect of the devaluation of generosity as a guiding social principle was truly a bleak one for Hobbes's aristocratic contemporaries. Hobbes himself recorded patiently, albeit critically, the dimensions of a social world in which sensitivity to reputation was matched only by a fierce obsession with pridefulness. Men would lose their lives rather than suffer slander because the loss of reputation was the loss of the "immortal part." Reputation could be more precious than blood ties. How essential was an understanding of human vanity in all things! Men were prepared to engage in money-making not from radical acquisitiveness but from vanity, "for their treasures serve them but for a looking-glass wherein to behold and contemplate their own wisdom." "All men naturally strive for honors and preferment: but chiefly they, who are least troubled with caring for necessary things." How easy it is to slip into the "gallant madness of Don Quixote" or to deceive oneself into believing that one is playing a part in a chivalric romance.[28]

Hobbes recognized that in a state of nature courage was the greatest virtue of all—if not the only one. In a "civil state," however, "courage inclineth men to public revenge." How readily the "royal virtue" of fortitude "can be employed to overturn states as well as to defend them." How dangerous is the cult of military glory for its own sake! How easily the vainglory of princes could lead to needless, costly, and bloody wars. Hobbes was consistent in his desire to present a systematized "civil philosophy" for "tame men." He felt keenly the imperative to write for those "tame men" who sought to prosper and survive in what he was to term "civil society." He understood how powerful and pervasive were the claims of honor: some valued them more than survival or property. Indeed, there was an ample context in which generosity and mutuality could be viewed as norms rather than aberrations. As an ethical ideal their principles could be appealing, but Hobbes was unwilling to make them an essential element of his political structure—that is, of civil society.[29]

To Hobbes's literary contemporaries society itself hardly seemed a likely prospect without the ample play of the virtues of generosity and beneficence. Relationships were endorsed by the multiple acts of benefiting and reciprocity. Society was created, as we have observed, from the quotidian exchange of courtesies and rituals of liberality and hospitality. Lord Clarendon (Edward Hyde) was among the many who excoriated Hobbes for his putting down of the greatness of the human heart. In his *A brief view and survey of the dangerous and pernicious errors to Church and State in Mr. Hobbes's book Leviathan* (1676), Clarendon advised that Mr. Hobbes not take "ill, that I observe his extreme malignity to the Nobility by whose bread he hath bin alwaies sustain'd who must expect any part, at least any precedence in His Institutions. . . ." Hobbes had injected a dart in the tender literary psyche that could not easily be dislodged by an *ad hominem* argument. In Hobbes's political vision there was little room for generosity or noble heroism. As much as he might personally admire these virtues, they counted for little when he presented a systematic account of his civil philosophy.[30]

Roger L'Estrange prepared an English précis of Seneca's *De beneficiis* and it was well circulated. The essential business of humankind was set under the literary rubric of "benefiting." Again the judgment was rendered that benefiting was the cement of all communities binding king and subject, husband and wife, parents and children, and masters and servants. A single abstract of Seneca's *On Benefits* went through ten editions in 21 years. Tirelessly, readers were reminded of the many evils, both psychic and material, that would befall them if benefits and gifts were not acknowledged. Charles de Saint-Evremond, in his *Miscellanyeous Essays* (1692), observed that if there was a dispute about the acknowledgment of a good turn or favor, the standard procedure was to refine the argument found in the "Discourses of Seneca." French moralists from Descartes to Senault and Courtin were translated by Walter Charleton, the friend of Dryden. Charleton's *Natural History of the Passions* (1674) projected a vivid conception of a heroic society. He, along with Dryden and others, sought to yoke beneficence with an enlightened version of self-interest. True generosity insured the so frequently sought-after good—a tranquil mind. There were of course many foxes among the grapes, and the more intent a writer like Charleton was to defend the noble passions, the more firmly situated in political discourse was the vocabulary of jealousy, envy, and betrayal. Schemes, fears, and plots were rampant in projections of a political universe serving to explain all disorders and failures of heroic virtue.[31]

Audiences appeared more interested in problem-posing than in problem-solving. The opposition between private and public roles held center stage and in the best heroic tragedies (the plays of Dryden), conflicts paralleled one another. The contest between love and duty or revenge and honor, or the passions of jealousy against the claims of friendship and kinship, took a fierce toll on the characters. As in the French tragedies of Corneille and Racine (translated into English and often performed in London and Dublin), characters competed to outshine one another in gestures of generosity and delicacy. But often virtuous warriors and selfless rulers were trapped in a web of malice and treachery; heroic actions were regularly located in an imperfect world of plotters and schemers. In Dryden's most serious work, the principal dramatic figure "is a dying emperor in the midst of a dying empire—Montezuma, Boabdelin, Maximin, the Old Emperor, Cleopatra and Antony, Muley Moloche, Cleomenes. The images are of sunsets, twilight, entropy, extinction, and exhaustion." Ideal kings are set against false leaders, the threat of mob action and the political nightmare of faction and feuding. In the last plays of Dryden the passions become more destructive and intrusive. Private stresses debilitate the psyches of public figures. One is reminded of Wordsworth's comment: "Whenever Dryden's language is poetically impassioned, it is mostly upon unpleasing subjects such as the follies, vices and crimes of classes of men and individuals."[32]

The libertines in Dryden's plays, unable to subordinate their natural desires to moral promptings, have encouraged literary critics to view them as spokesmen for Hobbes' minimalist ethics. A survey of Dryden's entire run of dramas indicates, however, that only the arch-villains are invested with Hobbesian attitudes. In fact, the heroic play with its rhymed couplets in the French style was losing its dominance with or without the Hobbesian villains. Dryden, a once-resolute champion, abandoned the heroic couplet for blank verse in his *All for Love* (1678). Subversion of the dramaturgy of heroic virtue led to the substitution of the emotional responses of pity and compassion for the plight of characters rather than admiration and awe. Pathetic tragedy held center stage dramatizing the interior state instead of highlighting social relations or public gestures. In the first of the sentimental dramas, Nathaniel Lee's *Princess of Cleve* (1681), taken from the French novel by Mme. de Lafayette, we observe the extension of a range of moral preoccupation and emotionality. Like the French theater, English drama was now eager to register a luxuriance of passion and an inwardness of being.[33]

Samuel Johnson, in his *Preface to Shakespeare* (1765), offered a critical perspective the applicability of which extended far beyond the literature of drama:

> The contest about the original benevolence or malignity of man had not yet commenced. Speculation had not yet attempted to analyse the mind, to trace the passions to their sources, to unfold the seminal principles of vice and virtue, or sound the depths of the heart for the motives of all. All those enquiries, which from that time that human nature became the fashionable study, have been made sometimes with nice discernment, but often with idle subtilty, were yet unattempted.

Thus did Johnson write in his grand and arresting style of the arc of change in dramaturgy from the time of Shakespeare until his own times in eighteenth-century England. Contemporary literary historians of our day have judged Johnson's overarching speculations on the mark.[34]

In the drama, the new literary form of the novel, the periodic essay, the sermon, mock epic poetry, and in numerous other forms of representation, we witness a protracted debate concerning human nature and the passions. The general outcome was to provide support, however modest, for the human talent or capacity for benevolence. Ethical theory had become a matter of grave concern and systematic attention. Thomas Hobbes, so often misread, was the single individual to deliver the deepest wound to those arguing for benevolence, innate or otherwise. He appeared to have dueled in so deadly a fashion as the champion for human depravity, that his name became synonymous with his Italian forebear, Machiavelli. Hobbes's most formidable work, *Leviathan* (1651), was mentioned in Parliament as a telling example of a blasphemous book. Modern-day scholars may well speculate as to why this ethical theme was pursued with so much single-mindedness in seventeenth-century England and France. Answers to this question are familiar and run the gamut from increased secularization to the rise of absolute monarchies. One might also take the route of featuring market economy and the diffusion of consumerism.

For present purposes, however, our concern will not be with this question—at least for now. Suffice to say that in general heroic ideals were being miniaturized, and the archaic bonds of a culture of obligation were no longer celebrated so robustly. Drama was not so likely to be located in the moral landscape of conflicting claims of public obligation or private satisfaction. Nor was reason to be defined through the heroes in Corneille's plays (for example, by the character Horace) as the just evaluation of duty toward the self and allegiance to others. Instead, a knowledge of the world and its complexity prompted moralists and playwrights to ponder the high cost of treating the problem of conflicting loyalties in such a decisive and stark fashion. Less exacting was the newer view that reason was given us in part to modify our customs and manners.[35]

Charles de Saint-Evremond (1613–1703), that elegant adornment of Franco-Anglo society (he spent years in exile in England), was altogether precocious in his anticipation of the philosophes. His *Sentiments d'un honnête et habile courtesan* (1666) presents an early and impressive appreciation for the intellectual prospects of the present historical moment. For him this was a time when reason was no longer "austere and rude." In his world, and in the fullness of time, reason itself had been civilized:

> Je sais que la raison nous a été donnée pour régler nos moeurs; mais la raison, autrefois rude et austère, s'est civilisée avec le temps, et ne conserve aujourd'hui presque rien de son ancienne rigidité. Il lui a fallu de l'austérité pour établir des lois qui puissent empêcher les outrages et les violences; elle s'est adoucie pour introduire l'honnêteté dans le commerce des hommes; elle est devenue délicate et curieuse dans la recherche des plaisirs, pour rendre la vie aussi agréable qu'elle était déjà sûre et honnête. . . .

The challenge of events bared the inadequacies of an archaic culture. La Fronde in France and the civil wars in England revealed that the dangers of "l'extremisme spirituel" had brought both kingdoms to the brink of dissolution. The times were ripe for *l'honnête courtesan* to reply to the extreme moralist (*vertueux*):

> Comme il y a peu de ces pleines vertus qui puissent tout à fait vous satisfaire, il y a peu de vices extrêmes qui doivent vous aigrir avec raison. D'ailleurs si on trouve des défauts au plus honnête homme, quand on l'étudie bien, on découvre quelque chose de bon en celui qui l'est le moins, quand on se donne la peine de le connaître. On voit rarement dans les hommes que tout soit vertu, tout soit vice: les bonnes et les mauvaises qualités sont confondues, et un discernement délicat peut faire la séparation de ce mélange.[36]

Parenthetically, one can speculate on the significant differences between England and France beginning at mid-seventeenth century with La Fronde as opposed to the English Civil War. French nobles opposed to the crown never elevated their opposition to a program of reform. They were supporters of the Divine Right monarchy; what they resented was the arbitrary use of royal power. They never contemplated a state not presided over by the crown. Recent scholarship has argued persuasively that the French nobility under Louis XIV were much advantaged by the crown's policy, having ample reason to be domesticated. Elites submitted to the monarchy, not because of the king's resolute will, but because there was much to be gained. Of course it was otherwise in England. There civil strife occurred on a monumental scale, and although the storm settled, seas remained rough and dangerous. Anxieties and bitter historical memories made the search for repair and consensus an imperative. In France a court-dominated society with a relatively stable "polite" culture was secure and historical memories less bitter. A more independent and critical literati plied their pens without fear of tipping the political balance. French literary experimentation and daring might be contrasted with the cautious and modest tone of English essayists and journalists who distrusted and feared political and religious enthusiasms. Incidentally, an analysis of French literary culture and the French press of the eighteenth century suggests the prevalence of aristocratic norms. This stance differed markedly from that of the English press which voiced the values and aspirations of middling classes; their reading public was filled with shopkeepers, craftsmen, merchants, professionals, gentlemen farmers, and their ladies.[37]

VI

Francis Bacon's skepticism concerning classical philosophers called into question their characterization of the "nature of the good" and their proclivity for offering "heroical descriptions of virtue, duty and felicity." Traditional philosophy did not, in Bacon's view, provide material about what men actually did but rather what it was they ought to have done. These materials must come from "history, poesy and daily experience." Especially valued were the materials from history where "receipts might be made for the use of life." The scholastics were specifically charged with neglect of the study of history. The key for Bacon in ethics as well as in the sciences was practical application. The study of man as he is—his character, temperament, humours—had been scandalously inadequate. Hobbes recapitulates this theme in his earliest work, the introduction to his translation of Thucydides' *Pelopennesian Wars*. Although Hobbes's interest in history diminished over the years, he continued to share two of the illustrious Bacon's judgments: first, he would scale down heroic descriptions of virtue, duty, and felicity, commonplace among classical philosophers; secondly, he would construct "laws of civil life" predicated on man not as an *animal sociale* or a *zoon politikon* (political animal), but rather on man as a self-regarding, egoistic creature. The proper object of man's will was some good for himself. Compassion and benevolence—those noble virtues—were reduced to self-pity and self-love.[38]

The quest for an ethic based on the study of human nature was intended to go beyond Machiavelli's achievement: more was required than an appreciation of the skills needed for holding power. Investigations now initiated would have a higher relevance for the general society and its governance. Critical for an evaluation of Hobbes's contributions is an understanding of the denizens he posited for his civil society. They were "tame men," and it was for them that he often wrote. This order depended upon sovereign power to protect them; tame men required security and "commodious living." This requisite should not obscure the fact that men, as Hobbes viewed them according to the lights of his day, were more concerned with honor and reputation than survival or property. The monarchy was itself more likely than the aristocracy or the *demos* to produce that peace for which civil society was instituted. Given security and safety enough, the citizen must forgo the excuse of acting on the suspicion of peril or of waging preventive warfare. Hobbes indicates that the conception of civil society is no older than his own book *De cive*. The novelty, according to Hobbes, is that he deals with "the matter, forme and power of a commonwealth."[39]

Civil philosophy, when applied to civil society in Hobbes's view, should aim to settle the causes for its genesis. Artificial in nature, civil society is itself a work of art, and its generation emanates from the force of numerous individual wills. The word "civil," in his vocabulary, signifies *artificial* in that it stems from more than one will. Civil history is thus distinguished from natural history which arises from the involuntary action of man. Civil authority originates from an agreement of wills, whereas natural authority, such as a father over a family, has no such origins. Essential for our purpose is Hobbes's distinction between civil society and mere gregariousness:

> Wherefore I deny not that men (even nature compelling) *desire* to come together. But civil societies are not mere meetings, but bonds, to the making whereof faith and compacts are necessary; the virtue whereof to children and fools, and the profit whereof to those who have not yet tasted the miseries which accompany its defects, is altogether unknown; whence it happens that those, because they know not what society is, cannot enter into it; these, because ignorant of the benefits it brings, care not for it. Manifest therefore it is, that all men, because they are born in infancy, are born unapt for society . . . wherefore man is made fit for society not by nature but by education.[40]

Man is indeed, then, not born for society, and civil philosophy must begin with a "realistic" description of the nature of man. For Hobbes such a portrayal features man as competitive, contentious, and endlessly questing for power. Enmity among men leads inevitably to "a perpetual contention for Honours, Riches and Authority." Man is civilized only by his abiding fear of mortal danger. The natural condition of humankind is one of endemic conflict. Fear of violent death is the only motive powerful enough to overcome man's profoundly antisocial nature. Only man's reason can raise him out of this state of nature—the war of all against all. This natural condition suggests how men would behave if not subject to a single sovereign authority. We have seen that the monarchy is most likely to produce the peace and security which man's reason acknowledges as essential for protecting him from violent death.

Hobbes's depiction of the transition from a state of nature to a social state or civil society emphasized scaling down the claims of the heroic and separating virtue from politics. The Aristotelian argument that a *polis* must care for the virtue of its citizens else there would be mere association and no community within the walls of the city had little appeal to Hobbes. The laws of nature were essentially maxims of prudence. Man reflecting on his own experience discovers that if he is to have peace, he ought to obey certain rules and regulations. Civil society emerges out of the contest between the "compulsion of natural desires and the commandments of natural reason." In his Epistle Dedicatory to *De Cive* (1642), he states:

> And I found the reason was, that from a community of goods there must needs arise contention, whose enjoyment should be greatest. And from that contention all kinds of calamities must unavoidably ensue, which by the instinct of nature every man is taught to shun. Having therefore thus arrived at two maxims of human nature: the one arising from the *concupiscible* part, which desires to appropriate to itself the use of those things in which all others have a joint interest; the other proceeding from the *rational*, which teaches every man to fly a contra-natural dissolution, as the greatest mischief which can arrive to nature: which principles being laid down, I seem from them to have demonstrated by a most evident connexion, in this little work of mine, first, the absolute necessity of leagues and contracts, and thence the rudiments both of moral and of civil prudence.[41]

Indeed, Hobbes illuminates the antisocial nature of man and neglects the prospect of his benevolence. Certainly man is not companionable nor is he a civil animal or social being; nor is society the innocent by-product of his gregariousness. Yet, whereas man is self-regarding and radically egoistic, Hobbes will not invoke the burdensome notion of Original Sin. Hobbes denies man's essential wickedness when he writes that "the Desires, and other Passions of Man are in themselves no Sin. No more are the Actions that proceed from those Passions till they know a Law that forbids them." In the state of nature "experiences are dreadful, so that passions which incline men to seek security are more compelling than those driving them to war." Nor does Hobbes despise the achievements of flawed and antisocial human beings. Instead he is rather prideful: "And this much for the ill condition, which man by mere Nature is actually placed in; though with a possibility to come out of it, consisting partly in the Passions and partly in Reason."[42]

The Hobbesian covenant prevails only because the "Desires and other Passions of men" such as the ruthless pursuit of wealth, glory and dominion are countered by those "other Passions which incline man to Peace." The civil victory is prompted by "Fear of Death: Desire of such things as are necessary to commodious living, and a Hope by their Industry to obtain them." For Hobbes this triumph was a one-time thing. Once the state was founded, men would somehow remain tamed and their pride held in check. There was no need for Hobbes to think in an ordinary fashion about the predicament of society when confronted with the aggressive pursuit of riches, fame, and power on the part of arrogant citizenry. For him all of society was political; the state of nature was no kind of society. Since man was not a social animal, he had little aptitude for society. But he must be divested of qualities acquired in a state of nature by being subjected to social discipline; without government man's lot would be intolerable. Covenants involving mutual confidence and trust were deemed unreasonable—that is, without prospect of being adhered to unless there was a power strong enough to enforce them. Hobbes's bleak estimate of human nature highlights man's antisocial proclivities. He viewed the species "man" with appropriate detachment, as a subject fit neither for tragedy and pathos nor for dignified regard. His aim was to investigate the movement of social relations with the same literal method and figurative telescope employed by a Galileo to chart motion in nature:

> For as in a watch, or some such small machine [an analogy by which nature as a whole was interpreted at that time—J.H.], the matter, figure and motion of the wheels cannot well be known, except it be taken insunder and viewed in parts; so to make a more curious search into the rights of states and duties of subjects, it is necessary, I say, not to take them insunder, but yet that they be considered as if they were dissolved; that is, that we rightly understand what the quality of human nature is, in what matter it is, in what not, fit to make up civil government, and how men must be agreed among themselves that intend to grow up into a well-grounded state.[43]

This detached stance allowed Hobbes to retain poise as he mapped the transition from a natural to a civil society. His distrust of similes and metaphors was a striking feature of his rhetoric, allowing for self-control and an impersonal, authorial voice. Unlike his thoughtful literary contemporaries, many of whom took an even bleaker view of human nature than did he, the author of *Leviathan* did not set himself above the human condition. That a paltry reckoning of man's capacity for generosity or benevolence (heroic social attitudes) was widely shared is itself one of the dominant features of the seventeenth-century literary scene. A pessimistic view of the human propensity for good was an essential element of that century's tragic vision. Hobbes might share part of this vision but not its dramatic posture. Civil society was surely not the creation of virtuous sociability or the result of sinful depravity: "We do not . . . by nature seek Society for its own sake, but that we may receive some honor or profit from it; those we desire primarily, that secondarily." The basic human drive is epitomized thus: " . . . all free congress ariseth either from mutual poverty or from vain glory. . . ." The causes for which men and women come together and take delight in each other's company are readily found:

> How, by what advice, men do meet, will be best known by observing those things which they do when they are met. For if they meet for traffic, it is plain every man regards not his fellow, but his business; if to discharge some office, a certain market-friendship is begotten, which hath more of jealousy in it than true love, and whence factions sometimes may arise, but good will never. . . .

Men and women band together for their own advantage, relating as it does either to the mind or the senses:

> But all the mind's pleasure is either glory (or to have a good opinion of one's self), or refers to glory in the end; the rest are sensual or conducing to sensuality. . . . All society therefore is either for gain or for glory. . . . But no society can be great or lasting which begins from vain glory. Because that glory is like honour; if all men have it no man hath it, for they consist in comparison and precellence. . . . Though

the benefits of this life may be much furthered by mutual help, . . . yet those may be
better attained to by dominion than by the society of others.

In scaling down human sociability and the play of heroic virtue Hobbes was not
attracted, as others were, to moralizing or to depth psychology. Instead he would
reflect on what was natural—dominion, not society. Without fear no society was
possible, only a bitter contest of each individual for power over others: "We must
therefore resolve, that the original of all great and lasting societies consisted not in
the mutual good will men had towards each other, but in the mutual fear they had
of each other."[44]

A reluctance to endorse the cult of heroic ideals was shared by many literati of
the first and second rank. They did not, however, participate in Hobbes's preoccupation with the examination of prospects for a new political ethic. Instead they
were concerned with depth analysis of the passions of an honor community and its
social ethos. Aristocratic pride was dissected and the quest for glory atomized
along with the numerous spectacles which gave these passions opportunities for
ample public expression. Already we have noted that Corneille's portrayal of the
play of heroic virtue was so extreme and its consequences so costly to its champions
that his tragedies may have contributed to the demotion of these very ideals among
subsequent dramatists. Racine evoked the aristocratic virtues only to find them de-
meaning rather than ennobling. In the French tragedies of the seventeenth century
the hero with his noble designs often brought catastrophe. And of course there was
Cervantes' Don Quixote who was a fool, if not a glorious madman.

VII

In France, the country in which the heroic ideal was most advanced, the literary
effort to record its derelictions was soon matched by sustained attempts to chronicle
the unforeseen consequences of vainglory, vanity, and the quest for reputation.
Ironically, the historical outcome of these so-called vices might yield social benefit.
Arguments against the cult of glory were shifted from the familiar terrain of theology and politics to that of psychology—both personal and social. A version of
human nature was postulated asserting that the craving for esteem and fame was
itself boundless and a constant of human nature. Not only was this thirst unquench-
able but, as we have noted, its outcome was unforeseeable. This riveting of literary
attention on the inexhaustible need of men and women for the approval of their
fellows led to a different charting of the ethical map. Perhaps those who deplored
this hunger for approbation had failed to realize that this so-called vice was itself
important for "the good order of society." Increasingly, literati defended this human trait as a vital source of energy without which men and women were likely to
be enfeebled. An ancient and honorable tradition of moral philosophy was retrieved
and augmented this inquiry into "human frailty." The twists and turns of these investigations were evidenced in dialogues concerning the sin of pride. The moralist
Jean la Placette, in his *Traité de l'orgueil* (1643), indicted pride as follows:

Everyone conceives of what others think of him as a second existence which he has in the public mind, the good and evil of which belong to him no less than the good and evil of the real and veritable being which he has in himself. Everyone is greatly occupied with adding all possible perfections to this second being; and this is the immediate object of all that we do to please [others] and to make ourselves esteemed. It is this that makes us so much love praise and manifestations of respect, as so many proofs of the perfection and the happiness of this imaginary being outside of us.

La Placette probably borrowed something of his critique from Blaise Pascal. Arthur Lovejoy, the premier twentieth-century historian of ideas, quotes Pascal's view of approbativeness as a type of "living-at-second-hand":

We are not content with the life we have in ourselves and with our own existence; we wish to live an imaginary life in the thought of others, and we consequently force ourselves to *appear*. We labor incessantly to embellish and preserve our imaginary being, and neglect the real one. And if we have tranquillity of mind or generosity or loyalty, we try to have it known, in order to attach these virtues to our *other*, imaginary being; and we would be willing to detach them from ourselves in order to attach them to the other. We should cheerfully be cowards in order to get the reputation of being brave.[45]

The desire not to live life "second-hand" appears to have been prompted in part by a recognition that the public self depended upon the esteem and approbation of others and was entirely imaginary and inauthentic. The critic and poet, Boileau, diagnosed this malady as the root cause of human misery. La Bruyère perceived that men wished to acquire virtue not for itself but for advantage. Similar judgments informed French vernacular prose and poetry from François La Mothe Le Vayer to La Rochefoucauld, yet there was a general problem: namely, there seemed to be no known cure for this malady. Boileau, in his *Epistle to Arnauld,* admitted that although a poet can make an audience conscious of this illness, he knows no prescription for its cure. To lament and decry the human passion for approbation was far simpler for authors than disproving its universality and social utility. Pascal, visiting the famous school at Port Royal, had the opportunity to witness an educational experiment in which an appeal to the pupils' pride was to be eliminated. He was compelled, after much reflection, to acknowledge that the trial had been a failure. In theory he despised the spoiling of children by telling them, "Oh, how well he speaks! Oh, how well he did that! What a good boy he is!" But the facts of human nature betrayed his lofty ethical stance: "The children of Port Royal, to whom this spur of envy and glory is not applied, *tombent dans la nonchalance* (fall into listlessness)."

Approbativeness, or the love of praise, and its derivative, self-esteem, may well have been an ignoble and irrational desire, but to say so in too bald a form posed impossible difficulties for Pascal and his paradox-loving contemporaries. The dilemma posed by an analysis of the moral implications of *noblesse* mesmerized seventeenth-century French literati. The *recherche de la gloire* was the basest thing in man, but it was just this which was also the mark of excellence. The explanation was complex: the desire for approbation signified that one did acknowledge an implicit appeal to reason; reason in this case being located in the impersonal judgment of others. Mistaken or not, the quest suggested a belief in the existence of a publicly validated norm. Ironically, this craving for praise implied an irrepressible and involuntary recognition "both of the authority of reason and its presence in some degree in other men; and it is also the unconscious disclosure of a desire to conform to it in oneself." Pascal observed in the *Pensées,* at what personal cost it is impossible to know:

> The greatest baseness of man is the pursuit of glory. But it is also the greatest mark of his excellence; for whatever possessions he may have on earth, whatever health and essential comfort, he is not satisfied if he has not the esteem of men. He values human reason so highly that, whatever advantages he may have on earth, he is not content if he is not also ranked highly in the judgment of man. This is the finest position in the world. Nothing can turn him from that desire, which is the most indelible quality of man's heart.[46]

Would it be overbold to suggest that *la recherche de la gloire*—that *plus grande bassesse*—was being converted by some mysterious chemistry into a mark of excellence, thus rendering a quality intrinsically evil into one of social worth? It is well to remember that Pascal in his *Pensées* was addressing a worldly audience composed in part of skeptics and *libertins,* and, therefore, spoke their language when discussing heroic virtues. One might invoke yet another paradox advanced by Pascal to suggest the unforeseen consequences of the play of human passions born of the mixed nature of man: "The greatness of man even in his concupiscence, to have known how to tease from it an admirable arrangement and to have drawn from it so beautiful an order." Contemporary followers of Pascal such as the Jansenists Pierre Nicole and Jean Domat proffered the religiously disquieting insight that a society could adhere round the sinful passion of self-love and its offspring, self-interest. Self-interest could be more efficacious than charity or benevolence in holding society intact. Indeed, the terms "interest" and "interests" and "self-love" now occupied primacy of place in the writings of French moralists. An ever more detailed analysis of the human passions was also the object of tragedy, comedy, and romance; there too *intérêt* and *amour propre* were matters of abiding concern. The quest for the many ways in which *les vertus* lost themselves within the public world of varied interests was to be compared with the ways in which mighty waves are dissipated in the sea.[47]

Descartes in his *Traité des Passions,* with its naturalistic determinism, highlighted the role played by the "humours" on the human will. For Descartes, unlike Pascal, God and divine providence were not players in this great drama. Nor did Descartes make a strenuous effort to underline the misery of the individual so that he or she might be inspired to place themselves into a state or condition whereby they could profit from God's grace. Moralists such as La Rochefoucauld worked to establish a context for this naturalistic determinism. One can argue that La Rochefoucauld was prompted by his own experience to undertake a wide-ranging approach to the play of the passions as a consequence of involvement in the political and religious controversies of the time. His *Mémoires* disclose a tangled and troubled personal odyssey. As a Frondeur caught in the civil wars at mid-seventeenth century, he witnessed infidelities and betrayals, cowardice, and victory through military accident sufficient to disabuse him of chivalric explanations of history and the ways in which political battles were won and wars lost. His *Maximes* provided a social context for the naturalistic, deterministic account of the passions.

Descartes's heroism of the spirit served to activate his almost military plan aimed at the conquest of wisdom. Like others of his time he simplified moral philosophy by centering morality on magnanimity. The heroic *vertu* of generosity set apart a *race* of great souls from *races des âmes basses.* For La Rochefoucauld, acts of generosity were suspect: always at the base was *amour propre,* not so much a vice as a "biological factor in the human make-up." La Rochefoucauld saw little likelihood for the exercise of any such heroic virtue of generosity that would separate the *race* of great-souled men from their small-minded inferiors. His study of the passions was at best illuminated by a darkling light. What set the passions in motion in human society and what were the consequences was concisely diagrammed by this bitter-sweet moralist: "That which men have called friendship (*amitié*) is but *une société, un menagement reciprocque d'intérêts et qu'un echange de bons offices: ce n'est enfin, qu'un commerce* where self-love always gains something for itself." One cannot readily escape self-serving gestures and relationships: "*L'intérêt* speaks in all sorts of languages, even that of disinterestedness." He compares "self-love" to a body "deprived of vital spirit, blind and deaf to the world which comes to life almost miraculously when touched by the right stimulus of its *intérêt.*"[48]

Since social life was a war of multiple deceptions, little space remained for disinterested feelings. Love was little more than a passion to dominate and possess. Courage, goodness, and humility were but refinements of egoism. Vanity and interest, not generosity, were the motives for the bestowal of charity, praise, favor, and gifts. The passions had a depth not to be fathomed. *La civilité* was a desire of the individual to be esteemed as "polished." Gratitude concealed secret envy. The language of the marketplace was employed by La Rochefoucauld to contrast the "apparent integrity of an even social exchange and the real incommensurability of the hidden motives of each of the parties to the transaction." Intelligence was no longer at the service of truth but was a form of *habileté.* One's worldly advantage was furthered by planning one's actions in a careful and orderly manner. This was not to be confused with finesse which, in the author's view, was a rather contemptible variety of "intellectual nimbleness." Vice could be an asset if used in the service of the "commerce de la vie."

The paradox was that from *amour propre* stemmed the alleged virtues of the desire for justice, love of truth and courage. Out of vanity and a desire for esteem one trafficked in noble gestures and seemingly altruistic actions. At one level the individual was relieved of the burden of heroic virtue and claims of the cult of obligation. Yet, vaunting self-regard produced unanticipated consequences for the community. From so-called base motives emerged deeds of generosity and charity, but here, too, subtle distinctions were required: the "commerce" of the assemblage of "honnêtes gens" could best be compared to a harmonious piece of music—elegant and pleasing. The "arte de vivere" was ultimately an esthetic, and while it was true that private vices could be converted into public benefit, this moral chemistry was radically inadequate to insure the order of society. At best one might argue that elegance and harmony served to embroider the fabric of society, not to secure it. If society was that form of organization wherein lies, intrigue, and cheating triumphed—a world without honor or generosity—then constraints and royal authority were the only remedies. If men were dominated by their passions, how else to secure order?[49]

La Rochefoucauld, Hobbes, and a battery of moralists worked to reduce the virtues and passions through infinite regress into a form of *amour propre*. Men could be governed but certainly not reformed. Pascal had read Hobbes and reviewed the English philosopher's findings in light of the pessimistic views of the Jansenist Port-Royal circle. Pierre Nicole, a fellow believer, also followed the dark path blazed by St. Augustine into the heart of man, but with a twist. Pascal had grudgingly acknowledged that from the very vices of men emerged those self-interested arrangements which constituted a society. Nicole went further: in his "De la charité et de l'amour propre," he observed, paradoxically, that vanity so nearly imitates works of charity that there is no difference in their social effect. Such a society generated by vanity and self-interest was still in Nicole's eyes and in God's eyes corrupt. Yet it was a society organized on new principles and he would give a fuller account of it than did Pascal:

> Entirely to reform the world, that is to say to banish from it all vices and all the grosser disorders . . . one would only need, given the absence of charity, that men should possess an enlightened self-interest. . . . However corrupted such a society might be within and to the eyes of God, there need be nothing lacking to it in the way of being well regulated . . . and what is even more wonderful is that although it would be entirely animated and moved by self-love, self-love would nowhere appear in it, and although it is entirely devoid of charity, one would see everywhere only the form and characteristic of charity.[50]

Nicole was an essayist, an educator, a moral polemicist, and a Jansenist who taught and organized religious schools for children of aristocrats. His intellectual life was bound with this religious group and he composed, with the Jansenist apologist Antoine Arnauld, the textbook *Port Royal Logic* (1662), which was to remain in use for generations. Just before this, he had collaborated with Pascal in the preparation of his *Provincial Letters* (1656–57), which proved devastating to Jesuitical casuistry. The play of wit in this work startled and delighted its cultivated readers. The Jesuits were mocked for their easy morality and infinite talent for justifying the derelictions of human beings: Jesuit or Molinistic theology held a buoyant estimate of the human capacity to understand and select the good. But Nicole and Pascal were made of sterner stuff. Nicole was a reader of Hobbes, taking to heart the English philosopher's version of what St. Augustine's fallen man would be like if there were neither political restraint nor sovereign authority to hamper vicious ambition and twisted desires. Hobbes, however, proffered no vision of what men might achieve with God's grace. The Englishman was perhaps more in tune with the founder of Jansenism, Cornelius Jansen (1585–1638), bishop of Ypres, whose views on grace and salvation were stern and rigorous. But for Nicole and possibly Pascal, these bleak conclusions were unattractive for political reasons.

It goes without saying that such a pessimistic doctrine was contrary to contemporary Catholic teaching, but more relevant was the fact that this harsh assessment of man in spiritual bondage placed the adherents of Jansenism in political danger. The Hobbesian argument was strong medicine, contending that in order to counter man's selfish and depraved nature, it was essential that he be held under the thumb of royal authority. If Nicole accepted this diagnosis, this would require that the Jansenists submit to a crown most unfavorable to their cause; therefore, he was required to do a quick-step. What Hobbes had failed to appreciate was that despite the dominance of self-love in human nature, divine providence was benevolent. Although few souls were saved, self-love did ape the work of grace-given charity. This replication, as was suggested in the above quotation from Nicole, is so precise that none were in a position to perceive the exact motive at its source—not even the actor himself. Since this was so, it was possible to have a form of governmental authority less authoritarian than that posited by Hobbes.

Nicole was perhaps the first to offer a theory of what has since been called "unintended consequences." Succinctly put, the theory adumbrates the notion that the actions of selfish persons have results far distant from those intended by the historical agent. By embracing this position, he translated Hobbes's conception of society, which was purely political, into something very different: that something occupied a zone between state and individual and might properly be deemed Civil Society. Leo Strauss, the modern-day political philosopher, defined civil society as that whole within which men and women lived life. This was, then, the zone or space in which humans conducted their social transactions, commerce, business, and the varied negotiations of ordinary life. Here exchange and ritual of family life, and all forms of social interaction, as well as property transactions, were initiated and consummated.[51]

Unintentionality, while pursuing selfish ends, allowed men to contribute to the welfare of others despite base motives. As we observed, human selfishness mimicked Christian charity, thereby reducing the need for absolute monarchy. A civil society could then be described as one in which public order and civic decency were leading features. Nicole was to write:

> The fear of death is thus the first tie that binds together *civil* society and the first check on self-love; this is what forces men, whatever they may say, to obey the law and makes them forget those grand schemes of domination to the point that in most people they almost cease to arise, as it is obvious that they cannot possibly succeed.
>
> Open violence being thus out of the question, men have no choice but to search for other means and to use artifice instead of force; and all they can do is to attempt to satisfy the self-love of those whom they need, instead of tyrannizing it.

Some try to serve [self-love's] interests; others use flattery to win it over. One gives in order to be given. This is the mainspring and foundation of all business transacted among men, which is now taking a thousand forms; for trade is not only a matter of merchandise given for other merchandise or for money but also one of labor, services, attentions, and civilities; all of this is exchanged either for things of the same nature or for more concrete goods, as, for instance, when one obtains actual advantages through mere friendly words.

By means of this trade, then, all of life's needs are somehow met without involving charity. Hence there is no reason that in states that have no place for charity because the true religion is banished from them one would not live as peacefully, safely, and comfortably as if one were in a republic of saints.

Fear of violent death was, as Hobbes had contended, surely the first principle of civil society and the premier check on blatant egoism. Yet self-love was resourceful, learning to make itself useful to others through civility, flattery, and services; in this way it was able to achieve its ends. Material interest and cupidity were, then, the secondary ties of civil society. Finally, neither fear nor interest would suffice and human sociability would be triggered by the concupiscent motive—strongest of all the social passions—the quest for the love and esteem of one's fellows. This was the most strenuous, the subtlest and finest social impulse of them all. Self-love, as we have noted, imitates perfect charity yielding a morality of "human decency" (*l'honnêteté humaine*). Sanctity and *l'honnêteté* appeared to mirror one another. If one listened to the self-effacing accounts of the great commanders Condé and Turenne of their military successes, rendered with the same modesty and forebearance as St. Louis's description of his holy crusade, the listener would discern how close was the resemblance of decency to saintliness. Although Nicole, as we have seen, never pronounced the play of *amour propre* morally good, he did not deny that enlightened self-love and concupiscence worked to weave social bonds necessary to any civil society. The flawed miracle of civil society required an ample landscape for the passions, not just the narrow territory of fear that Hobbes had reconnoitered.[52]

Nicole's *Moral Essays* were widely admired and widely read. Appreciated by Mme. de Sévigné, they were translated by John Locke for the Countess of Shaftesbury. We noted that Locke, in the initial sentence of *Two Treatises of Government* (1690), praised the generous temper of the English nation but concluded that such generosity was not to be presumed upon. Already in La Rochefoucauld's writings we see an awareness of the narrowing of the definition of "interest." In his preface to the second edition of his *Maximes*, he offers "Advice to the Reader":

By the word interest I understand not always an interest concerned with wealth (*un intérêt de bien*), but most frequently one that is concerned with honor or glory.[53]

This was the single point the author made in the short preface suggesting that he was concerned that readers were all too likely to associate interest with material economic advantage rather than with the quest for acclaim and concern for reputation. This was a worry for La Rochefoucauld because it disvalued his relentless and generalized exposé of the vanity and illusion filling wretched man with fantasies of greatness. His savage descriptions were in danger of being trivialized if "interest" was narrowly defined and not viewed in the harsh light of day as the motive for seemingly generous and valorous actions. Nicole, La Rochefoucauld and a legion of other French moralists recognized the siren call of *amour propre* as an ontological blemish inseparable from human nature itself. The human condition was a type of bondage not to be easily explained by any restricted devotion to material advantage.

For La Rochefoucauld an unpretentious wisdom and pride in facing truth, even at one's own cost, offset his loathing and anguish at human wretchedness. By surveying the defects of man with such astonishing lucidity, it was possible to be persuasive on the necessity of certain traits for human preservation and the constitution of human society. In the very act of scaling down heroic virtues and obligations of benevolence and charity, one was required to explain that most beguiling of all paradoxes: How then were the bonds of society forged in the face of radical selfishness? Secondly: What was the genesis of civil society if altruism, benevolence and sympathy were so limited? Hobbes and the French moralists questioned ancient and modern formulations of the nature of sociability. Of course they were not the first to do so, nor were they alone in dissecting conceptions of self-interest in which all voluntary actions were perceived to be for the benefit of the agent. They relied on near contemporaries as varied as Machiavelli and Montaigne. For Machiavelli the central political question involved the development of tactics for converting citizen self-regard into concern for the common good. For the Montaigne of the earlier *Essays,* it was necessary to have a deity or Nature itself demonstrate what one should do or be required or induced to do "to live together decently." In his later *Essays* he took a more optimistic view: men were less wretched and less weak than he had supposed. Indeed, they were so constituted that it was possible for them to lead decent private lives "without external direction by expressing their own nature." Germane to our argument is the fact that Montaigne did not explore the possibility that this same experience of men would enable them "to constitute a morally satisfactory society."[54]

VIII

The insistence on the primacy of self-love had been a leading feature of classical natural-law thinkers from Aristotle to the Epicureans. In their judgment ethical theory could not gainsay this and remain convincing. In general there was agreement that self-love reflected the moral good of "responsible independence." Self-love did not undermine sociability but it was precisely because of the frailty of human existence that it served as a prop and support. Scottish "common sense" philosophers lauded Hugo Grotius (1583–1645) as the "immortal Hugo Grotius," and Adam Smith (1723–1790) hailed him as one of the great innovators in the field of natural jurisprudence. The Dutch lawyer, diplomat and humanist was also awarded this accolade on the grounds that he had "systematized the common-sense moralizing of the human race with the aid of the civil law's technical apparatus." Grotius had reviewed natural law jurisprudence and drew an innovative and crucial distinction between "perfect" and "imperfect" rights. Ordinary moral duties were demoted to the second rank. The quintessential right was marked as that of property. The restriction of the purview of government to the primary end of protecting this property culminated in a rearrangement of the theory of justice so that it gravitated around the planet of commerce rather than that of politics.

Two generations after the death of Grotius, Jean Barbeyrac (1674–1744) translated and annotated his principal writings into French and this rendition proved widely popular for legal studies and moral philosophy. The translator advanced the view, soon readily accepted, that the Dutch scholar had shattered the frozen wastes of the bootless disputes of Aristotelian scholasticism. He had prepared the path the science of morality was to follow even unto this day. Barbeyrac was correct, for Grotius's influence on state legislation and its enactment lasted well into the eighteenth-century. Grotius offered a compelling theory concerning basic human desires. Like Hobbes, he perceived men and women as self-interested yet capable of enjoying each other's company for its own sake. Grotius, like Hume of a later day, observed that human beings looked out for themselves, but against Hume, he held out for the persistent and natural (rather than acquired) human traits of sociability; all was not sweetness and light, however, since these traits might be social or antisocial. Society should be organized to take into consideration man's proclivity for engaging in conflict as well as his innate sociability. The guide to such an enterprise of social construction was natural law considered as the dictate of right reason and predicated on the human truth of sociability. The law of nature was founded on this essential trait, and for humans sociableness does not bear the requirement of blending all individuals into a social whole. Grotius contended that society aims at preserving what belongs to a person. He spoke in favor of "private ownership according to positive law." This included an individual's "life, limbs, and liberty." Through an elaborate argument he distinguishes between perfect moral qualities and imperfect moral qualities. The former are rights and give rise to legal rights. These include the following:

> . . . power, now over oneself, which is called freedom, now over others, as that of the father and that of the master over slaves; ownership either absolute, or less than absolute, as usufruct and the right of pledge; and contractual rights, to which on the other side contractual obligations correspond.

At the other pole are the imperfect moral qualities and these are "associated with those virtues which have as their purpose to do good to others, as generosity, compassion and foresight in matters of government." Therefore, while natural law is founded on the natural sociableness of men, this trait is delimited:

> . . . it is not . . . contrary to the nature of society to look out for oneself and advance one's own interests, provided the rights of others are not infringed.[55]

In general we notice a move away from stern duties and compelling obligations as legally enforceable. Grotius, for example, rejected an adage redolent of the "most humane sentiments of the medieval world": that property has its duties. The position of influential jurists such as Grotius indicated commitment to a less "interdependent social world." The right of necessity had been defined in part by positing a dilemma: "If not starvation, then crime." This terse judgment now required qualification: property was secured unless dire need forced the impoverished to appropriate that which belonged to another. The right of necessity was therefore limited to dire need and did not apply if the necessity was avoidable.

It should be noted, however, that Grotius did concede that the systems of property had a natural limit. Private property represented the final stage in the conversion of that complex form of stewardship termed "use right." Since the system of private property was designated for the more efficient preservation of humankind, it would still be essential to recognize the right of necessity. This ancient prerogative, to make use of things belonging to another, further atrophied with the influential jurist and moral philosopher, Samuel Pufendorf, and of course John Locke. Finally, it was virtually eclipsed as David Hume and Adam Smith rejected the natural law framework. A point we shall return to subsequently is the growing confidence of leading jurists and moral philosophers in the virtues and benefits of commercial society—highest of all being the remarkable capacity of business and industry to diminish economic necessity. This optimistic forecast was subscribed to by students of political economics who predicted that if property holders' rights were strengthened, and a panoply of customary obligations and duties made voluntary, then such traditional claims as those emanating from the right of necessity would become obsolete. Again we observe a reduction of requirements of generosity, charity, mutuality, and the many other demanding virtues. These were considered "aptitudes" and, as such, were not enforceable at law. Imperfect rights embellished life and society but were not indispensable to it. Further implications of the demands for beneficence and their softening will be considered shortly. For present purposes, it might be well to recall that the moral treatises pertaining to this subject were themselves undergoing transformation from a collection of aphorisms to a comprehensive and ordered survey. Finally, we might note that a marked tendency was evident in the seventeenth and early eighteenth centuries to transform the language of duty into a vocabulary of rights. Here we notice telling examples of the strain between the familiar and the novel ethos—the old and the new. Premodern natural law doctrine instructed men and women in their duties. Where they dealt with rights (which was seldom), they reckoned them to be derivative from the duties of men and women. Clearly, the accent shifted from natural duties to natural rights. Classic monographs by historians of political thought, such as Otto von Gierke and J. N. Figgis, have underscored the increasing attention given to rights in the late seventeenth and early eighteenth centuries. This they judged to be unprecedented in the history of Western political thought. The message had its heralds in Hobbes, Grotius, and Pufendorf. By the late eighteenth century with Immanuel Kant the question had become: Why is moral philosophy referred to as the doctrine of duties and not the doctrine of rights? Edmund Burke was to add, with his customary sharpness, "The little catechism of the rights of man is soon learned; and the inferences are in the passions."[56]

IX

The debate on the nature of obligation then took center stage among seventeenth-century jurists and moral philosophers from Grotius and Samuel Pufendorf to Gershom Carmichael (1672–1729) and John Locke. Moral philosophers endeavored to shed the prolix style of their recent forebears; the latter had shown little reluctance to catalogue a vast array of duties of which they claimed direct knowledge. Natural law jurists such as Pufendorf reduced all moral obligation to one comprehensive duty posited by the law of nature: ". . . that each man ought, so far as in him lies to promote and preserve a peaceable sociableness with others." This obligation of sociability was deduced by Pufendorf from man's needs, insecurity, and undeniable talent for mischief. The worst mischief would prevail if stubborn, selfish, and quarrelsome men were not united in society under an absolute power. Soon strong opposition to this stark judgment was voiced even by Pufendorf's keenest admirers. That sociability required the absolute power of a ruler over subjects was a proposition to be rigorously contested.[57]

Scottish and English criticism on this issue was strenuous and persistent. The duty of sociability tended to be defined in terms of the obligation to respect the natural rights of others. Gershom Carmichael, regent of the University of Glasgow under the old system (before 1694), and then the first professor of moral philosophy at that thriving intellectual center, was a great admirer of Pufendorf and was to translate and annotate the continental natural jurist's *On the Duties of Men and Citizens* (Glasgow, 1724). In the main, he was satisfied with the text's central arguments, but he did dissent on the vital issue: Natural right was not based on obligation to a superior; nor must human rights be given over to a higher power in order for citizens to secure the benefits of social life. Sociability was, then, as we have noted, defined in terms of the obligation to respect the rights of others. Variations on the theme of sociability were advanced predicated upon natural instincts, affection, empathy, sympathy, or sentiment. Locke of course had influenced Carmichael and many others in that generation when challenging absolute authority and the duties of subjects. Civil society had, in general terms, come to signify relations between rulers and subjects. Locke contended that absolute monarchy and the exercise of absolute royal power over subjects was inconsistent with the existence of civil society. For this he was to be attacked by David Hume, a great appreciator of French life and culture. Given the Terror and the Jacobins, Locke's views on this matter may hold up better than Hume believed. Carmichael, whose writings have been judged "the bond which connects the old philosophy with the new in Scotland," was, as we have noted, the most expert commentator on Pufendorf. He introduced *On the Duties of Men and Citizens* as a centerpiece of Scottish moral philosophy and was insistent in urging his readers and students to appreciate the text in the light of improvements in political philosophy introduced by

Locke. Especially favored was the Lockean defense of the individual against the magistrate:

> In his discussions of the state of nature, of the family, of master and servant relations, of the causes of civil society, of the duties of magistrates and the rights of subjects Carmichael amended Pufendorf's texts by notes, supplements and appendices which provided the reader with an understanding of the duties of man and the citizen which was much more insistent on the rights of individuals and less indulgent towards the power of magistrates than the text of Pufendorf; the authority most frequently invoked for these amendments was Locke's *Second Treatise.*[58]

Lockean improvements continued to shape revisions of Pufendorf's text and other juridical writings. The work of Carmichael was continued by his successor, Francis Hutcheson (1694–1746), who was in the Chair of Moral Philosophy at Glasgow. Especially influential in this intellectual endeavor was Locke's definition of civil society and its legitimation:

> Hence it is evident, that *Absolute Monarchy,* which by some Men is counted the only Government in the World, is indeed *inconsistent with Civil Society,* and so can be no Form of Civil Government at all. For the *end of Civil Society,* being to avoid, and remedy those inconveniences of the State of Nature, which necessarily follow from every Man's being Judge in his own Case, by setting up a known Authority, to which every one of that Society may Appeal upon any Injury received, or Controversie that may arise, and which every one of the Society ought to obey; where-ever any persons are, who have not such an Authority to Appeal to, for the decision of any difference between them, there those persons are still *in the State of Nature.* And so is every *Absolute Prince* in respect of those who are under his *Dominion.* (italics mine)

An absolute prince judges his own case, as indeed must all men in "the State of Nature." He substitutes the rule of will and force for that of reason. These societies were structured by force, not by right. This did not signify, however, that there would be no peace, no justice, no means for political and social cooperation. That was not true to human nature, even in a society ruled by a prince. The state of nature with its "immanent sociability" and play of human interdependence places Locke closer to Aristotle than some of his critics believe. This is not to suggest that Locke had confidence in man's beneficence or capacity for disinterested action. But it is important to recognize that society never totally transcends the state of nature, nor is that condition without its social impulses toward cooperation. If civil society (its synonym for Locke was *political society*) is dismantled, men will still live in an organized community and custom, habit, and education will promote mutuality. Indeed, when civil society comes into being, citizens will bring their prior social understanding and experience into new areas of political life. Locke conjectures as to the reason why accounts do not survive for that time when men lived in a state of nature: "Government is every where antecedent to Records, and Letters seldome come in amongst a People, till a long continuation of Civil Society has, by other means necessary Arts provided for their Safety, Ease, and Plenty."[59]

When men have no appeal against any individual, no matter what his station, this society is out of "Bounds of the Civil Society which they are of." They cannot be protected against any harm they might receive and there is no appeal. It is then that they are likely to consider themselves to be "in a State of Nature, in respect of him, whom they find to be so; and to take care as soon as they can, to have that Safety and Security in Civil Society, for which it was first instituted, and for which only they entered into it." In the state of nature men might find a "good and virtuous individual of Natural Authority" to arbitrate disputes and quarrels. He might be himself upright, wise, and impartial, but in the next generation his successor could be of a very different stripe. ("No man in Civil Society can be exempt from the laws of it.") The people would find that their properties were no longer secure "under the Government, as then it was (whereas Government has no end but the preservation of Property) could never be safe nor at rest, nor think themselves in Civil Society, till the legislature was placed in collective Bodies of Men, call them Senate, Parliament, or what you please."[60]

When one comes to define property, the range is wide and not simply confined to material goods. Man belongs to himself and thus is not subject to the arbitrary will of another. The field of definition is extended to "Life, Liberty and Estate." The idea of property includes one's person, "the labour of his body, the work of his hands." One's life and liberty belong to oneself: "Every one is bound to preserve himself." Property has a dynamic quality; in order to grow and survive, individuals must acquire particular material goods. Like Grotius, Locke believed that legal relations mimic or mirror natural law. If the world had been given to humans in common by God, how did private property come about? How did it arise in the original community? The answer for Locke was that it emerged through the improving acts of human labor and this in turn resulted in benefits conferred upon economic life. Through the self-preserving activities (labor) of humans, private property originated: "Labour in the beginning gave a right of property." Civil or political society developed in order to avoid mischief and contests over property. Men "by Compact and Agreement settled the Property which Labour and Industry began." Conceptions of property were an extension of this natural process.[61]

Locke offered a historical account of the origins and development of private property. The social and economic import of this narrative disclosed that the poor as well as the rich were benefited by this process of transformation. True, the introduction of money in the form of precious metals made large estates possible. Great landholders produced vendable surpluses. This did make for great inequality in wealth; however, this did not harm the poor but advantaged them. By working the estates of the rich they were better clothed and sheltered than they had been in the free but impoverished state of a "pre-money society." Increased productivity resulting from liberating the enormous capacity of humankind was itself the consequence of the removal of the restraint whereby only the most immediate needs were satisfied. Apportioning of property was linked in general to some type of material improvement. Here Locke's narrative breaks, for modern legal relations were to be determined by legislatures which were themselves constituted by the consent of the governed. No radical alteration of the ownership of private property would

gain consent, since the productivity and wealth of the people depended on possessions being secure and safe.

Locke believed that the introduction of money was the mark of an advanced civilization. The commercial society of his day had the inherent capacity to improve
the condition of its poorer members: witness the increased productivity when
wasteland was converted to farming for profit. In a celebrated passage from *The
Second Treatise,* Locke compares the Americas with the England of his day:

> There cannot be a clearer demonstration of any thing, than several Nations of the
> *Americans* are of this, who are rich in land and poor in all the Comforts of Life;
> whom Nature having furnished as liberally as any other people, with the materials of
> Plenty, i.e. a fruitful Soil, apt to produce in abundance, what might serve for food,
> rayment, and delight; yet for want of improving it by labour, have not one hundreth
> part of the Conveniences we enjoy: And a King of a large and fruitful Territory there
> feeds, lodges, and is clad worse than a day Labourer in *England.*[62]

Efforts to triumph over the "right of necessity"—which Locke understood in
terms of charity and limitations placed on property—involved new strategies. Like
Pufendorf and other jurists and moral philosophers, Locke believed that incentives
must be given to promote industriousness and avoid laziness, carelessness, and in-
competence. To this end civil society was to ensure private property and justice so
that the fruits of human labor would be safeguarded. This in itself was encourage-
ment enough to stimulate human efforts. Human beings are vulnerable and therefore easily hurt and must have material goods in order to survive. The duty to
preserve oneself was justified by holy writ and reason. Locke derived human actions from self-love (the desire for pleasure and avoidance of pain), while simultaneously disposing of the notion of innate ideas. In their stead he elaborated a
"sensational" psychology and epistemology. This, in the view of influential contemporaries, including Shaftesbury, his own pupil, signified a denial of moral virtue. Locke contended that men were not born actually knowing a certain number of
truths: for him, morality was not given but discovered. In *An Essay Concerning
Human Understanding* (1690) Locke avers that

> . . . the Goodness of God hath not been wanting to Men without such Original Im-
> pressions of Knowledge or Ideas stamped on the Mind: since he hath furnished Man
> with those Faculties, which will serve for the sufficient discovery of all things req-
> uisite to the end of such a Being.

Moral laws can be discovered by reason, and by reason Locke meant not intuitive
reason but "the discursive faculty of the mind which advances from things known
to things unknown and argues from one thing to another in a definite and fixed
order of propositions."[63]

Locke's critics were legion: there must, they argued, be a system of moral truths
which men accept simply "by virtue of the make up of the human mind." One of
these early challengers, Henry Lee, compiled a catalogue of duties, from preserving one's life to honoring promises and contracts. Practical principles were perceived as moral precepts, and only if the former were innate could one be certain
of a moral law governing all individuals:

For, if the Author of Nature has contributed nothing to our gaining the Knowledge of them in the original Constitution of our Souls and Bodies; but left us wholly in the dark, wholly at liberty to gain our Knowledge of them from *Experience* and *Conversation;* then the *Laws of God,* may be words interpreted to signifie only such Rules of Action as every man voluntarily makes to himself, and shapes by the mutable Sentiments, and exemplary Practice of his own *Familiars* or *Superiors.*[64] (italics mine)

Thomas Burnet also contended against Locke's dismissal of innatism. He argued that by means of the "natural conscience," the mind was capable of apprehending at an instant the moral worth of things:

This I am sure of, that the Distinction, suppose of Gratitude and Ingratitude, Fidelity and Infidelity, Justice and Injustice, and such others, is as sudden without any Ratiocination, and as sensible and piercing, as the difference I feel from the Scent of a Rose, and of Asso-foetida . . . it rises as quick as any of our Passions, or as Laughter at the sight of a ridiculous Accident or Object.

The anonymous *Dialogues Concerning Innate Principles* announced that "conscious internal sentiments on which such moral propositions are based is innate":

When we are told that *benevolence* is *pleasing;* that *malevolence* is *painful;* we are not convinced of these truths by reasoning, nor by forming them into propositions: but by an appeal to the innate internal affections of our souls: and if on such an appeal, we could not feel within the sentiment of benevolence, and the peculiar pleasure attending it; and that of malevolence and its concomitant pain; not all the reasoning in the world could ever make us sensible of them, or enable us to understand their nature.[65]

Locke does concur that there are certain common notions clearly true and to which a rational person must assent. It is so that "men must repent of their sins" and that "virtue is the best worship of God and that sin is the contrary." But these tell us nothing about the type of acts which fall under the rubrics of virtue and vice.

Locke aimed at a science of morality, and to this end he believed that an account of the psychology of moral action must be rendered. The issue to be resolved was: what drove humans or impelled them to moral action? And what were the wellsprings? All humans strive only for their own pleasure; this they do sometimes by an indirect and zigzag flight from "painful uneasiness." However, since humans desire praise for their acts, this brings into play what Locke termed the "Law of Opinion." Concern for reputation and esteem can lead to the disinterested pursuit of the "sociable." This was something of a maxim of natural law. In general, natural law posited the centrality of self-love, but sociability was perceived as not incompatible with self-love. There was of course a tie-in: human nature mirrored the laws of nature.

However susceptible humans were to the "law of opinion," and whether self-love was the initial trigger for action, remained issues for lively debate. Whether self-regard and egoism were compatible with sociability remained a matter of persistent interest and even "scientific" inquiry. Locke was accused by his adversaries of stinting the pull of the social and reducing its circumference when he rendered it congruent with life, liberty, and estate. This triad, they argued, was only the meagerest representation of the domain of human sociability.[66]

Locke's favorite pupil, Anthony Ashley Cooper, the third Earl of Shaftesbury (1671–1713), while acknowledging the debt to his mentor, proved to be an effective critic. Locke's efforts to do away with innate ideas and thus derive all human action from self-love were judged by Shaftesbury to be pernicious in the extreme, for he was more of a Platonist than an empiricist in his epistemology. Since Locke denied that vice and virtue were naturally implanted in human minds, they could not be anything in themselves. Locke subverted the force of all moral virtue, cancelling sociability and altruism; in its stead he would substitute the bleak winter of blatant self-interest. For Shaftesbury virtue was something innate in the human mind and was to be perceived by "a special sense"—the moral sense. The reality of moral sense or fundamental benevolence was a principle in human nature. In Shaftesbury's view, Locke would account for morals through mere fashion and experience, thus denying their objectivity.

Shaftesbury understood the risks inherent in spawning a vocabulary of fellow-concern and sociability. In a recent study of eighteenth-century common-sense moralism, David Norton sums up Shaftesbury's reactions to the dangerous deflation of the language of virtue:

> Such words as *courage, friendship, love,* and *public interest,* words which seem to denote altruistic acts or tendencies, are found to mean [on the self-love view] nothing different from their apparent opposites, for all acts and tendencies are similarly motivated and hence all are at bottom alike.[67]

The power of natural affection and generosity, along with a multitude of teeming social passions, was under siege. In particular, man's natural bent toward benevolence had been challenged by that foe of virtue—John Locke. Shaftesbury was to write:

> It was Mr. Locke that struck the home blow: for Mr. Hobbes' character and base slavish principles in government took off the poison of his philosophy. 'Twas Mr Locke that struck at all fundamentals, threw all order and virtue out of the world and made the very ideas of these . . . unnatural and without foundation in our minds. . . . virtue, according to Mr Locke, has no other measure, law, or rule, than fashion and custom; morality, justice, equity, depend only on law and will. . . . And thus neither right nor wrong, virtue nor vice, are anything in themselves; nor is there any trace or idea of them naturally imprinted on human minds. Experience and our catechism teach us all.

Shaftesbury contended, then, that moral distinctions were rendered not by reason but by moral sense:

> No sooner are actions viewed, no sooner the human affections and passions discerned (and they are most of them as soon discerned as felt) than straight an inward eye distinguishes and sees the fair and shapely, the amiable and admirable, apart

from the deformed, the foul, the odious or the despicable. How is it possible therefore not to own that as these distinctions have their foundation in nature, the discernment itself is natural and from nature alone?[68]

The charges against Locke devolved around the issue of his failure to appreciate the abundant ramifications of the social nature of human beings. In the view of certain of Locke's leading critics, social passions were irreducible, serving as springs for the psychology of action. Sociability itself was a construct of the social passions. The passions need not be destructive or archaic forces, Hobbes ("that ablest and witty philosopher") notwithstanding. Yet at the same time, Shaftesbury himself was open to the charge that moral obligation and a sense of duty resolved themselves or, better still, dissolved into, nothing more than "social affection and natural temper." Shaftesbury was to be regularly vulgarized by novelists and moralists with his psychology of "good affections," translated into an evasion of sterner ethical requirements. Sir John Hawkins (1719–89), a very "unclubbable" but knowledgeable literary critic and musicologist, scorned Shaftesbury's ethics:

> His [the novelist Henry Fielding] morality in respect that it resolves virtue into good affections in contradiction to moral obligations and a sense of duty, is that of Lord Shaftesbury vulgarized, and in a system of excellent use in palliating the vices most injurious to society. He was the inventor of the cant phrase, goodness of heart, which is every day used as substitute for probity . . . in short, he has done more towards corrupting the rising generation than any writer we know of.[69]

Locke himself had distinguished clearly between moral obligation and duty on the one side and one's reasons for fulfilling them on the other. The decisive reason for performing an act was that it would contribute to the agent's happiness or lessen his pain. Since the demands of morality may have an outcome negating the agent's pleasure, it was essential to have the moral law supported by sanctions promising reward or punishment. If moral notions were of the agent's making, did it not follow that if one did the right thing for reasons other than the right one, that the act would nonetheless be virtuous? If the reasons for acting were non-moral, why should one take into account the moral worth of an act? Locke's reply drew on theological considerations: even if acts in harmony with the moral perspective caused the agent to be unhappy, it would be reasonable for him to act virtuously because God had ordained that vice should be punished and virtue rewarded. Furthermore, in Locke's principal argument he will contend that conduct is right or wrong by dint of law promulgated by God and binding on all humankind. This law is objective and evidenced in God's creation—that is, human nature itself.

At the same time as Locke invoked a theological ethic, he also opted for legal sanctions to enforce obligation. He did not, however, strain after the higher reaches of moral notions, but rather distinguished between the ways in which an obligation bound a person: first, obligation bonds "effectively" when imposed by a rightful lawmaker; this is the formal cause of obligation. Secondly, the binding is a form of delimitation which dictates the "manner and measure of the obligation and our duty is nothing other than the declaration of that will [of the lawmaker], and this declaration by another name we call law. We are bound effectively by God, but His declaration of His will in natural laws delimits the obligation.'' Locke makes crucial distinctions. The duty not to commit murder or theft is absolute. Other obligations stand forever, dealing with sentiments ensconced in natural law, such as reverence for God, ''affection for parents [and] love of neighbours.'' Charity and its obligations emerge from special circumstances and are binding only when these are present. Finally, there are acts in which ''contingent preferences are expressed and which involve no direct obligation.'' An individual may talk about his neighbor as he pleases but is obliged not to lie when doing so.

Locke does not push for higher-level moral notions. True, human happiness is the end of morality but he does not argue that this translates into a requirement that the agent choose a course of action maximizing the well-being of the greatest number of his fellows. There are areas of conduct that are in themselves morally neutral. In the final reckoning, however, obligation and duty depend on the formal and material elements of the divine will. God has implanted the natural law in the hearts of men and women but He did not write it in their minds. Natural law is no mere bundle of innate ideas and must be discerned by rational cogitation and the experience of the senses.[70]

Shaftesbury had reflected on his teacher's opinions concerning morality and was dismayed by Locke's voluntarism. His reading of Locke confirmed the judgment that his mentor believed that God was totally free to fix moral laws for humans according to His unfettered will. This voluntaristic conception of God was vigorously repudiated by Shaftesbury. That there was no measure of morality except the will of God was a proposition he shunned. While in Amsterdam in 1698, Shaftesbury had met Pierre Bayle, then a French Huguenot refugee living in Holland. The Calvinist Bayle had been among the first to argue for the seeming paradox that a community of atheists could in the City of Man appear as virtuous and maintain the good order of society as well as a body constituted by the godly and religiously committed. As we have noted, this was in the spirit of Pascal and the rigorist tradition. The familiar question was raised: to what extent was the good order of society (to the degree that it existed) attributable to reason and virtue? The Augustinian mode of appraisal of human nature could not vouchsafe a confident ''yes.''

Did not atheism have its martyrs and did not atheists lead virtuous lives? Hence, given that law punished crime, a society of atheists could endure. A perfect Christian society could not sustain itself when in tight geographic proximity with its less upright neighbors. Spinoza was a virtuous atheist and the harmonious life of Epicurus and his disciples demonstrated that religion was not a necessary bond of society. It was not religion but law and self-interest that held society together. One recalls the controversial conjecture of Hugo Grotius in his ''Prolegomena'' to *On the Law of War and Peace* (1625), section 11, with its Latin ''etiamsi daremus,'' translated as ''even if we concede . . . that there is no God,'' and this is unthinkable, human society is indeed possible. Historians of political thought have charted the beginnings of this epochal change back to Hobbes. Some have contended that no pre-modern, ''so-called political atheist'' would deny that social life demanded the worship of and belief in gods or God. Edmund Burke highlighted this transformation with a pointed observation:

> Boldness formerly was not the character of atheists as such. They were even of a character nearly the reverse; they were formerly like the old Epicureans, rather an unenterprising race. But of late they are grown active, designing, turbulent, and seditious.

The defense of a society of "speculative atheists" ran counter to Locke's views. He would have tolerated pagans but excluded atheists as bad citizens on the ground that they could not be trusted to keep their oaths and sacred promises. For him, the very core of political society was trust. For Bayle and for Shaftesbury human actions were prompted more by social feeling than opinion. These passions or feelings need not be either destructive or archaic forces. Feelings, if not manipulated, need not divide the community; in fact, from them social affection could emanate. There was no theoretical justification for persecuting non-orthodox believers, since it was not possible to have a sure knowledge of the truths of faith. Men's opinions on matters of belief had no theoretical base. In any case, religious beliefs were of little significance in shaping morality, thus diversity was no substantial threat. Men do not live according to their principles but despite them. For example, Christians persecute other religions in the name of God although their principles proclaim fraternal love. Mohammedans, on the other hand, are more tolerant of religious diversity although their principles are less fraternal and more militant.[71]

Shaftesbury championed religious toleration and a moral psychology in which social feeling and natural affection displaced sterner and more heroic virtues. From these social passions, he argued, were knit the bonds of general society. He was among the first in England to broadcast the civilizing influence of literature, the arts, and philosophy. These engaged men's minds not toward separatist tendencies of sectarianism or political factionalism but toward a harmonious and cooperative style of life. The theme of culture in a civil society will be considered shortly, but for the present it should be noted that the role of the arts was enhanced at a historical moment when English political culture had only recently been sorely tested by civil war and religious strife. Again Shaftesbury led the way in stressing the place of art in civilizing society. For him modern discursive practice was to be modeled on the paradigm of the "urbane" conversation of gentlemen. A central objective of his *Characteristics of Men, Manners, Opinions, Times* (1711) was to demonstrate that neither the royal court nor the Anglican Church was an institution suitable for governing discursive practice. Nor was the one or the other looked to as a center of cultural production. The discipline necessary for good conversation between equals had been explicated over the sixteenth and seventeenth centuries in an abundance of manuals and pamphlets on civility. But by the late seventeenth and early eighteenth centuries in England, the cultural environment was no longer ordered by traditional institutions. New social and civil disciplines favored a model of politeness in which political partisanship and the zealous religious spirit would be tamed. Religious institutions were brought under civil control, and while religious sensibilities did not decline, they were subjected to social and civil restraint. New cultural forms and agencies were taking shape as the English elites abandoned the university.[72]

Questions pertaining to the definition of good and evil might well be translated from the idiom of theology and the discourse of civic humanism into the vocabulary of esthetics and psychology. For example, *virtù,* in the Machiavellian sense, was converted by Shaftesbury into *virtuosity,* with the ethical paragon represented by the virtuoso. A century earlier "virtuoso" meant someone who explored the secrets of nature. With Shaftesbury it became synonymous with good breeding. The esthetic dimension of morality was highlighted. Just as art ceased to be defined as a skill and came to be viewed as a special form of sensibility, so too *virtue* became a taste for the beautiful, the decent, the just, and the amicable—that which gave perfection to the character of the gentleman and philosopher.[73]

X

To reduce morality to self-love as Hobbes had done was repugnant to Shaftesbury. Such philosophical sleight-of-hand rendered fine moral distinctions meaningless. "Common sense" informs us of the value of benevolence, generosity, love, and friendship. These are real and to be prized as ethical features of everyday living. Locke had argued that the ultimate determinant of morals was the will of God. The laws of equity and standards of moral rectitude change at His pleasure. The voluntarists would have it that God would not be omnipotent were he not at liberty to dispense of these legal and ethical norms. When one peruses the corpus of Locke's writings, however, especially his discussions of education, this stern picture does not seem to hold. In fact, the philosopher speaks to and for a world in which moral ideas are governed by fashion and custom. His message appears to be one of adjustment to the norms of the society to which an individual belongs. What is esteemed as virtue and what is decried as vice are fixed by the standards of societies, clubs, or tribes. Convention and custom are the guide; therefore, ideas of order and virtue have no innate foundation in our minds. Thus, despite his invocation of God, Locke has denied the objectivity of morals.

Shaftesbury argued for the existence of a cognitive moral sense rather like that of man's esthetic sense of beauty. This innate moral faculty brings inner order to the mind and thus is like the order imposed on the world when one is composing a work of art. Each individual is an independent artist. In addition to Shaftesbury's confidence in a cognitive moral sense, he also trusted human sentiment to guide individuals to act appropriately. Self-awareness would alert the individual as to whether these sentiments were sufficient to direct actions into suitable or unsuitable channels. Stoic rather than Christian in language and spirit, he regarded the solution to ethical problems as resting in an interior space replete with human sentiment and charged with reflective self-awareness. The consequences of his "sentimentalist" stance, with its heavy emphasis on the internal movement of the psyche, led to an acceptance of external, social, economic, and political circumstance. The battleground, or better still the contest, was waged in the human soul, which was optimistically tilted toward the better parts of human nature. Against Shaftesbury, other moralists entered the lists, so that many different variants were added to the discourse concerning self-interest or *amour propre* on the one side and "natural affection" and altruism on the other. In this torrent of social discourse we observe a sustained critique against the Hobbesian view that all voluntary actions were self-interested. Shaftesbury's moral-sense theory and his buoyant trust in the power of "human sentiments" to prompt individuals to take a suitable course of social conduct drew the praise of British philosophers, even those who on other points dissented from Shaftesbury. David Hume conceded his debt to his forebear in his first versions of "Of the Dignity or Meanness of Human Nature":

> I shall observe, what has been prov'd beyond Question by several great Moralists of the present Age, that the social Passions are by far the most powerful of any, and that even all the other Passions receive from them their chief Force and influence. Whoever desires to see this Question treated at large, with the greatest force of Argument and Eloquence, may consult my Lord Shaftsbury's Enquiry concerning Virtue.[74]

The code and claims of human sociability were being relaxed. Strenuous allegiance and exaggerated conceptions of largess were reduced in favor of less heroic and more middling ideals of social virtue. Instead of highlighting the traditional world of self-denial and obligation, Shaftesbury digressed fondly on "social affections." Speaking for the power of "common sense" in his "Sensus communis: An Essay on the Freedom of Wit and Humour," he was to contend that

> A public spirit can come only from a social feeling or sense of partnership with human kind. Now there are none so far from being partners in this sense, or sharers in this common affection, as they who scarcely know an equal, nor consider themselves as subject to any law of fellowship or community. And thus morality and good government go together. There is no real love of virtue, without the knowledge of public good. And where absolute power is, there is no public.[75]

Shaftesbury goes on to argue that those living under a tyranny have no notion of what is good and just other than the will and power of a ruler. But even among those unfortunates there is a "natural affection" toward a government and order. If men have no magistrates to protect them, they will imagine that they have some "public parent." The "Britons," however, were bequeathed a "better sense of government delivered to us from our ancestors." They have a conception of "a public, and a constitution," and know how a legislature and executive are modeled. They are able to reason fairly on the balance between power and property. The maxims they deduce are as clear and cogent as those derived from geometry: "Our increasing knowledge shows us every day, more and more, what common sense is in politics; and this must of necessity lead us to understand a like sense in morals, which is the foundation."

For Shaftesbury and his followers, natural law was grounded in moral sense. The doctrine of moral sense was the bedrock of civil society. How to understand it? How to investigate moral philosophy as an enterprise fundamentally naturalistic, that is, free (at least in aim) not to depend upon metaphysical or religious beliefs? The intention was naturalistic though not always achieved. Locke had offered in his *Civil and Ecclesiastic Power* (1673–78) contrast and comparison between civil and ecclesiastical society. The end or purpose of the former was the present enjoyment of the world. In the view of Shaftesbury and others, this world as diagrammed by Locke had failed since it did not reckon with the full nature of human beings; yet Locke's contribution toward an understanding of the causes of civil society and the duties of magistrates had gained their full approval. Locke had been more insistent as to the rights of individuals and less indulgent toward the power of magistrates than his illustrious forebears among moral philosophers and jurists. This is a point to which we shall return.[76]

Gershom Carmichael, Francis Hutcheson, and his student Adam Smith began their analysis of civil society by defining the relationship between citizen and magistrate. Civil government represented a decisive move toward the "modern" legal conception of property. As to beneficence and the other wholesome virtues, they were not felt to be as capable of forging social bonds on which "mediocre man" ought to depend. Pufendorf's text *De officio hominis et civis juxta legem naturalem* (1673) had proven influential. Moving in a "modern" direction, he had distinguished between law and morals. Laws were shaped in accord with the observed facts about the "human constitution." Self-interested and also fragile by nature, man's need for sociability was fundamental. The disposition toward a common life stemmed from the very essentials of the human condition. Duties and obligations originated in large measure from laws which were binding by virtue of the facts of our nature. There were also positive duties: men must treat each other as equals and be helpful, even benevolent. These duties, however, did not have the force or scope that might be wide-ranging or precisely detailed. They were limited when compared with the derivative obligations and rights originating from agreements men make with one another. Property rights and contractual rights were to be located here. While men ought to be bound together by "kindness, peace and love, and therefore mutual obligation," the word *ought* was normative and therefore lacked legal force. These benevolent imperatives might be termed "positive duties" but "imperfect obligations." Therefore, they ought to be performed upon a volitional basis, not under legal compulsion. These were matters of conscience and here was the source of imperfect obligation or intrinsic obligation. For Scottish moralists from Hutcheson to Hume and Smith, this ethical mapping was to hold with the key word "ought."

This does not signify that imperfect obligations were trivial or not to be acted on. Locke, for example, placed a heavy cargo of philanthropic and charitable imperatives on the property holder. Further, he set up the workmanship model whereby the impulse to appropriate was tied to the imperative that the owner engage in some form of improvement. Many ethical burdens were placed upon the "haves," but the fact was that an erosion in the force of that time-honored adage that "property has its duties" was apparent. Though this maxim was hedged with numerous human concerns, it did not impose on holders of property "a general duty to secure the welfare of the less fortunate.'' Grotius had written and it was often cited: ''It is not . . . contrary to the nature of society to look out for oneself and advance one's own interest, provided the rights of others are not infringed.'' This harsh and stark statement does not do full justice to his concern or that of Pufendorf, Locke, and others for the weak and impoverished. It does, however, underscore the projection of a version of a less interdependent social world than had been traditionally posited.[77]

Grotius's harsher view had then been ameliorated, but arguments in favor of limited sociability proved durable and were generally appealing to jurists. As to the issue of property, a conjectural historical account of its origins became increasingly popular. These beginnings were located in the naturally self-preserving activities of human beings. Grotius, Pufendorf, and Locke essayed a ''natural history of property'' linking the different rules of property to a stadial view of society with divisions between the nomadic, the settled agricultural, and commercial phases. This perspective was more fully explicated by Adam Smith, forming the basis for his *Lectures on Jurisprudence.*[78]

Locke charted the transition from ''original appropriation'' (pre-money community) to the post-money society with its advanced notions of property. Such sophisticated conceptions of property could be realized only in a civil society. Had humans been content to live in mutual affection and simplicity, there would have been no reason for civil society. Locke was in agreement with Grotius that it was as a result of the discontents rampant in this first stage that the transition from pristine to sophisticated notions of property emerged. Recently, Grotius's views and Locke's concurrence on this theme have been summarized by James Tully:

> However, men soon increased their knowledge and this could be put to either good or evil uses. Agriculture and grazing developed, men became crafty rather than just, and the age of giants, given over to murder, rivalry and violence, followed. The Flood ended the age of giants and ushered in an age of pleasure, incest and adultery. Ambition, 'a less ignoble vice', emerged and it became the major cause of disharmony in the next age. For Grotius, as for Locke, vice is a product of history. To avoid disharmony, division of things took place. Men divided into separate countries and private property was introduced, first of moveables, and then of immoveable things.

It was money that furnished the main motive for the individual's entry into political society. Civil society, a concomitant of this transition, was defined by its capacity for securing the life, liberty, and goods of the individual. Men had entered the political community in order to resolve problems generated by this new form of exchange into what had constituted a state of nature. The right to property was prior to entry into political society:

> For the preservation of Property being the end of Government, and that for which Men enter into Society, it necessarily supposes and requires, that the People should have Property, without which they must be suppos'd to lose that by entering into Society, which was the end for which they entered into it, too gross an absurdity for any Man to own.[79]

The above did not, however, signify any absolute right to property; only those rights vouchsafed for the individual by law obtained. Furthermore, the distribution of property was based on the agreements made at the time of the individual's entry into political society. There were serious moral dilemmas that revolved around the individual's responsibilities as an owner of property. Ethical problems were clustered around the issue of ownership of property so extensive that its return far exceeded the possessor's needs. It was true that men entered society not merely for self-preservation but to enjoy it per se and for "the enjoyment of their Properties." These pleasures were not to justify the sin of acquisitiveness nor to negate the Christian duty of charity. Locke was keenly aware of the possible conflict between considerations of justice and the right of charity. When conflict between these two virtues arose, charity might supersede justice in a given particular instance. But charity, while useful and desirable, was essential only in well-defined situations. For any society to exist, the requirement of justice was central. If the right of charity had to be invoked frequently to sustain the social fabric, the level of economic and social life would indeed be low. In Locke's view this was not so: in his world the relatively high "productivity of the system of private appropriation keeps cases of necessity rare. . . ." Furthermore, Locke limited the operation of charity to cases of "extreme want" or "pressing wants," in which there were no other means of survival available.

In Locke's system of justice, the right of charity has been termed a "buffer" against extreme necessity. In the pre-monetary age of simplicity, what was not consumed immediately was soon to spoil, and this limited the productivity of land and labor. In a sophisticated money economy, the capacity for improvement and labor found ample play. Locke in his *Two Treatises* indicates that a static economy and its zero-sum game were transformed by the introduction of money, which released productive forces from the strict limits set by spoilage. The theory of prosperity introduced by Locke as a consequence of this transition worked to weaken traditional obligations and duties, since virtually all citizens could prosper in some measure. As noted earlier, Locke was eager to compare the felicitous condition of the English worker or peasant to that of the denizens of that new continent—the Americas.[80]

Locke appears to allow full play to self-interested behavior provided it does not have a deliterious effect on society. The creation of wealth and the general increase in living standards, he argues, have operated to make the social world, if not an Eden, at least no treacherous mine-field. Those tense moments and situations in which the right of property and the right of charity intersect are few. Furthermore, Locke was confident that "mediocre men" could navigate the shoals of ethical responsibility. In his *An Essay Concerning the Understanding, Knowledge, Opinion and Assent,* he writes: "Our Business here is not to know all things, but those which concern our Conduct." Our essential search is to "find out those Measures, whereby a rational Creature put in that State, which Man is in, in this World, may, and ought to govern his Opinions, and Actions depending thereon." This quest can be completed successfully since men "have Light enough to lead them to the Knowledge of their Maker, and the sight of their own Duties." Not only did God give men light enough to know their duties, but He also provided His abundance for them to enjoy. Enjoyment was not indulgence in the sin of acquisitiveness; instead, in seventeenth-century terminology, enjoyment was constituted by the activity of consumption. Satisfaction of needs and even pleasures in moderation did not foreclose the liberality and charity to be expected from a Christian. In his late work *Some Thoughts Concerning Education*, Locke called for the instruction of the young about use of property:

> As to having and possessing of Things, teach them to part with what they have easily and freely to their friends. . . . Covetousness, and the Desire of having in our Possession, and under our Dominion, more than we have need of, being the Root of all Evil, should be early and carefully weeded out, and the contrary Quality of a Readiness to impart to others implanted.

Locke's appeal to Scripture undergirded the case he made for the transition from a negative or pre-monetary community to a monetary society of positive laws. This transition was a direct result of human labor, and Locke notes God's commandment to Adam that he labor. Locke's maxim that "labour makes the far greatest part of the value of things we enjoy in this world" was to gain assent, though not necessarily within his theological frame. He asserts in his *Two Treatises:* "I think it will be but a very modest Computation to say, that of the Product of the Earth useful to the Life of man 9/10 are the effects of labour."[81]

XI

Francis Hutcheson followed Locke almost word for word in his panegyric to labor, but without an appeal to Scripture and the divine command to Adam. Instead, his argument was grounded in the material benefits accruing to humankind from the power of labor to add value to land and goods. Essential for the increase of human productivity was the knowledge of laborer and cultivator that they would be secure in the fruits of their industry. Without this protection they would be "a constant prey to the Slothful and Self-love against Industry." Cultivators and the industrious must be more than protected; they must be rewarded. Moreover, they must have the right to dispose of the surpluses beyond their needs. Of course there were limitations: one person must not acquire the right to land beyond his power to cultivate. But the system of property was justified on the grounds that it brought benefits to society at large. Hutcheson may have been the first to elevate the idea of utility to the level of the principle of utilitarianism. He anticipated Jeremy Bentham (1748–1832) with his formula: "That action is best, which procures the greatest Happiness for the greatest Numbers."[82]

Although Hutcheson did not explicate this principle in the modern spirit or in detail, it was manifest in his practical outlook on property ("compleat unlimited property"). He followed Locke in recognizing that it was not the "spontaneous fruits of uncultivated earth" which sustained humankind, but industry and diligence. The will to work could not be sustained through affection or self-love, unless one was secure in one's property. As we have noted, Hutcheson placed few restrictions on property: he perceived that its origins were a natural result of population growth. With the advent of scarcity, competition for resources became intense.

> . . . when once Men become so numerous, that the natural Product of the Earth is not sufficient for their Support, or Ease, or innocent Pleasure, a necessity arises, for the support of the increasing System, that such a Tenour of Conduct be observ'd, as shall most effectually promote Industry; and that Men abstain from all Actions which would have the contrary effect.

The origins of society for Hutcheson were like those of Locke: to be found in the lineaments of a social contract whereby individuals in their natural state rendered mutual promises to live together as a community. A civil society was forged by individuals from a condition judged pre-civil. This political or civil society was in Hutcheson's view not, as Shaftesbury had contended, an instinctive development stemming naturally from the sociable nature of human affections. True, the benevolent affections of the "moral sense" were the base for sociability, but they alone could not furnish the instinctual foundation for civil society. Hutcheson had been influenced by the Stoic conceptions of "citizen of the world" and "universal good," and indeed defended Shaftesbury's theory of the reality of a "moral sense": from the original benevolent impulses in human nature were to be derived beneficent behavior. But Hutcheson differed from Shaftesbury in that he detached the moral-sense doctrine from the theory of innate ideas: "We are not to imagine that this moral Sense, more than the other Senses, supposes any innate ideas, Knowledge, or practical Proposition." Questions can of course be raised: How did this virtue come into being? What were its limits? How stable was it? Did sociability depend on fellow feeling entirely or only to a limited degree? In all this there was a conflict: the key virtue, justice—respect for another's life, liberty and property—was predicated on a principle of rational utility which must clash with impulses toward beneficence. These problems were difficult to resolve. Hutcheson worked toward illumination of the psychology of social action, affirming the strength and amplitude of the social passions. Like Shaftesbury he resisted reductionist definitions of self-love as the single and compelling motivator. Whereas Shaftesbury converted Hobbes, Locke, and Mandeville into a dangerous opposition, Hutcheson assumed a more tolerant and nuanced perspective. He located the failure of their social psychology in its inability to render a full account of the facts of human nature. One had only to look at the details of everyday behavior and ordinary human transactions, he argued, to perceive how simplistic was the explanation proffered by self-love theorists. One could easily find generous and kindly acts in daily relations:

> . . . we are determin'd to common Friendships and Acquaintances, not by the sullen Apprehensions of our Necessitys, or Prospects of Interest; but by an incredible variety of little agreeable, engaging Evidences of Love, Good-nature, and other morally amiable Qualities in those we converse with.[83]

From Hutcheson's experience of social life, he learned that "many have high Notions of Honour, Faith, Generosity, Justice, who have scarce any Opinions about the Deity, or any Thoughts of future Rewards; and abhor anything which is Treacherous, Cruel, or Unjust, without any regard to future Punishments." But in fact, could these virtues (now secularized) be counted upon to anchor society? Could a sense of duty be grounded in any doctrine of benevolent affections? How did selflessness work in specific situations where legal claims obtain? The right of the poor to charity, or benefactors to gratitude, or the doers of good offices to appreciation—were these not imperfect or weak rights? Transgression of imperfect rights might be tolerated whereas violations of perfect rights could not be. Distinctions had to be made between the right to avoid injury (a strong right), as opposed to the conferring of succor. In Hutcheson's view rights tended to improvement and increase of the good in any society. Perfect rights were absolutely essential to prevent misery; imperfect rights brought benefits but were not indispensable to the survival of community. Certainly, the moral sense worked to form sociability, but what were its limitations? There was weak benevolence and strong benevolence. One could hope that a rich man would not demand restitution of a loan from an impoverished friend, but he did have an "external right" to do so, and this right took precedence over an imperfect one. Justice itself was an artificial rather than a natural right, since it was perforce arbitrary and did not depend on the moral sense. Justice evolves from "some previous act of man"; each must give the other his due; this entails protecting rights to the fruits of an individual's labor as well as the requirement of "performance of contract." The original pre-political society was in Hutcheson's view a peaceful one since people possessed naturally sociable affections. But civil society depended upon rational artifice. The most fundamental virtue, that of justice, was grounded in rational utility and therefore came into conflict with fellow feeling. Thus, though the generous affections of the moral sense were indeed the foundation of sociability, they could not provide an instinctive beneficence for a civil society. As we have observed, Hutcheson limited the sway of the beneficent affections of the moral sense; they could not sustain civil society. Moral sense was a passive determination of the mind serving to ratify acts of benevolence by the individual. Therefore, it is not possible to anchor a sense of duty or obligation in a theory of moral sense.[84]

Hutcheson, Adam Smith's teacher, came close to anticipating his pupil's position, albeit reluctantly. Not only was there tension between virtue and nature (benevolence and self-preservation), but also between virtue and society. This seemingly irreconcilable conflict between the claims of virtue and obligation of duty on the one side, and the requirements for preservation of life on the other, set the stage for a protracted analysis by prose essayists, novelists, and moral philosophers. Many ventured responses to the writings of the moral theorist Bernard de Mandeville (*Fable of the Bees*, 1716), who in jeering and mocking tone sought to release the denizens of what he characterized as "civil societies" from those conflicting demands. This he would do by invoking the familiar psychological motives of *amour propre* and self-interest. The secret of the education of citizens was to direct their vanity to proper objects. Mandeville argued that civil society was made possible not by the grand virtues, but rather by "private vices":

> . . . that what renders him [man] a sociable animal consists not in his desire of company, good nature, pity, affability, and other graces of a fair outside; but that his vilest and most hateful qualities are the most necessary accomplishments to fit him for the largest, and, according to the world, the happiest and most flourishing societies. . . .

Hutcheson challenged Mandeville's and his fellow moral theorists' single-mindedness determination to enfold moral distinctions and human sociability in the mantle of self-love. (His caveat pertaining to oversimplification was not to be lost on Hume.) Mandeville's explanation, he argued, was too parsimonious and reductive. In the preface to *An Essay on the Nature and Conduct of the Passions and Affections* (1728), Hutcheson wrote: "Some strange love of simplicity in the structure of human nature . . . has engaged many writers to pass over a great many simple Perceptions which we may find in ourselves." This impoverishment is summed up by Hutcheson thusly: when considering "our Desires or Affections," these theorists of radical egoism have been compelled to render "the most generous, kind, and disinterested of them, to proceed from Self-Love, by some subtle Trains of Reasoning, to which honest Hearts are often wholly Strangers." These writers have subscribed to the simplistic thesis that "all the desires of the human Mind, nay of all thinking Natures, are reducible to Self-Love, or Desire or private Happiness. . . ." This is the teaching of "the old Epicureans," only recently "revived by Mr. Hobbes, and followed by many better Writers."[85]

The Sentimental school of English and Scottish moral philosophy was working toward the colonization of a middle ground in its analysis of human nature. Questions raised concerned the origins of moral sentiment and how it operated to move individuals towards action. How to explain the propensity of individuals to enter deeply into the sentiments of another or seek to communicate their own? Definitions of sympathy were being extended beyond the bounds of pity or kindly feelings. Shaftesbury's achievement had been to rehabilitate benevolence and generosity, which he characterized as "natural affections." He was careful to delineate the effect of these natural affections as forces for private and public good. Certain of these sentiments worked well in both realms, whereas others needed to be classified as advantaging the private but not necessarily the public good. These were separated from the admirable affections and termed "self-affections" or "self-passions." Of course there were "unnatural affections" such as inhumanity, greed, envy, and others from which neither public nor private good resulted. He then subdivided these classifications to distinguish between immoderate and moderate passions. Finally, he further refined certain of these categories when he was required to place human economic activities into his conceptual framework. These are considered under the heading of "self-passions," but soon he blunts the force of the argument to exculpate them:

> If the regard toward [acquisition of wealth] be moderate, and in a reasonable degree; if it occasions no passionate pursuit—there is nothing in this case which is not com-

patible with virtue, and even suitable and beneficial to society. But if it grows at length into a real passion; the injury and mischief it does the public, is not greater than that which it creates to the person himself. Such a one is in reality a self-oppressor, and lies heavier on himself than he can ever do on mankind.

Hutcheson reduced Shaftesbury's elaborate ethical scheme to distinctions between "selfish" and "benevolent" passions on the one side and "violent" and "calm" "motions of the will" on the other. Among the few illustrations offered on this simplified mode of classification, one is rooted in economic life:

> . . . the calm desire of wealth will force one, tho' with reluctance, into splendid expences when necessary to gain a good bargain or a gainful employment; while the passion of avarice is repining at these expences.[86]

Hutcheson's distinction between the "calm desire of wealth" (the French *doux*) and avarice does not rest in the intensity of the desire but instead in the "willingness to pay high costs to achieve high benefit." A "calm desire" corresponds to the seventeenth-century conception of "interest," whereby one behaved with rationality and calculation. A patient explication of the distinctions between calm and weak passions and strong and violent ones was a hallmark of early eighteenth-century moral philosophy. Paralleling the French experience, the British worked to validate the calm or *doux* passion for the love of gain over those emotions rooted in love of pleasure. Shaftesbury's optimism concerning the advantages to be gained by commercial development and refinement of the arts was shared in the next generation by Hume and others. The conversion of the vestiges of the once malignant desire for gain into a benign human impulse attracted the attention of the best moral philosophers.

In the introduction to his *A Treatise of Human Nature (1739–40)* Hume paid special tribute to Shaftesbury for rendering more scientific the study of human nature. In his *Characteristics of Men, Manners, Opinions, Times* (1711), Shaftesbury had not only presented moderate views on the beneficial effects of the acquisitive instinct on society as a whole, but he also served as a spokesman for moderation in many areas of cultural and political life. He defined a political stance for "men of moderation." This outlook was not surprising coming, as we have noticed, from a generation so close to the year 1688 and the Glorious Revolution. Duncan Forbes, the modern historian of eighteenth-century English political thought, observes that especially prized by Shaftesbury and his ilk were "men who were too secure of their temper and who possessed themselves too well 'to be in danger of entering warmly into any cause, or engaging deeply with any side or faction'." The politics of the "moderate man" were characterized as being "the science of man united in society and dependent on each other." At the same time, contemporary commentators on the British scene dwelled upon the impact of specialization and the division of labor as a deadly threat to the traditional bonding of society. Further, they highlighted the risks of depending upon the altruism of others. Moral principles derived from human nature instructed individuals that reliance on the benevolence and self-denial of others was a risky choice. Would the industrious feed the idle?

Finally, these critics concluded, albeit reluctantly, that human expectations must be moderated, and therefore it followed that public space must be allowed for the play of egoism and human vanity.[87]

The limits of human powers and excellence became a favored theme. The pervasiveness of pride and its unintended benefits to society attracted some of the best essayists and poets of the time. Similarly, heroism in its many guises was brilliantly satirized. Commercial society and its law codes were working to limit the liability of business. Specialization and division of labor were often recognized as essential for the growth of commerce; but these developments promoted a decline in sociability. More complex social and economic relationships in turn demanded greater cooperation and forbearance, yet it had become increasingly difficult to rely on older forms of solidarity and group identity. Throughout the period we observe a decline in the advocacy of theories of society prompted by the human propensity for fellowship. Indeed, what we notice is the very antithesis of this version of sociability. Social space between individuals in this ever more commercialized world is judged to be more impersonal. The call of duty and the claims of individuals on one another were weakening. Recent scholarship following the lead of Norbert Elias has characterized this social space, perhaps a bit overboldly, as something of an emotional void. Indeed, the professions were becoming the new "theater of virtue." The idea of talent was displacing older notions of merit; the latter had carried the heavy charge of gift-giving and reciprocity. Virtue signified a "habit of the soul which inspired it to do good things." Now *talent* became the operative word indicating a quite definite capacity or set of capacities:

> It was a 'gift of nature,' disposition, natural aptitude for certain things. Moreover, talent was something that demanded to be put to use. It is said figuratively: 'Make the most of talent,' that is to say, 'usefully employ one's mind, one's skill.'[88]

XII

The term "society" was losing something of its active and immediate sense. An advanced thinker such as David Hume employed the term in a variety of ways: in his *Enquiry Concerning the Principles of Morals* (1751), he used it both with its ancient meaning, "company of his fellows," and the more modern notion, "system of common life." The newer usage does outnumber the more traditional by some 110 instances to 25. At critical points in Hume's argument, the intermediate use of the term surfaces, so that the meaning can be located somewhere between the immediacy of fellowship and company and the more formal notion of society as a distant object. Yet, despite his appreciation for the ambiguities, Hume presents a clear representation of the more modern conceptualization. Not only is the active and immediate sense of old being shunned, but Hume uses the alternative word "company" very much as we would:

> As the mutual shocks in *society,* and the oppositions of interest and self-love, have constrained mankind to establish the laws of justice . . . in like manner, the eternal

contrarieties, in *company*, of men's pride and self-conceit, have introduced the rules of Good Manners or Politeness. . . .

There is something perplexing here: we observe that the semantic range of the word *society* was being extended to run from the familiar meaning of indiscriminate gregariousness and fellowship to a newer definition wherein it denoted an entity abstract and distant, with a life of its own. Society in this latter sense was conceptualized as having laws pertaining to its own being. What is more, it was now likely to be regarded as being durable and not merely the incidental outcome of human sociability. Yet such an entity existing independent of benevolent impulse, generosity, and the exchange of courtesies ran the risk of being defined, in the words of Adam Smith, as a "Society of Strangers."[89]

There appeared to be less space in this social world for the play of gallantry or heroic virtue. In the early eighteenth century there were signs of an inclination to relinquish the strong definitions of this grandiose vocabulary. In its stead was substituted a less ambitious array of qualities that might be subsumed under the rubric of "manners." The virtues still highly prized were modest and of the middling sort, those David Hume was to term "aldermanic"—that is, pertaining to the alderman who steadfastly served community or church. Writers worked in the middle range of social experience; language moved away from the rich variety and freedom of an earlier time with its license, excess, obscurity, and crudity. A comfortable tactic of communication prevailed with stability in language mirroring stability in society. In the theater, movement from the sparkling wit of Restoration comedy toward genteel, sentimental drama took hold. The realistic novel emerging in the first part of the eighteenth century explored narrative verisimilitude in its attempt to secure a commonly held view of everyday life. Samuel Johnson in *Lives of the Poets* (1779–81) proffered a by-now standard explanation of the widespread anxiety prevalent in England with the civil wars and Restoration. Reflecting on these troubled times and the factions and sects spawned by divisions in society, an identification was made between license and language on the one side and the forces of civil unrest and disruption on the other. The result was that in matters of language there was a heightened suspicion of extravagant metaphors and literary enthusiasms. In fact, the word *enthusiasm* had become a pejorative. As we have seen, grandiose terms such as "virtuoso," which once identified that individual who had, by arcane means ("the chemical fire of enthusiasm") penetrated the darkest secrets of nature, lost most of its flavor. Around 1700 the word had come to signify a person of myriad cultural talents. In the writings of Shaftesbury we have already recognized that notions of virtue can barely be distinguished from notions of good breeding. Definitions of virtue were now more easily to be bracketed with the refinement of manners. There was a distrust of imaginative poetry: not inappropriately, the literary culture of early eighteenth-century England has been characterized as an "age of prose"—some would say prosaic. Relations between court and country based on consensus tended to replace the adversarial relationships of the seventeenth century. Hume was quite pleased to employ clubs as a paradigm for the moral history of society itself: "But why in the greater society or confederation of mankind, should not the case be made the same as in particular clubs and companies?"

The idea of a consensus view gained strength from the time of Hutcheson to that of Hume and Smith. The first of these maintained that a moral consensus obtained concerning virtue, just as a natural consensus held about what was sweet or sour or colored. Hume extended the idea, arguing on his own a position close to that of Smith's construction of the "impartial spectator." He contended that

> . . . to prevent those contradictions and arrive at a more stable judgment of things, we fix on some steady and general point of view, and always in our thoughts, place ourselves in them, whatever may be our general situation.

From John Locke to David Hume and Adam Smith, there were thoughtful spokesmen opting for epistemological modesty. They spoke to their audience in a language not freighted with technical terms. Locke in his "The Epistle to the Reader," introducing his *An Essay Concerning Human Understanding,* injected this cautionary note: No need to scale the skies with the theologians nor descend to the dark depths with metaphysicians. Instead, one should study one's own nature, and if this is done scrupulously, it will serve to dismantle the structure of "vanity and ignorance" long bricked up with meaningless words. In this way the path will be cleared for a secure ground on which to construct a science of man. The key and indeed modest questions to be posed run thusly: What are the materials with which the human mind is furnished? What can it make of them? A psychological account of human nature was to be constructed in ordinary language out of ordinary experience.[90]

XIII

The term "society," as we have noted, had lost something of its active and immediate sense. In this new social space one was to remain distant from political faction as well as from religious enthusiasms, fanaticism, and superstition. Instead, one was to cultivate moral refinement and good taste. Furthermore, morality was more important than doctrine and less likely to be divisive. One registered a concern for what in contemporary parlance was described as "the minute decencies and inferior duties." These were vital since they regulated daily converse and material exchange. The word "conversation" in 1700 had a broader concern for manners than in later-day idioms. The matter and manner of conversation was under regulation. Already Jonathan Swift's *A Tale of a Tub* (1704) demonstrated an appreciation for conversation which would deflect political zealotry. The periodical essay in Samuel Johnson's view presented general knowledge appropriate for circulation in common talk. This accomplishment had only rarely been achieved in an earlier time and now was to contribute to political harmony by introducing "subjects to which faction had produced no diversity of sentiment such as literature, morality and familiar life." Singled out for special praise were *The Tatler* and *The Spectator:*

. . . to minds heated with the political they supplied cooler and more inoffensive reflection, and it is said by Addison . . . that they had a perceptible influence upon the conversation of the time, and taught the frolic and the gay to unite merriment with decency . . . they continue to be among the first books by which both sides are initiated in the elegances of knowledge.

That principal literary genre of the early eighteenth century—the periodical essay—often sought to persuade the reader of its own triviality. The author of *The Tatler* spoke of his essays as "lucubrations." Even papers of considerable gravity were published by Sam Johnson under the titles "Ramblers" and "Idler." The favored moral crusades of *The Tatler* were deflated in self-mocking tone:

Never hero in Romance was carried away with a more furious Ambition to conquer Beasts and Tyrants, than I have been in extirpating Gamesters and Duelists.

We notice efforts to scale down language. If one breaks faith, one might be charged with *inconsistency*. How different this is from the more dramatic charges of perfidy or treason once so commonly applied to even minute infractions of a demanding social code. A favored creation of the new journalism was the fictional Sir Roger de Coverly, whose genial rhetoric was designed to avoid contest and harsh recrimination. The experience of the French at the early eighteenth century might prove instructive. We observe that the semantic field of terms such as *judgment, discernment, sentiment, bienséance, bon sens,* and *honnêteté* was much enhanced. A lexicon of terms denoting shades of sensibility impinged on the traditional idiom of stoicism in order to give an account of human nature. The passions were analyzed in endless detail and, as we have noted, were often legitimated. Pride or vanity or *amour propre* became identical for all practical purposes. And if in fact they were vices they were regarded as dissolute rather than as signs of spiritual weakness. Virtue itself was often reduced to social virtue, particularly to benevolence or kindness. These "liberal virtues" challenged "the severe virtues of self-restraint." At the end of the eighteenth century, Edmund Burke attempted to strip away the disguises of "the new morality" with this polemic:

The Parisian philosophers . . . explode or render odious or contemptible, that class of virtues which restrain the appetite. . . . In the place of all this, they substitute a virtue which they call humanity or benevolence.

The risk, in Burke's view, was that in the easy conversion implicit in the optimistic maxim "private vices may promote public benefits," there would ensue a reckless "political hedonism." The "severe virtues" were rivaled by those virtues measured by the yardstick of culture and taste. Instead of more demanding criteria for measuring truth, the English vocabulary favored the looser usage derived from "common sense" and "good sense," both of which became hardy staples in literary and philosophical discourse. Furthermore, *sentiment,* which had formerly meant little more than the capacity to feel strongly, now conveyed the meaning of a quick sense of right and wrong in all human actions. *Virtue* extended its boundary of meaning to include matters of personal judgment beyond the earlier definition of moral responsibility. The decline of a more aristocratic view of a life of duty and obligation was in prospect. The problematics of this relaxation were dramatized in the novel from Defoe and Richardson to Fielding and Stern. The middle-brow virtues were at the center of Stern's enormously popular and highly disturbing *Tristram Shandy*. The meaning of such words as responsibility, duty, and obligation was extended to include both legal ethics and social mores. The individual must behave in what was reckoned to be a "responsible manner," that is, in keeping with the standards promulgated by society. The rules governing society were themselves the product of unintended consequences and the accretion of customs and habits embodying the fruits of generations of wisdom. Even philosophers as skeptical as Hume were accepting of the rules of the game. To the first meaning of the word "propriety" (the owner of something), another was added in the eighteenth century. It came to signify conformity with good manners; propriety had shifted from ownership to correctness of behavior. The word "sympathy," as we have seen, was once largely limited to the emotions of pity and compassion; now, in the eighteenth century, it came to play a commanding role as the key emotion allowing one person to experience the feelings of another. It was as if sympathy replaced the sterner ties of duty and obligation. This was part of a process by which ties and bonds among the citizenry were being psychologized. One might argue, perhaps a bit too over-assertively, that a deep-sea change from empathy to sympathy was at center stage in the eighteenth century. The play of sympathy might well counterfeit, and therefore function in society in a manner similar to, charity and benevolence. Indeed, sympathy was widely held to be the very cause of civil society. James Beattie (1735–1803), a most royally favored and popular Scottish moralist, rendered a classic account of sympathy in underscoring the indisputable fact that its effect was "to bind men more closely together in society and prompt them to promote the good and relieve the distress of one another."[9]

XIV

The classical idea of virtue sanctioned by the centuries-long tradition of civic humanism drew upon Roman models for inspiration and knowledge. A demanding ethic, it called for self-knowledge and self-command. Its theater was a public domain generated by civic action and buttressed by a prejudice in favor of agriculture. A determinism was established between commerce and the decline of public virtue. The growth of luxury was regarded as a political menace. Republicanism and republican society were supposed to serve the state. The virtues of course were in themselves civic—liberty, valor, frugality, and military prowess. Not surprisingly, the vices were chauvanistically designated as feminine: luxury, sexual indulgence, and cowardice. The discourse of civic humanism readily converted political and economic preoccupations into a moral vocabulary. Economic issues were treated as ethical problems to be resolved by the right distribution and use of wealth. This wealth was assumed to be directly available rather than considered as a problem relating to production and consumption. The workings of the economy were of course part of a larger debate about the nature of the state and the conduct of social policy.[92]

Against a time-honored mode of discourse featuring an edifying classical past, we find the gradual articulation of an idiom framed to illumine the day-to-day, less heroic workings of a civil society. The vernacular present was no longer so likely to be perceived as compatible with the classical past. The rhetorical tactics of civic humanism with its advocacy of political virtue now tended to be challenged by a less demanding code. Was the real choice between a society grounded in some inexplicable way on "principles of virtue" or one based on some substitute—commerce, for example?[93]

Perhaps one of the more telling responses was that of Immanuel Kant. At the end of the century he observed that the founding of the right social order did not require a nation of angels: "Hard as it may sound, the problem of establishing the state (i.e., the just social order) is soluble even to a nation of devils, provided they have sense. . . ." Sense, in Kant's view, signified the ability to be directed by "enlightened selfishness." There was something of a consensus: the way to maximize the social and economic benefits of freedom was to minimize the extent to which public demands could be made upon private lives. Society is separate from the state and functions according to its own laws. The principle of voluntary association (voluntarism) thus came to the fore and was championed with exceptional fervor. In an increasingly urbanized world, traditional structures were either absent or inappropriate, and it was here that this voluntarism found expression in a wealth of new institutional forms. Patriotic societies, reading clubs, masonic lodges, academies of science and the fine arts are but a sample of the numerous manifestations of these practical social initiatives. In the main they were committed to the general improvement of the individual, his society, and economic life. Geographically, they were located in assembly halls, concert halls, lecture halls, museums, lending libraries, coffee houses, public walks, and theaters. The separation of society and the state enhanced and fortified that public space aptly termed "civil society." The bonds of associative life were slackened in favor of this voluntarism, and contemporary definitions of civil society took this into account. These developments might be a matter of pride or perturbation. Adam Ferguson, the Scot Highlander of whom we have spoken before, was among the first to explore in depth the genesis of civil society. For him, as for so many others, it was a cause of concern, if not anguish. For his contemporary, Adam Smith, it was to be the occasion for many a rhetorical flourish. Specialization and the division of labor had reduced interdependence among groups so that when Ferguson came to define civil society, he classified it as being "made to consist of parts, of which none is animated by the spirit of the whole." He was concerned with the "animated spirit of society" in an "age of separation." For him the dilemma was framed thusly: modern civil society needs a sovereign in order to survive. A centralized constitutional state coupled with manufacturing and commerce, as well as a powerful ruler, shatters "the bonds of society," menaces the liberties of citizens and the free expression of independent associative life. Ferguson's resolution of the dilemma of big government and big commerce was at best halting. He was to advocate the strengthening of citizen associative life as a buffer against political despotism and economic tyranny. Within public space humans, differing from animals in their capacity to consult, persuade, oppose, could kindle the embers of society in their fellows.[94]

Journalists and literati concurred that there had been a decline of generalized sociability, gregariousness, and the propensity for fellowship. John Locke's belief that government depended on trust seemed archaic even at that moment in the late seventeenth century when he sounded it. The idea of society expressed in terms of social contract, in which humans in the natural state made mutual promises, also came under attack. Mounting historical criticism challenged this mythic construct over the first part of the eighteenth century. At best, this benign thesis might be considered a pleasant working fiction and no more.

Hume exposed the inadequacies of any "original contract" theory as explanation for the foundation of political society. Instead, he sought for origins in the experience of history. His influence, coupled with that of Montesquieu (*Spirit of the Laws*, 1748), emphasized that it was essential to understand historically the ways of life of a people if political science and philosophy were to flourish. Their skepticism about the theory of contract was then predicated upon a reading of history, but in Hume's case, he was willing to modify his earlier harsh views of the doctrine of social contract. In a new edition of his essay "Original Contract," he made the following insertion:

> My intention here is not to exclude the consent of the people from being one just foundation of government. Where it has placed it is surely the best and most sacred of any. I only contend that it has very seldom had place in any degree, and never almost in its full extent.[95]

XV

The zone of voluntary sociability might be located between the dictates of family life at the one boundary and the growing public authority of the state at the other. In this mapping we observe a growing disjunction between private and public life. This area of "lived life," as Jürgen Habermas has termed it (it does sound more impressive in German), attracted the critical attention of men of letters from the time of Montesquieu to that of Hegel. (The latter was to offer the fullest and most persuasive analysis in his *The Philosophy of Right*.) Adam Ferguson, whose work was both early and highly influential (read by Kant, Hegel, and Marx), experienced fatal fascination, as well as a certain repulsion when addressing himself to the social and economic opportunities and perils afforded by a civil society. There were steep prices to be paid by citizens of such a society of alienation and loneliness. He decried, like many of his contemporaries, the decline of civic virtue and the martial spirit attendant upon the victory of avarice and the pursuit of luxury over public interest. Certainly he was not persuaded that the onset of civil society signified progress. It did not appear to offer "the best gratification for a just and happy engagement of the mind and heart.'' Nor was the psychological burden to be dismissed even by a radical explicator of the benefits of the free play of the market. Bernard Mandeville, himself a medical man and author who constructed the classic representation of the economic advantages of the rigorous pursuit of self-interest, also authored *A Treatise of the Hypochondriack and Hysterick Diseases in Three Dialogues.* According to his diagnosis, hypochondriasis (or old-fashioned melancholia) was caused principally by accumulation of wealth and leisure. This was a disease most likely to strike scholars and men of business.[96]

Indeed, at the core of social life historians have observed a general move at the top of society toward a withdrawal into privacy. For the great, the near great, the gentry, and the well-to-do of commerce and finance, a less demanding and more intimate style of domestic life was in prospect. The great were no longer expected to pass their days in public parade and tiring display, freezing and uncomfortable in vast apartments. Withdrawal from marble halls and antechambers to warmer rooms with furniture, to bedrooms with cabinets, where intimacy and comfort held, was much in fashion. Furniture itself was now more likely to be designed for ease and not for splendor. The success of intimate memoirs and epistolary novels, as well as the diffusion of solitary reading habits indicate the expansion of this domain. Pleasures were to be derived from friendships and shared taste, with a minimum of obligation and protocol. Definitions of ''friendship,'' such as that of Jaucourt's in his article in the *Encyclopedia,* rejected the demanding ''all or nothing stoic tradition'' in favor of a more modulated series of definitions varying ''according to degree and character.'' Unprecedented was the rise of the ''man of fashion'' who gave expression to the community of the esthetic presentation of self. The expanding of the rights of privacy for the well-born and well-to-do allowed for freedom and innovation. Sometimes these were moments for celebration, but on occasion they were cause for scandal. For those upon whom work and family imposed severe constraints, no such turning away from common life was possible.

One can set George Sturt's observations of society alongside those of Adam Ferguson. In the former's *The Wheelwright's Shop,* he presents a picture of a traditional and archaic society that might be paraphrased as follows:

> Thought, behavior, and exchanges of goods and services were so ritualized that each individual life reflected the underlying and animating common life. Yet each had his or her own jobs, responsibilities, and feelings. One person was much like another, yet everyone had personal attachments. Private life did exist, but it was inseparable from the indispensable community.

Against this one can posit Mandeville's or Ferguson's definitions of civil society as being characterized by fragmentation, specialization, professionalization, division of labor, and the play of the market. Hume was to write: ''There are two principles which induce men to enter civil society which we shall call the principles of authority and utility.'' The conception of society as a generalized system, no part of which was animated by the whole, was gaining ground. Both the motives for engaging in social relations and the very processes of the formation of such a distant and abstract entity were now the subjects of heated debate.[97]

Hegel judged the formation of civil society in the West to be of world-historical significance. He was perhaps the first to lend the term its full definition. The *sine qua non* of civil society was the right of the ownership of property. This ownership was recognized by one's fellows, and this implied the concept of contract by which property transactions were regulated. Here judges and courts were necessary to adjudicate disputes between property owners. Such a society of property owners called for a market in which exchanges could be made. Here human ingenuity and inventiveness were enhanced and the individual could better realize his or her freedom. Yet Hegel, like so many of his historically minded contemporaries, harbored certain profound caveats: he was not persuaded that the market should be allowed full play. A balance must be struck between the marketplace and the rights of corporations like guilds. The latter must be afforded legal recognition. Furthermore, the state must work to preserve a hereditary agrarian class. Representation, in Hegel's view, should be corporate, not individual. Some regulation and control was to be exercised over capitalism itself. Here a fine distinction was made: the beneficent modernizing effects of capitalism were to be allowed their play but under certain controls. Like so many of his thoughtful contemporaries, Hegel, the father of the full-blown definition of civil society, was well aware of the problematics of this revolutionary form of economic organization.[98]

Francis Place (1771–1854), the "radical tailor of Charing Cross," remarked that as recently as the late seventeenth century, "there had been no disposition to pry into the state of society." An analysis and historical understanding of the play of human relationships beyond the personal, and the possibility that these emerging relationships might have laws and a life of their own independent of the individual, were matters of abiding philosophical concern. At one time it had been sufficient to recognize that policies of state and formal institutions were "embedded in the thick, informal social matrix of intimate relations and rituals of familie, dependencies, and clientels." Now it was possible to hypostatize society and confer on it an ontological status, thus distancing it from private life. The very veins and arteries that formerly had allowed for the full flow of lifeblood between private and public realms were themselves narrowing. Mediating ties such as those generated by neighborhood, corporation, guild, trade association, vocation, kinship groups, youth organizations, religious confraternities, and a spate of what Edmund Burke had referred to as "little platoons," reached their zenith and were now in decline. Forms of associative life (corporate and communal), once essential for lending structure to politics and the economy, now lost primacy.[99]

At the level of the quotidian we observe that solemn public events involving entire communities in their ceremonies now became an "intense and introverted family affair." For example, rituals surrounding the funeral were no longer a public occasion but rather a private happening. Indeed, we notice something of a change in emotions and attitudes expressed toward death:

> The last will and testament became a family document, rather than a public and religious manifesto: the details of funeral ceremonies and, even, of masses can be left to the affection of the heirs—the important question is, has generosity and fairness

been shown within the family circle? The deathbed becomes the centre of family loyalties, a scene of sorrowful leave-taking unsuited for the curious, or, even, for the pious onlooker from outside the close circle.

Changes are observed at the upper reaches of society as emotions and sentiments grew more likely to be indentured to private concerns than in the past. Assessments were made as to the extent of the withdrawal of feeling and engagement from that once magnetic middling zone of promiscuous sociability. Declines in god-parenting between elites and commoners, as well as declination in open hospitality were statistically reckoned. Segregation of elites from the *menu peuple* were cited after extensive analysis of the diminution of urban festivals and city-wide processions. Communal forms of activity and expressions of proverbial wisdom, familiar as collective possessions of small-scale societies, were now targets for ridicule by men of wit and fashion.[100]

Recreation and leisure-time activities of the well-born and well-to-do appear to demonstrate a withdrawal from public space into exclusive balls, private repasts, and race tracks where admission prices soared. As noted earlier, ostentation and the quantity of food were challenged by the preoccupation with quality. In the fine arts pleasure was achieved through appreciation and connoisseurship; no longer was knowledge of the mechanics of the process essential. Cookbooks devoted to the gourmet followed the general line of cultivating good taste and refinement, and this was another form of exclusivity. An erosion of the support for ceremonial display and open entertainment has suggested to modern historians a declining allegiance to that middling zone between a circle of intimates at the one boundary and the distant collectivity (society) at the other. Furthermore, obligation toward that distant entity was vague and frequently unenforced. Concentration of affection in the family circle was now normative, calling for more intense relations between husband and wife, and parent and child. The tone of family life in France and England at the late seventeenth century has been assessed as more affectionate, or at least more intense among both Protestants and Catholics. The last wills of French-Catholic couples do testify to this psychological change. A public campaign was initiated during the following century in England and France exhorting mothers to breast-feed the infant rather than house it with a wet-nurse. New ideas of child rearing and education for the young highlighted the need for intimacy and tenderness.[101]

A literature attempting to reappropriate the family from its narrow sphere in order to blend it into a larger Christian community had once been widely popular. In England it had its last and most splendid literary example in John Bunyan's *Pilgrim's Progress* (1678–84). Separation or, better still, emancipation of the well-to-do family from the rituals of a corporate, hierarchical society is suggested by researches into the decline of penitential sodalities in France. The new attitudes toward death regarded grief as an intimate concern for the family as the rituals of mourning were privatized. The heyday of prayers and masses for the dead was passing, as was the idea of hope for a collective salvation. Responsibilities of the living Christian for the dead slackened as did the threat of hell. Michel Vovelle, the modern historian of eighteenth-century French emotive life, writes of a "profound modification of feelings," noting the decline in monastic vocations, the number of Easter communions in Bordeaux and Paris, the practice of giving infants a saint's name, depiction of saints in paintings, and in the proportion of religious books being printed over the eighteenth century.[102]

XVI

A sense of withdrawal from the communal round of religious life is suggested by the growing professionalization among the ranks of musicians. (Parenthetically, it should be noted that painters were beginning to view aristocratic patronage as restrictive and to recognize the value of gaining a wider reputation. Comparable developments have also been observed in the provincial theaters of England and France where amateurs were being displaced by semi-professionals and traveling companies who staged long sessions of drama.) Returning to musicians, we discover full-time performers and semi-professionals competing successfully with amateur musicians. In England this led to the presentation of religious music more showy and extroverted, allowing professionals to display their high skills. A craze for "brilliant compositions" brought a spate of French and Italian music and musicians to the British Isles. A new type of church music gained popularity, and it was both more dramatic and less devotional. Soon the oratorio combined sentiments stemming from the English choral tradition with the verve and "public appeal" of the musical theater. Passionate expressions of emotion gained intensity as the oratorio was no longer exclusive to the church but found its voice in the public concert hall. The genre had always been "public," of course, yet now it served commercial rather than liturgical purpose; Handel's *Messiah* in particular revealed the commercial possibilities of sacred music. Cantatas had likewise been an integral part of the liturgy placed next to the sermon; they too followed something of the path of the oratorio.

If we assume music to be an index for general cultural trends, we might postulate a certain displacement in the arts from their time-honored function of communal and ceremonial representation: this was to result in creative tensions. Yet, on balance, the social function was gradually losing its dominant role. Previously, music had been rooted more firmly in religious life, enhancing as it did the integrity of worship. Furthermore, it had been frequently attached to communal purpose, adding glamour to the community event. Fixed to the splendor of the courts of prelates and princes, it accentuated the solemnity of ceremony and advertised power. Music for the occasion was congratulatory (the wedding) or commemoratory (the funeral) or celebratory (military victory or act of homage). Where these roles continued to be called for, they now did so under the influence of changing fashions in English church music. The choral set pieces were now less devotional and more dramatic, with the broad public appeal of musical theater.

The ideal of the autonomous composer free from restrictions was in sight, and here again we observe tension: on one hand the composer was free from restriction, but on the other, loss of patronage was a threat. An argument was made against the traditional view of performing and composing as a type of service: was this not degrading? "Polite culture," for that is what it was called by contemporaries, brought those refinements to the arts which encouraged the formation of public venues and even an art market. Were not the prospects such that writers, musicians, and artists could be released from many of their traditional obligations to the patron and his coterie? Simultaneously, traditional rural fêtes and urban carnivals within easy access of the populace were domesticated, policed, or even suppressed. Elites who had once subsidized these collective rituals withdrew support, and by the end of the eighteenth century, commonfolk were defenders of these traditional recreations and customs which now were shaped into something resembling a popular culture.[103]

Musical journalism and criticism proliferated. Taste in music and the other arts became a matter of a knowledge of history and stylistic development. Tastes were not to be determined individually or by exclusive groups of people. Whereas the virtuoso of the seventeenth century was known by the variety of his interests, the connoisseur was designated by the quality of his interests. Judgment on the inherent quality of the work was a prime requisite. The ideal connoisseur was identified as a first embodiment of the esteemed *philosophe*. Culture had a general significance in that it was now possible to apply "detached absolute standards" to an object under view. All of this led to a correct appreciation by the connoisseur who was termed both "unprejudiced and liberal." The standards were deepened by a knowledge of history. Further, they were verified by a new critical vocabulary owing less to the supervision of institutions—the Church, universities, and the court. In fact, a new cultural environment (highly urban) was in the making. Philip Skelton, the Irish theologian, remarked toward the end of the eighteenth century that novels "for half a century have made the chief entertainment of that middle class which subsists between court and the spade."[104]

The traditional legitimation of landscape painting with its mythological associations, biblical titles, and allusions designed to ennoble this genre were rejected by a Gainsborough. Rural scenes and life no longer served to inspire the viewer's search for the celestial. Figures did not transcend the limits of ordinary humanity nor was a courtly Arcadia to be in prospect. Instead of Claude Lorraine's golden horizon, we have a simple scene with no effort to break the vault of heaven. The aristocratic dreamworld of the nobility was receding, with painters more often portraying daily routine as a series of amusing episodes from which emerged the stories of the life and times of ordinary men and women.[105]

II

CIVIL SOCIETY AND THE CASE OF ENGLAND AND SCOTLAND

Taste in the arts and an appreciation of nature were now benchmarks of civility. Indeed, definitions of civility leaned toward a more generalized conception of culture as well as of society. In an earlier time instruction in civility worked to modify extravagant behavior; these lessons were directed at the membership of an honor community. Atavistic cravings for revenge were to be sublimated, as was conspicuous consumption and the reckless gallantry of a nobility. At the late seventeenth century, the mission of civility underwent alteration, moving far beyond the domestication and taming of a recalcitrant order. No longer were its roots deeply embedded in the need for repression of promiscuous sociability; instead it was becoming synonymous with that politeness which allowed men and women to overcome their differences. Civility was subsumed under the rubric of a grander process whereby whole societies were to be transformed from crude to polished, from barbarous to civilized. The word *civilization* was now assuming its newer and more ambitious meaning. The general theme of the movement from barbarism to civilization (or civil society) became the spine and scaffolding for historical writing. Human development was charted through common stages and, in this historical mapping, a new orthodoxy was being propounded.[1]

"I believe," wrote David Hume, that "this is the historical age and this the historical nation." The characterization was fitting and the impulse to historicize was strong. Montesquieu's *The Spirit of the Laws* endeavored to relate the politics and governance of a society with its mores, climate, and social institutions using, throughout, comparative materials. He did not, however, employ his evidence to structure any progressive view of the different stages in the development of human society. This was to be the major contribution of the Scottish school and their version of the human past. Possibly the first to offer this view was Sir John Dalrymple: his *Essay towards a General History of Feudal Property in Great Britain* (1757) posited three diverse stages of property ownership, but no solid conclusions were drawn. He was followed by Lord Kames (Henry Home) who, in his *Historical Law Tracts* (1758) divided social development into four distinct stages, employing this stadial perspective on the past to illuminate the transformation of legal institutions. It is possible that both these jurists were anticipated by Adam Smith whose lectures on jurisprudence at Glasgow in the early 1750s provided the blueprint for an understanding of society from hunting to pastoral to agricultural to the commercial of his own day. This vision of change had considerable cultural and ethical import. Smith's predecessor at Glasgow, Francis Hutcheson, had spelled out the moral obligations of men and women in society. In Smith's lectures on jurisprudence he took the revolutionary step of locating these obligations in their proper historical context. Changing personal and property rights were themselves the product of historical movement from one stage of social development to the next. The proper historical context was to be defined principally through the explication of the framework of economic structures. The present age in which commerce had a large role, then, was the appropriate backdrop for comprehending personal obligation and property rights.[2]

Traditional notions of civility were judged by eighteenth-century critics as an impoverished form of politeness. Worse yet, they were considered unfashionable— that is, replete with affectation and mindless formality. "The dream of governance of the soul" was perceived as degenerating into "ridiculous posturing." Now a more informal brand of sociability was championed.

In an age of rising living standards and economic advance, sentiment had a special appeal to middling folk preoccupied with the quest for property and riches. The rules of genteel behavior, encompassing the nature of duty and obligation of individuals toward one another, must be sufficiently flexible to allow for the differences in background and education. The emphasis on sentiment or feeling permitted this flexibility in the face of a narrow aristocratic code positing social discrimination.[3]

The old aristocracy had been caricatured in the person of the proud Duke of Somerset, who would not permit his own daughter to sit in his presence. Now the resources of intimacy and privacy were on the increase; inner life and sensibility counted for more. Against the tyranny of custom was evoked the authority of the human heart and of reason. Educational ideals were changing both for children of the traditional elite and for the growing middling ranks. More detached from collective life, lessons in social ease and naturalness were to be garnered from the immediate family, kinfolk, tutors, and neighbors. Sensibility, sentiment, and sincerity were the values to be cultivated, rather than mastery of the recipes of old-fashioned politeness and civility. The social ideals of ease and informality as essentials of politeness challenged the endless bowing and scraping. Nature itself appeared to dictate an informal approval of everyday social ties, thus rendering restrictive courtly etiquette outmoded. The public wearing of the sword was less common and when donned was more likely to be decorative than martial. The poet, publisher, and proponent of new styles of social behavior, Robert Dodsley, intoned the following:

> Honour!—What's honour? A vain phantom rais'd, To fright the weak from tasting those delights, Which nature's voice that law supreme, allows.

Movement was away from the "protocol infested seventeenth century." The oft-repeated account of Beau Nash's removal of the feathers and finery of the Duchess of Queensbury at the Bath Pump Room lent force to the now fashionable requirement that the nobility, when mixing in public with those of different rank, should appear like the others and submit to the same conventions and rules so that they might be judged on their "intrinsic merits." The delights and dilemmas of a more liberated age were favored topics for literary and philosophic inquiry. The contemporary commitment to congenial and convivial relations was endorsed; frequent social intercourse was prized as an educative tool. Implicit in this evaluation was the idea of civility as leading to the reform of society. Traditional forms of civility were now to be refined and unified. Furthermore, reform of manners was to be achieved without giving offense. Sir Roger de Coverly, the journalist Joseph Addison's most popular creation, was exemplary of malleability in politics. A sage observation was recorded in *The Spectator,* 126 (5 July 1711): "I find, however, that the Knight is a much stronger Tory in the Country than in Town which as he told me in my own ear, is absolutely necessary for keeping up his own interest." The call to reform or, in the parlance of the eighteenth century, "improve" society without giving offense, was nowhere more evident than in the literary campaign to reduce antagonism between town elites and country gentry. Bitter satire against rustic squires was now accounted dangerous to the equilibrium of society. This literature of ridicule, in which Tory gentlemen heaped invective upon their country brethren, was a hardy staple of the Restoration theater. By the early eighteenth century, however, it was perceived as contributing to subversion of authority and thus weakening the governance of society. The editor of the *Gentlemen's Magazine* wrote under the name of Sylvanus Urbanus, suggesting the goal of a happy synthesis: ideally, the Tory gentleman and rustic squire were to exchange views and opinions and share taste in landscape gardening, fashion, architecture, and connoisseurship. Once again the esthetic jostled the rudely political. Finally, the language in which these exchanges were to take place was itself to be standardized.[4]

Surely the flashpoints of the recent past—the Civil War, the Interregnum, and the trying events of 1688 with the aftermath of the Restoration—still scorched historical memory. Civil culture served to dampen the flames of controversy still smoldering from these bitter happenings. Contacts between town and country, elites and middling folk, and gentry and professionals called for greater opportunity for conversation and easy exchange. Moreover, communication was to be consummated on the basis of greater equality and in the name of common interests. The *Encyclopedia Britannica* confidently opined that "nothing renders the mind so narrow and so little . . . as the want of social intercourse." Philip Dormer Stanhope, fourth Earl of Chesterfield, prized highly the rank and dignity of birth; he also valued the privilege (not the duty) of mixing with those whose social origins were entirely modest:

> There are two sorts of good company; one which is called the beau monde, and consists of those people who have the lead in courts, and in the gay part of life; the other consists of those who are distinguished by some peculiar merit, or who excel in some particular valuable art or science. For my own part, I used to think myself in company as much above me, when I was with Mr Addison or Mr Pope, as if I had been with all the Princes of Europe . . .

Oliver Goldsmith's kindly Vicar of Wakefield would remind his contemporaries:

The order of men which exists between the very rich and the very rabble . . . in this middle order of mankind are generally to be found all the arts, wisdom and virtues of society. This order alone is known to be the true preserver of freedom and may be called the People . . .

Apart from traditional corporate forms, new bodies and groups now colonized public space. The formation of innumerable types of voluntary association has been counted as a leading feature of emerging civil society. (An eighteenth-century contemporary has estimated that 20,000 Londoners met in various clubs each night.) If we single out a city such as Edinburgh in order to illustrate this thesis, we notice that members of the learned professions (especially lawyers and clergy), literary folk, large and middling landlords, and later, physicians, practically minded farmers, and merchants assembled in a variety of clubs and societies for the improvement of all matters. All matters ranged from agriculture to commerce to vernacular culture to recreation and leisure time. Civic issues were certainly not neglected and scientific concerns were to be furthered. These voluntary associations went by the names of Philosophic Society, Musical Society, the Poker Club, the Select Society, Rankenian Club, The Honorable Society of Improvers in the Knowledge of Agriculture in Scotland, and dozens more. Allan Ramsay the Elder, poet, founder of the first circulating library in Scotland, and Edinburgh bookseller, whose shop became a mecca for the high-born and middling folk for exchanging ideas, wrote these lines in praise of the last-named society on the list:

> Continue, best of clubs, long to improve
> Your native plains and gain your nation's love.
> Rouse every lazy laird of each wide field
> That unmanured not half their product yield.
> Show them the proper season, soils, and art,
> How they may plenty to their lands impart,
> Triple their rents, increase the farmer's store,
> Without the purchase of one acre more.[5]

In the collected works of the same Allan Ramsay the Elder appears the following entry from the *Journal of the Easy Club* (founded in May, 1712). It speaks eloquently to trust in improvement of sociability through the banishment of protocol, pedantry, and all forms of antisocial behavior. Well chosen was the adjective "easy" as affixed to this club:

The gentlemen who compose this society considering how much the unmaturity of years want of knowing the world and experience of living therein exposes them to the danger of being drawn away by unprofitable company to the waste of the most valuable part of their time, have resolved at some times to retire from all other business and company and meet in a society by themselves in order that by a mutual improvement in conversation they may become more adapted for fellowship with the politer part of mankind, and learn also from one anothers happy observations to abhor all such nauseous fops as are by their clamorous impertinences the bane and destruction of all agreeable society, and also to ridicule these pedantic coxcombs who by their unthinking gravity peevish preciseness or modest folly demonstrate themselves the apish counterfeiters of such perfections as God by nature has utterly denied them the capacity of ever attaining to, which sorts of people are so industriously avoided by the Society and others of free tractable and ingenious tempers so carefully encouraged that on the second day of their meeting, after some deliberation it was unanimously determined their society should go under the name of the Easy Club, designing thereby that their denomination should be a check to all unruly and disturbing behaviour among their members. To prevent which also each of them are styled with a particular name taken from some eminent person whose character though they are sensible of their own insufficiency fully to maintain yet everyone knowing something of his patrons history have him before them as an example which as the wise say is more prevalent in reformation than precept. And each member being always called by his patron's name at the meeting makes it impossible he should forget to copy what is laudable in him and what is not so to reject.

The next entry offers pseudonyms for the membership. Some are historical figures and others taken from Addison and Steele's *Tatler* and *Spectator:*

> May 12, 1712. Those who founded the Club called one another by the names of Rochester, Isaac Bickerstaff and Tom Brown—they were in a few days joined by three who assumed the names of Sir Roger L'Estrange, Sir Isaac Newton and ——— Heywood.

In 1717, the editor of the *Northern Tatler* (a spin-off from its London forebear), calling himself "Duncan Tatler," proclaimed his high purpose "to instruct, rectify, and reform the North Country." Remaining within the cultural bounds of Edinburgh, we have the *Scots Magazine*—a heavy literary journal—announcing: "That the Caledonian muse might not be restricted by want of a public echo to her song." Public libraries follow soon after Ramsay's patronage of the circulating library. The specialized legal library (Advocates Library) became the principal reference tool for leading Edinburgh scholars. A copy of every book in Scotland was to be deposited there, and within a generation after 1722, its holdings had increased sevenfold. Music societies abounded and, while religious resistance to the establishment of a theater was bitter, it did come at the mid-eighteenth century.[6]

I

Recent studies of eighteenth-century urban planning in the British Isles have highlighted the conscious effort to generate new forms of public space. Edinburgh's New Town was a prime example. A pamphlet was published in that city in 1752, ostensibly written by Sir Gilbert Elliot but owing its inspiration to the civically minded George Drummond (1687–1766). This gifted politician, six times Lord Provost, had been responsible for an elaborate building program including the Royal Exchange and the Infirmary. The aforementioned pamphlet entitled "The Proposals for carrying on certain Public Works in the City of Edinburgh" commenced with a general statement of intention:

Among the several causes to which the prosperity of a nation may be ascribed, the situation, conveniency, and beauty of its capital, are surely not the least considerable. A capital where these circumstances happen fortunately to concur, should naturally become the centre of trade and commerce, of learning and the arts, of politeness and refinement of every kind. No sooner will the advantages which these necessarily produce, be felt and experienced in the chief city, than they will diffuse themselves through the nation, and universally promote the same spirit of industry and improvement.

In the provincial towns of England, promotion of the efficient operation of the market and free commerce between landed elites and the middling ranks was to be coupled with efforts to make the townscape a center of "politeness and refinement of every kind." The public concert, the race meeting, and that proudest symbol of extended sociability and easy exchange—the assembly room—was no monopoly of a single order. Families of town gentry mixed with squires from the neighborhood, professional men, clergy, and merchants. At Sheffield and Birmingham we see assemblies of ironmongers, goldsmiths, wealthy "hardwaremen," physicians, parsons, lawyers, and others. This motley group was joined by squires who traveled to town from their great houses in the country. A recent survey of the social scene at Leeds during the first half of the eighteenth century concludes that "not only did the close association between gentry and merchants . . . create a society that was far more open than any on the Continent, but also there was a perfect mutual understanding of each other's world." The opinion is rendered that this was indeed a privileged social moment. In the 1770s and 80s, new manufacturing would produce social segregation, but for the time being, social stability and the mix held.[7]

In framing the townscape, the message of classical architecture with its rules and standard building forms proclaiming the virtues of uniform street architecture proved decisive. Local vernacular tradition and baroque fantasies were displaced in favor of simplicity, restraint, and moderation. Extravagant imagination and decorative impulses were domesticated in the English townscape. Reaction was strong against the "picturesque." Private travel and inland trade called for broad, straight thoroughfares. Demands for personal mobility were matched by requirements for the efficient shipment of goods. Private homes were subsumed under a grander configuration of architectural units. These of course were the square and street; both came to depend upon architectural uniformity:

> The development of the street and square contributed much to the emerging elegance and amenity of the town's built environment. It also, by emphasizing the collective rather than individual treatment of structures and spaces, suggests a new contemporary concern with the form of the town *as a whole.*

In English provincial towns there was a persistent demand for high-status leisure. Cultural facilities were developed for music and theater around the performing arts. Fashionable leisure involving spas, coffee houses, literary societies, and dozens of other clubs was perceived as a means for encouraging neighboring country gentry, squires, retired merchants and army officers to spend their winter season profitably in a provincial town. Of course the most innocuous forms of fashionable culture might only exacerbate prejudice and partisan politics; but contemporaries believed that the new pastimes, both intellectual and social, would inhibit political partisanship and factionalism. John Toland's thoughts are representative of this optimistic forecast. In his *Description of Epsom* (1711), he wrote:

> I must do our coffee-houses the justice to affirm, that for social virtue they are equalled by few, and exceeded by none, though I wish they may be imitated by all. A Tory does not stare and leer when a Whig comes in, nor a Whig look sour and whisper at the sight of a Tory. These distinctions are laid by with the winter suit at London.

Shortly after the accession of George I to the throne, John Macky (d. 1726), author of *Journey Through England* and memoirist, paid a visit to the north England city of York. Here he found the town's "polite" society considerably embarrassed by the continuation of a convention fixed in the bitter atmosphere of the late Queen Anne's reign. The convention dictated holding to assemblies during the week. Monday was the day for Tories and Thursday belonged to the Whigs. This type of antisocial practice would not do in the more tranquil reign of King George. The loyal Whig, Lord Carlisle, himself took the initiative to alter custom by "carrying mixed company" to both assemblies. Later, Macky learned that "the officers of the army" played a crucial role in the process of healing old wounds by "making no distinctions." In 1730, long after the competing gatherings had united in harmony, a fitting epilogue was played out. In that year work began on the construction of Lord Burlington's grand assembly rooms, which were to be "urban showpieces" of north England. A recent historical commentator has written: "Of a thousand bricks such as these, small though each may have been, was much of the solid edifice of early Georgian political stability constructed."[8]

Doctor Samuel Johnson was among the many literati who singled out the civilizing influence of Addison and Steele. *The Tatler* and *The Spectator* were both praised for being congenial and moderate in substance and tolerant in spirit. Like his literary confreres, Johnson contended, "to minds heated with political contest, they supplied cooler and more inoffensive reflections." Addison's writings were singled out by British and Continental contemporaries for contributing to social cohesion and creating trust among men where once suspicion reigned. This he did by coining a *lingua franca* of politeness permitting individuals to resolve their differences amicably. Although the journalist Addison was closely tied to the Whig point of view, he castigated "the rage of party." When strife between Whig and Tory was at white heat (1711), he cautioned his readers that "a furious party spirit, when it rages in its full violence, exerts itself in civil war and bloodshed . . . it fills a nation with spleen and rancor, and extinguishes all seeds of good nature, compassion, and humanity. . . ." He continues this theme, suggesting to the wide readership of *The Spectator*, "We should not any longer regard our fellow subjects as Whigs or Tories, but should make the man of merit our friend and the villain our enemy." Again we take note of Samuel Johnson, who in *The Lives of the Poets* reflected on the widespread and deep anxiety in the aftermath of the civil wars which led to suspicion of "enthusiasm" and the language of extravagant metaphors. Political license and grandiose language were thus identified with civil unrest and social disruption.

In *The Spectator,* Addison constructed a literary persona—that of the spectator. Using this voice, the author fixed himself at a benevolent distance from politics, observing rather than engaging in this heated activity. The same rhetorical tactic was to hold for Francis Hutcheson and David Hume with their conception of a benevolent observer and Adam Smith's idea of an impartial observer. This imaginary, unprejudiced spectator of our actions proved the standard by which individuals might learn to judge themselves. Through these rhetorical strategies journalists like Addison were able to create an ample cultural space in which morals, refinement, and taste might themselves be cultivated. Furthermore, it would be possible to have critical discourse on these matters. Politeness entered that domain of behavior where civility had once been dominant and, in turn, was integrated into a moral framework. Addison and Steele distrusted politeness as a thing in itself, for it could be reduced to nothing more than a notion of social strategy or a veiled opportunity for license. Politeness adrift of its ethical moorings could make England a polite nation at the expense of good sense and religion. In *Rambler,* number 187 (7 January 1754), Samuel Johnson voiced the worries of many of his readers:

> The artful and fraudulent usurpers of distinction deserve greater severities than ridicule or contempt, since they are seldom content with empty praise but are instigated by passions more pernicious than vanity. . . . The commercial world is very frequently put into confusion by the bankruptcy of merchants, that assumed the splendour of wealth . . . [until they] drag down into poverty those whom their equipages had induced to trust them . . .

The dilemma commerce posed for Johnson and legions of others was not one to be resolved merely by keeping out the nouveau riche or Johnny-come-lately. Awareness of complex relations and exchanges not easily negotiated by entering claims of merit, duty, or obligation, prompted the need for new forms of accord or agreement. Social interaction involving the exchange of opinion required more than virtue. "Agreeable negligence" had been the high recommendation of Addison. Where would the world be without agreeableness? Informality of style—itself a style—might bring method and order to literature and life without calling attention to itself. Esthetic forms of cultural expression had just such power. Taste became part of a discursive revolution encouraging readers, listeners, and viewers to alter their conviction or even take a new perspective. Ideally, taste was egalitarian—independent of class, birth, and rank: good taste would produce "good society." The capacity of individuals to transcend their private predilections to reach the entitlement of judgment was a key. The shared nature of their judgments rendered taste social rather than a private phenomenon.[9]

Shaftesbury's essay entitled "Sensus Communis" (common sense), already referred to, was in the familiar style—what he termed "the way of the chat"—and

was appropriate to "pleasurable reflections." Nothing was more certain to bring
satisfaction than ruminating on music and the arts. Taste in the arts allowed gentry
and middling folk to draw closer, defining the grounds and terms for membership
in a "polished or civilized" public. Culture was identified with intellectual and
artistic sophistication. The idea of culture did not exist in an absolute sense in the
eighteenth century; by "absolute sense," the individual would be judged as lacking
in culture. Instead, it was employed as a figurative term for the refinement of fac-
ulties, manners, and mind. Samuel Johnson wrote in *Resselas* of a certain woman
that "she neglected the culture of her understanding." The word "culture" signified a process of training, improvement, or refinement. That it was a process suggests that the context in which it was located was more socially assured than that
of the nineteenth century. One recalls a comment of George Eliot in her *Mid-
dlemarch* where, in appropriate nineteenth-century fashion, she speaks of one of
her characters: "He wants to go abroad again . . . [for] the vague purpose of what
he calls cultural preparation for he knows not what."

Again, on the matter of culture and nineteenth-century views we have Matthew
Arnold's celebrated comment in his *Culture and Anarchy:* "The great men of culture are those who had a passion . . . for carrying from one end of society to the
other, the best knowledge, the best ideas of their time." Finally, yet another spec-
imen of the "absolute" view of culture: J. A. Froude, the nineteenth-century historian, in his *Nemesis of Faith,* posits the following: "The End of all culture is
that we may be able to sustain ourselves in a spiritual atmosphere as do the birds
in the air."[10]

II

The movement of history was driven substantially by commerce, credit, and the
play of the market. Often an effort was made to integrate the changes affected by
these stimuli with advance toward a readily identifiable culture of polish and politeness—something approximating a civilization. The word "civilization" was
only now coming into vogue. Boswell relates a visit to Doctor Johnson who at the
moment was busy preparing a fourth edition of his folio dictionary. Johnson would
not admit the usage of the word "civilization"; instead, he insisted on the word
"civility." Boswell took up the new usage and with great deference to his mentor,
said, "I thought civilization from to civilize, better in the sense of opposed to barbarism than civility." Culture, then, was perceived as a process of refinement
prompted by a growing trade and manufacture. Montesquieu's analysis was influential, and *The Spirit of the Laws* was quickly translated into English and widely
read by Scottish and English literati and lawyers:

> Commerce is a cure for the most destructive prejudices; for it is almost a general rule,
> that wherever we find agreeable matters, there commerce flourishes; and that wher-
> ever there is commerce, there we meet with agreeable manners.

Let us not be astonished, then, if our manners are now less savage than formerly. Commerce has everywhere diffused a knowledge of the manners of all nations: these are compared one with another, and from this comparison arise the greatest advantages.

Commercial laws, it may be said, improve manners for the same reason that they destroy them. They corrupt the purest morals. This was the subject of Plato's complaints; and we every day see that they polish and refine the most barbarous.

Widespread was the belief that culture as a process of refinement was prompted by vital economic activity. Zeal for improvement and enthusiasm for generalized guides to this end rivaled older notions of duty and obligation. Virtue itself shaded into good manners and polish. From the vantage points of polite culture and commercial society, past ages were perceived as times in which the passions had not been appropriately socialized. These views were advanced against a backdrop of a growing economy and mounting prosperity. Civil society was highly prized since it operated to "ensure a safe and autonomous productive zone."[11]

Poised against these buoyant assessments was a vigorous discourse highlighting the worthiness of civic virtue and public eloquence. Reluctant to contemplate with satisfaction the growth of commerce, consumerism, the radical division of labor, and the free play of the market (all hallmarks of a civil society), except as evidence of historical decline, civic-minded humanists continued to champion models of politics based upon the select experience of small republican states. The idea of the virtuous and frugal citizenry of the republic (here of course Rome was much in mind) proved as durable as it was attractive. The decline of the martial spirit was attributed to an appetite for luxury which had been the undoing of societies in the past. The experience of republican Rome and many another political community demonstrated that agriculture was the natural school of civic virtue. The politics of virtue brought forth the shade of Cincinnatus: there must be agrarian roots for an active citizenry willing to relinquish power in the interest of the common good. An active citizenry should be largely amateur, and therefore, professionalism was no just part of this political culture. However, these formulations of civic humanism offered precious little practical guidance as to how the public world should be organized or society arranged.[12]

Over the eighteenth century, the nature of "polite" society was itself becoming increasingly porous. This was a world much enlarged and open to virtually all candidates possessing the required credentials. Voluntary forms of associative life served as a bridge to join professional men, middling tradesmen, and skilled artisans with their social superiors. Again we might refer to the experiences of Scottish cities such as Edinburgh to underline the extent to which clubs, lodges, fraternities, and academies permitted literate and affluent Scots to confront rapid change in economic and political life with a substantial degree of confidence. Hume writing to the painter Allan Ramsay the younger (1713–84), in May of 1755, tells how sought after was membership in the Select Society. It brought together the rulers of Scotland with the professionals and men of letters:

... Young and old, noble and ignoble, witty and dull, all the world are ambitious of a place amongst us, and on each occasion (of election) we are as much solicited by candidates as if we were to choose a Member of Parliament.

The divide between landlords on the one side and literati and moderate clergy on the other closed the gap between membership of this order of decision makers and their families. The breaching of the social divide was of special significance for the moderate clergy who tended to support the authority of the lay patrons of churches—so frequently landowners. This accommodation was essential for defusing religious issues which still threatened social stability. That the literati were also generally sympathetic to landowners lent further stability to contemporary culture and politics in Scotland. Less elitist than England, a "lad o'parts" could "wag his head" in the pulpit of a church of Scotland.

Hume in his *Essays, Moral, Political and Literary* [Political Discourses] was one among many who extolled the public advantages gained through the heightened sociability of his fellows:

> The more these refined arts advance, the more sociable men become: nor is it possible, that, when enriched with science, and possessed of a fund of conversation, they should be contented to remain in solitude, or live with their fellow-citizens in that distant manner, which is peculiar to ignorant and barbarous nations. They flock into cities; love to receive and communicate knowledge; to show their wit or their breeding; their taste in conversation or living, in clothes or furniture. Curiosity allures the wise; vanity the foolish; and pleasure both. Particular clubs and societies are everywhere formed; both sexes meet in an easy and sociable manner: and the tempers of men, as well as their behaviour, refine space. So that, beside the improvements which they receive from knowledge and the liberal arts, it is impossible but they must feel an increase of humanity, from the very habit of conversing together, and contribute to each other's pleasure and entertainment. Thus *industry, knowledge* and *humanity,* are linked together by an indissoluble chain, and are found, from experience as well as reason, to be peculiar to the more polished, and, what are commonly denominated, the more luxurious ages . . . [13]

After 1707 and the union with England, Scotland was a nation without a nation, and Edinburgh was a capital without a capital. As we have already observed, a myriad of private voluntary clubs and societies were founded to debate questions of economic improvement and cultural advance. In these voluntary associations, lawyers, landowners, university teachers, physicians, moderate clergy, and women assembled to ventilate public issues and express private anxieties. The quest for the improvement of everything from agriculture to manufacture to *belles lettres,* invested Edinburgh society with a dignity compensating somewhat for loss of political status. The proliferation of associations and institutions hospitable to a civil culture was an indispensable ingredient of the Scottish Enlightenment. Meanwhile, in both Scotland and England, a new vocabulary for the public life surfaced. Words such as "agenda," "chairman," "membership," and the very word "club" came into currency in its modern meaning. The term "association" now had a decidedly positive connotation.[14]

The Masonic Order originated in England and Scotland and is emblematic of the change. Its requirement that no private quarrels or piques were to be vetted at its lodge meetings was overmatched by the grander prohibition against initiating political and religious controversy. The need for tolerance and forbearance was a hallmark of this brotherhood. Masonic lodges held elections, required consent of "all of the brothers," and endorsed representative governance. The call was for self-discipline and leadership guided by constitutions and by-laws. Society had become more complex, more abstract, and more distant. Voluntary associations of those with power as well as those of meager strength were organized to act independently of household, family, neighborhood, and workplace. They brought a certain order to the exchange of ideas in the assembly and marketplace. The number of roles individuals were required to fill both increased and were more various. Furthermore, social change was far less predictable and its effects less familiar. New forms of associative life were housed in halls, institutes, and assembly rooms as professional men, merchants, middling tradesmen, clergy, and women joined reading and book clubs as well as societies for cultural and economic improvement. Broadly based groups were regularly meeting out of mutual interests rather than confessional affiliation. Ideally they might learn to cooperate with those holding rival ideas. One might entertain strong private convictions but they were not to serve as the springboard for positing social arrangements.[15]

The minutes of the Select Society of Edinburgh for 19 June 1754 and 7 August of the same year permit us to have a window into an exchange of views on vital issues. At the first meeting, Mr. Adam Smith was in the chair as president, and the questions to be argued were first, was it advantageous to Britain to permit general naturalization of foreign Protestants; second, whether bounties paid on exportation of corn would be advantageous to manufacture and trade as well as to agriculture? At the August session, the chairman of the Committee for Questions read several of these topics for debate into the Book of Questions and these were to be disputed at a future meeting. (Parenthetically, the chairman was Sir David Dalrymple (1726–92) and was the third baronet of Hailes. He had a distinguished career as a justice and was an accomplished historian, author of *Annals of Scotland.*) The issues to be tested have a range and historical pertinence which is most instructive: Were the numerous banks existing in Scotland truly useful to the trade of this people? Was paper credit advantageous to a nation? Should a bounty be continued on exportation of low-priced linen manufactured in Scotland? Were the Scottish practices of distributing money to the poor in their own houses or receiving them in hospitals or work-houses to be distinguished in terms of which would be most advantageous? In present circumstances is it most advantageous to increase tillage or grain? For a change of pace we have the old chestnut, did Brutus do well to assassinate Caesar? The matter of intemperence was to be considered, especially among the "vulgar." Did the increase of wealth enhance this vice? The self-serving question was raised: "May a lawyer of ordinary parts become eminent in his profession?" A delicate issue: "Whether it be advantageous to a nation, that the law of private property should be reduced to an art?" Finally, a matter of grave concern to public morals and religion: "Whether the repenting stool ought to be taken away?" All these queries for debate were then approved by the committee and entered in a book. The president of each meeting selected the appropriate questions to be debated.

Like so many other societies, clubs, lodges, and academies in Britain and on the Continent, the Select Society (in conjunction with the Edinburgh Society) offered a prize for the best essay ''relating to literature.'' Here again we observe the promotion of critical debate through historical investigation, analysis of economic change, and assessment of social policy—all of this ventilated in a public forum. Submissions were to be on the following topics:

I.   History of the extent and duration of the Roman and afterwards of the Saxon conquests and settlements in Britain to the North of Severus's wall in Cumberland and Northumberland.

II. Account of the rise and progress of commerce, arts and manufactures in North Britain, and the causes which promoted or retarded them.

III. The most reasonable scheme for maintaining and employing the poor in North Britain; and how far the scheme can be executed by the laws now in force.

Which being read and considered by the Society, they unanimously approved of the Report.[16]

III

Urbanity, with its accent on manners, prized a sociability that lived in public within defined social forms. That social and political compromises were effected against a backdrop of general prosperity is relevant. So too was civil society's allegiance to the sacredness of private property and the play of the free market. Without idealizing eighteenth-century associative life, it is plausible to suggest that it burgeoned at a ''privileged'' historical moment. Unlike the previous century, the public sphere was not torn by civil war and religious hatreds. As we have noted, the memory of this troubled time was not lost on subsequent generations; some profit was drawn by eighteenth-century men and women from the terrible lessons of the past. And unlike the succeeding nineteenth century, circumstances in the eighteenth were indeed more conducive to stability in the public domain. (We shall be returning to this matter shortly.) In that later time voluntary societies were themselves sorely embattled. Food scarcity, crime, public disorder, disease, labor organization, and the lack of a consensus over prices and wages were but a few of the seemingly intractable problems festering in the insalubrious industrial towns of Britain. Class division and the turn of middle-class culture away from public sociability were the mark of early nineteenth-century England. Already, between the time of the American Revolution and the French Revolution we observe ''among quality folk'' something of a departure from engagement with high culture, and a shift toward anxious preoccupation with the reform of political and economic problems. For the policy-making classes of Victorian England, at issue was the need to contain and control "the forces unleashed by the anarchical dynamics of capitalism and individualism." The breakdown of authority led to the agitation and excitement which market forces set free.[17]

To return to the late seventeenth century is to feature a very different set of social concerns. Political stability had been conspicuous for its absence in England and Scotland for most of the century. But after 1688 political feuding in England was for the most part confined within constitutional channels. This signified that they were to be contained within the frame of parliamentary elections and the regular meeting of this body. There was little enthusiasm on the part of the upper echelons of English society to resort to violent and desperate resolutions of problems. The politics of parliament revealed a pattern of sensible administration with a minority opposition as energetic as it was ineffectual. In Scotland the Moderate clergy gained increased support during the first half of the eighteenth century and the religious cauldron was no longer at a boil. In England the Glorious Revolution of 1688 was no disreputable enterprise, having as its objective the election of a "free parliament," so that political divisions could find a certain legitimacy. Further, there was little serious pressure from below: the plebeians did not seek to gain advantage from the protracted "rage of party" so toxic at the top of political society. Unlike the 1640s or 50s, or indeed the late eighteenth century, the political nation was stable from the late 1680s to the 1760s. Political issues, while arousing interest, did not prompt the resort to reckless gallantry or urgent reform.[18]

A strong case has been made for the generalization that by the early 1700s the higher orders of society were coming to acknowledge "common interests" and a "common identity." We have already reviewed the experiences of town life and the mingling of top-echelon folk. Moreover, the experience of town life was itself becoming increasingly familiar, with the urban population of England doubling over the eighteenth century. Of course close ties between town and country were of long standing. Functional bonds between local gentry, market, and country towns involving trade and justice went far back into the Middle Ages. It was, however, the multiplication and reinforcement of social links that would prove decisive.[19]

Between the 1690s and 1720s England continued to experience political and constitutional strains. But there were long-range trends—demographic and economic—operating to smooth the jagged edges. Demographic stability, coupled with increased prosperity and a modest expansion of opportunity in the professions for the sons of gentry, eased social tensions. After the 1660s a greater balance between resources and population was in prospect. Growth of population had been upward for the first part of the seventeenth century; now this trend was played out. Until the 1740s, then, population remained relatively stationary, increasing by only three or four percent in the two generations after the 1660s. This figure obtaining over an eighty-year period can be compared with the twenty-five percent increase registered between 1600 and 1640. Population figures do indicate heightened prospects for stability in the late seventeenth and early eighteenth centuries. This possibility appears to be enhanced by the remarkably low agricultural prices prevailing from roughly 1660 to 1750. England became a grain-exporting nation around 1670, and by 1700 seems to have been a meat-eating one as well. For this period England was no longer in danger of famine and this was a victory of no small magnitude. Cheaper imported commodities, especially inexpensive clothing as well as household furnishings, were available at the early eighteenth century. Between 1680 and 1720 wages appear to have been advancing more rapidly than the price of food and consumer goods. Without striking an easy equation between the decline of radical politics and mounting prosperity from the Glorious Revolution to the 1760s, we still should not ignore the possible correlation.[20]

This period after 1688 and just beyond the mid-eighteenth century was a time of lower temperatures for popular and spontaneous politics. Certainly this era was very different from that of the toxic politics of the first five decades of the seventeenth century. Likewise, the time of relative stability can be marked off from the radical agitation and unrest characterizing English political life in the late eighteenth century. The foremost historian of popular unrest, E. P. Thompson, has been influential for more than a generation in offering a very different portrait of plebeian politics and culture in eighteenth-century England. In recent years, however, critics have chipped away at his construct, laying bare its deficiencies. His characterization of the state as parasitic—the quintessential mechanism for patrician appropriation—has been effectively rebuffed. So too has his castigation of the Whig regime as criminal. His critics have demonstrated that participation in government extended further down the social ladder than hitherto believed. The electorate has been reckoned larger and its constituency humbler than previously affirmed. Furthermore, this electorate was growing in the last decades of the seventeenth and early eighteenth centuries at a rate faster than the general population. Opinions of the citizenry of more modest origin, although unpolished, served as something of a check to popular radicals. A sense of *polis* as well as politics has been underscored by recent research. Sentimental views on law and the state, casting each in the role of arch-villain, fail to acknowledge that the courts could benefit as well as work against the lives and interests of the laboring poor.[21]

The damping down of popular radicalism in the late seventeenth and early eighteenth centuries is evident when one compares its tepidness with the blazing temperatures of an earlier generation. The governing elites had learned hard lessons from the past and were not about to give the plebeians an opening to make political mischief. Economic interests bonded agriculture, mining, and manufacturing. Often the same landed individuals stood as owners and improvers in all three sectors. There were industrial disorders, press gang riots, cider tax riots, Mother Gin riots, turnpike riots, and a legion of other protests. Dissatisfaction and political unrest there was aplenty, what with the human cost of wrenching economic change. But these protests and disturbances did not threaten the ruling order. Jacobite insurrections in 1715 and 1745 did not significantly weaken the authority of government. Educated and propertied individuals who had given leadership to popular radicalism in the seventeenth century were now in short supply. Finally, the religious radicalism of the 1640s was little in evidence. Anglican clergy of the eighteenth century might whip up popular fury against Methodists and Dissenters (and there were always the Catholics and Jews) but none of these sects presented the likely prospect of revolution or political radicalism. Only in the late eighteenth century, when regeneration of popular Anglicanism created division among the ruling class, did political circumstance alter. For most of the eighteenth century, then, religious differences were contained. Until the middle years of the century Dissenters stood in an attitude of tense accommodation. Archbishop Thomas Herring, a cleric from a dissenting background, observed in 1748 that "nothing in the world is more contrary to my judgment of things than to make alterations in our establishment of which in some sense the toleration act is a part; and what I am determined to stick to, is the support of these two [the Test and Corporation Acts] in conjunction. I think philosophy, Christianity, and policy are all against changes."[22]

E. P. Thompson's casting of the laboring poor in so heroic a role as "popular radicals" is a bit romantic. Yet he is to be congratulated for his meticulous survey of popular resentment and discontent. Like a true historical detective, he has traced them out in ballads, threatening letters, and quotidian challenges to deference and hierarchy. Of course the laboring poor had ties to consumerism, to religious life, and were just as likely to be patriotic as middling folk. Still, his portrayal of the deep attachments of the lower orders to a world of habit and custom is worthy of regard. Their recreations and rituals carry the flavor of an archaic culture. One can observe how this culture was under threat, challenged as it was by more impersonal norms of commerce and a more abstract conception of society. Plebeian belief in the idea of just price for provisions and a regulated market in grain suggests something of the deep attachment to archaic notions of a highly moralized economics. So too was the value fixed to multiple land use rather than absolute ownership. Upholding the commons against the movement toward enclosure at the late eighteenth century was yet another manifestation of deep-seated and traditional views. Yet this was surely a complex game and movement was often crab-like rather than straightforward. Between 1715 and 1774, approximately 850 enclosure acts were passed by parliament, and the pace of adoption accelerated after mid-century. These went some distance toward ending "overlapping" customary agrarian rights. But change was far from linear. It is true that by obtaining parliamentary sanction landed proprietors could override local custom. A majority of landlords in a given area could force a reluctant minority to accept compensation in common fields, thus depriving cotters and their ilk of "use-claims." But the courts were indeed open to custom and traditional claims when these were supported by evidence and backed by men of substance. Determined tenants in Cumbria successfully defended their claims at law. The courts upheld their case on the level of entry fines as well as use-rights. The customary rights of rural poor were less likely to be sustained, as was evidenced in the Common Pleas judgment of 1788 against gleaning.[23]

Not just segments of the laboring poor dissented from the doctrines of economic improvers and the imperatives of a "polite and commercial society." A rich literature of didactic verse and mordant satire illuminated the dark corners of the antisocial quest for "superfluities"—the eighteenth-century term for luxuries. There was a strong primitivist component among writers and ethical philosophers; poets and moralists in great numbers repudiated the idea of the utility of superfluities. In its stead they invoked the archaic notions of simplicity and communion with nature. Rousseau, who had highlighted the deleterious effects of social refinement, had a strong influence on Scottish thought. He had extended the frame of reference of primitivism by superimposing an idealized past upon a rural present. Especially touching to the Scots was the romanticized portrayal of peasants and farmers: for certain Scottish authors of the Lowlands, their neighbors, the Highlanders, were living proof of the value of a culture that was being denigrated as passé. Of David Hume, a contemporary was to remark that his taste was a "rational act" rather than an "instantaneous feeling." But even the skeptical philosopher, whose historical sensibilities were so cool and whose literary tastes were neo-classical, was to write the following in a letter to his friend David Wilkes in 1754:

> If your time had permitted, you should have gone into the Highlands. You would there have seen human Nature in the golden Age, or rather, indeed, in the Silver: For the Highlanders have degenerated somewhat from the primitive Simplicity of Mankind. But perhaps you have so corrupted a Taste as to prefer your Iron Age, to be met with in London & the south of England; where Luxury & Vice of every kind so much abound.

Passé and archaic Highland civilization might be, but ideally it still carried the mark of an honor culture under threat of being overwhelmed by commercialism and consumerism. In Scotland, as indeed throughout Europe, the grand epic *Poems of Ossian* (*Fingal* and *Temora*) gripped the public imagination. Thomas Sheridan, teacher of Elocution and the English Tongue, was invited to lecture by the Select Society of Edinburgh. According to James Boswell, this expert

> thought [Ossian] excelled Homer in the Sublime and Virgil in the Pathetic. He said Mrs. Sheridan and he had fixed it as a standard of feeling, made it like a thermometer by which they could judge of the warmth of everybody's heart.

This forgery by the Scot James MacPherson took Edinburgh society by storm, dividing critics as to its authenticity. His representation of a lost Celtic world whose primitive denizens possessed those virtues of loyalty, bravery, and an exquisite talent for friendship proved singularly appealing to an increasingly urbanized readership. Literary critics and moral philosophers were eager to vouchsafe the historical truth of this rousing epic of primitive grandeur and tragedy against a battery of doubters. The dispute held center stage in Scotland, England, and Europe for better than a generation.[24]

Eighteenth-century rustics and peasants were endowed by Scottish poets with the virtues of the age of the patriarchs. The fall away from grace of rural life was adumbrated by scores of Scottish literati. Themes such as the disintegration of an age-old social structure in the countryside; the laird's abandonment of his tenants and severing of the feudal bond; the laird's withdrawal of financial assistance, guaranteed by custom; and finally, the laird's cruel alliance with the town lawyer to drive "gudemen" from their ancestral homes—all these were hardy perennials of Scottish prose and poetry. Robert Fergusson, the best of the Edinburgh poets writing in the mid-eighteenth century, treated the abdication of "good-lordship" among country gentry as a primal sin. The socially fragmented city and countryside, the misguided efforts at urban renovation, which obliterated ancient land-marks, and the rise of distrust and legalism among the masses—these were but a few of the mischiefs, misfortunes, and economic tragedies befalling contemporary Edinburgh. The Scottish novelist Tobias Smollett spoke for many when urging that the passion for utility be tempered by an appreciation for custom and historical con-tinuities. His fictional character Matthew Bramble journeys through the commer-cial cities of England and Scotland and back, only to return to the felicities of his native rural Wales. There he will assume his proper place as the benevolent and fatherly laird. The kindly laird will protect his tenants from the blistering winds of change. Such at least was the fragile literary construct.

In Allan Ramsay the Elder's highly regarded pastoral play *The Gentle Shepherd*, the character Sir William resolves problems for an overmatched peasantry incapa-ble of responding to changing circumstances. However, with the passing decades of the eighteenth century, the pastoral genre loses its glossy confidence and will turn upon itself to criticize the very ideals it was designed to celebrate. Characters caught in the torrent of change, having no comprehension of the forces raging against them, can only engage the reader's sympathy. Soon the novels of Sir Walter Scott and John Galt will deepen the reader's understanding of history—that "hard rock against which men and women break their heads." Increasingly, social change will be set against a backdrop of economic determinism. In this historical universe characters can do no more than understand the inevitable or, in a word, come to terms with history itself.[25]

IV

The framework of social arrangements was predicated on the norm of propriety rather than virtue. In an earlier archaic world the force of involuntary association (guild) had a dynamic role. Now voluntarist notions were proving more attractive. The impact of change found dramatic resonance in contemporary literature. Duty, mutuality, obligation, and a sense of responsibility were often shunted in favor of less demanding forms of emotional bonding. Virtue itself was judged as being in-separable from the capacity for and the expression of feeling or sentiment. From what the poet Keats later designated as the "heart's affection" sprang benevolence and those highly valued feelings of compassion and pity. The poet spoke glowingly of "the holiness of the heart's affection," and many in an earlier time had been moved to write and meditate on the symbiotic relations between sympathizer and sufferer. The identification was itself most therapeutic. An anonymous author (1735) made this tender assessment:

> Humanity, in its first and general Acceptation, is call'd by Holy Writers, *Goodwill towards Men;* by Heathens, *Philanthropy,* or *Love* of our *Fellow Creatures.* It some-times takes the Name of *Good-nature,* and *delights* in *Actions* that have an *obliging* Tendency in them: When strongly *impress'd* on the *Mind,* it assumes a *higher* and nobler Character, and is not satisfy'd with good-natured Actions alone, but *feels* the

Misery of others with *inward Pain*. It is then deservedly named *Sensibility,* and is considerably increased in its intrinsick Worth.[26]

The widely read and psychologically influential Scottish novelist Henry Mackenzie gives perfect expression to the boundless world of sentiment in his novel *The Man of Feeling* (1771). The absolute formulation of this ethos must culminate with the helplessness and death of the hero Harley when confronted with the anguish and pain of sorrows beyond human endurance. Harley is not distant from Goethe's Werther—that other hero who found a home in tender human hearts.

Francis Hutcheson in his *Concerning Moral Good and Evil* highlights the moral sense, which in his view was intuitive rather than rational. He sanctioned the immediate and hence "untested" responses of sympathy and fellowship. Hume and Smith, in their different ways, favored these untested responses against a more cautious rationalism. The man of feeling had Hume's support:

> No qualities are more readily intituled to the general good-will and approbation of mankind than beneficence and humanity, friendship and gratitude, natural affection and public spirit . . . and a generous concern for our kind and species.

It might be argued that the desire to believe in the force of sympathy and sensibility in human affairs was, ironically, directly proportional to the triumph of self-interest and property rights in the public world—that is, to Adam Smith's "society of strangers." In an advanced commercial world of abstract ties, civil society had considerable durability, so that the maintenance of social hierarchy no longer needed to be an antipode to social breakdown; nor was the exchange of gifts and courtesies so essential for cementing social arrangements. Images of the harmony of the cosmos with their implicit references to the body social were less fashionable. As if in compensation, emphasis was placed on the relevance of deep social feeling as a mechanism for repairing the raveled sleeve of society. Sympathy was at the center of Adam Smith's *Theory of Moral Sentiments* (1759), and this work should be read in conjunction with *Wealth of Nations*. The literature of sentiment commanded the field and like its immediate predecessor *politeness*, it tended to camouflage rather than reveal social differences and ideological breaches.[27]

Dissent, dissatisfaction, and resistance were vocal and intense but with only modest political dimension. Isolated from grander historical movements, these voices of disapproval were to become effective only late in the century. The American and French revolutions were to offer different paradigms of politics to the disaffected and disabused. As was indicated, the term "association" had a positive connotation, but this changed in the 1780s. Discontent and agitation among workers and plebes was now judged threatening and the term tended toward the pejorative. Earlier the political parties had no program for systematic reform; not until the beginning of industrialization were new models for social organization to be readily available. As we have observed, religion was not a force to energize the politics of eighteenth-century Scotland or England. Fear of popery as the harbinger of an "all-pervasive foreign tyranny" had shaped the seventeenth-century Englishman's conception of liberty. This menace of popery and Spanish intrusion struck at the triad of piety, property, and liberty. Now the threat had dissipated and danger to the commonwealth receded so that public anxiety found expression in bigotry and prejudice rather than fear of national disaster. The hangover from the dread religious wars of the seventeenth century and the religious enthusiasms had lifted. One could almost argue that civil society won by default. The fear of royal absolutism and Catholicism which held John Locke in thrall when composing *The Two Treatises* gave way to the more secure stance of the generation of Hume and then of Smith. The political opportunity for the various pieces (some old, some new) to coalesce was most favorable. The Jacobites had failed abjectly in 1715, 1744, and 1745–46. Neither the Tory party nor those on the Celtic outskirts of the kingdom nor ordinary folk intervened in a decisive manner on behalf of the Pretender's quest for power. Jacobite and Hanoverian were both drawn to commerce; each prized traditional English liberties, were mainly Protestant, and held comparable views on family life, property rights, and the law and its institutions. In the words of a recent reviewer, they were "too much part of their age to disrupt it." The Tory Samuel Johnson is exemplary of those of modest beginnings who were, likewise, assimilated.[28]

It has been suggested that the ideological norm of political society at the mid-eighteenth century was "determinism." Historical reflection reinforced the conclusion that commercial and civil society were together the wave of the present. The commercial society now in flower gave no hint to thoughtful contemporaries of the mass industrial society to come. Therefore the bold sociological and economic analysis of an Adam Smith was not accompanied by a call for new radical notions of morality. In fact, just the opposite was true: commercial society was not seen to require any reformulation or even rethinking of relations between elite and common folk or rulers and the ruled. Yet the emergence of a mass industrial society would demand just such a reformulation of moral imperatives; social and economic analysis would not be enough.

Civil society was that entity which protected life, liberty, and property. Its progress was to be charted by Hume, William Robertson, Lord Kames, and Smith. The stadial historical framework developed by these Scots was to be employed by English jurists such as William Blackstone to explicate transformations in the law resulting from economic change. Prescriptions for a healthy contemporary society were then confidently announced. Ideally under its aegis labor and commodity exchange were to conducted in that free zone apart from seigneurial and political direction. Moreover, the process of privitization created an autonomous sphere outside the reach of the state where public affairs could be debated by ordinary citizens. For reasons which we shall allude to momentarily, it was easier for historically minded Scots to argue for the relevance of commerce in shaping the form of government in an advanced society. Unlike their English confreres they could not rely on the idea of the "ancient constitution." This interpretation contended that England had inherited "the ancient Anglo-Saxon liberties," and these forged the constitution. Not even the pernicious efforts of the Stuarts could subvert these time-honored liberties. Scots, on the other hand, had no such sacred documents, rights, or memories. The union with England in 1707 put an end to facile discourse as a mode of upholding historical continuities. Instead, the Scots were now confronted with the need to come to terms with more generalized forms of social change. Moreover, these transformations occurred at a much accelerated rate. What had transpired to the south in England was of more than two centuries' duration; across the northern border structural change was telescoped within less than a century. Scots lived through many of the changes they came to record as chroniclers of the manners of their people. John Ramsay of Ochtertyre was one of these, and his observations may stand for many. He commented upon a "wonderful change upon female manners, in consequence of playhouses, assemblies and concerts." Previously, "the Scottish women made their most brilliant appearance at burials."[29]

Like a legion of other observers, then, Ramsay was preoccupied with the eighteenth-century transformation of Scottish customs, rituals, routines, and habits. Many concurred in his judgment that the attraction and pull of an emerging civil society precipitated certain of these crucial alterations. The new type of society deemed "commercial" was the venue for the decline of indiscriminate charity; old-fashioned tolerance for beggars, the homeless, gypsies, and wandering folk atrophied. A century earlier, according to commentators, courtesy, the exchange of good offices, and gifts of hospitality and gratitude worked to weave the threads of society. Status and honor were conferred on lairds who fed and housed batteries of retainers—so-called "idlemen." So, too, "kindly" or customary tenants were protected by good lairds from the frozen blast of the marketplace. Early in his career as a novelist, Walter Scott (1771–1832), who, above all the contemporary writers provided the fullest picture of this transformation, queried himself as to what he would do were he a great landlord supporting a raft of idlefolk: "It is the hardest chapter in Economicks." He then goes on to confess that he would be sorely tempted "to shuffle on with the useless old creatures." Scott's life and works offer us a singular opportunity to explore a highly articulated historical consciousness situated at the watershed of the turning of social tides between *auld* currents and new waves.

Adam Smith, like his socially minded confreres, explicitly contrasted his contemporary society with conditions prevailing in "pastoral countries." In that world even the remotest members of clan or tribe could lay claim to some connection implying a degree of obligation. In his *The Theory of Moral Sentiments* (1759) he recollects:

> It is not many years ago that, in the Highlands of Scotland, the chieftain used to consider the poorest man of his clan, his cousin and relation. The same excessive regard to kindred is said to take place . . . I believe among all other nations who are merely in the same state of society in which Scots Highlanders were about at the beginning of the present century.

Against a backdrop of limited resources these complex organisms (Highland clans) competed and even warred for advantage. The power of clan chiefs to lead or to adjudicate was crucial for the survival of an archaic Highland society. But to be released from the rounds of kin allegiance and clan loyalty with their steady claims upon an individual's property, time, and emotional resources was, and is, a mark of movement toward what Scottish historical moralists termed "advanced commercial society." Perhaps the most costly claims were those involving honor and the vendetta; these were still exacted in the eighteenth-century Scottish Highlands, Corsica, and the Caucasus. In the nineteenth century the price would be paid in Ireland, and in the twentieth century in North Africa and dozens of other regions. Where property was mortgaged to kin and chits could be called in at any time to avenge insult, the bonds of society were immediate and concrete.

When Boswell and Johnson visited the Highlands in 1773 (*Journey to the Western Islands*), each voiced his disappointment at the passing of a noble race and a heroic way of life. The learned Doctor Johnson perceived with his usual astuteness, however, that historical events and the economy dictated the triumph of a new social structure: "The chiefs, divested of their prerogatives, necessarily turned their thoughts to the improvement of their revenues, and expect more rent as they have less homage."[30]

V

The English thought of their realm in terms of immemorial and autonomous usage: authority was highly institutionalized. The Scots, by contrast, tended to talk of their society in terms of "covenants" and "kindness." Scots law possessed much more restricted authority, and therefore concepts such as *desuetude* (discontinuity of a use or practice) and learned custom had weight. Yet over the eighteenth century it was precisely "learned custom" that came under review. James Boswell, speaking as the lawyer, not the biographer, discoursing on the transition from rudeness to refinement and civil society, remarked that a civil jury trial would provide a better system of justice than "our ancient aristocratic court."

The young Sir Walter Scott entered his father's law office and attended the University of Edinburgh studying civil law. The high point of his student years were the lectures of Dugald Stewart and Baron Hume. The former had been a pupil of Adam Smith's at Glasgow, writing a life and works of his mentor for the Royal Society of Edinburgh; the latter was the nephew of David Hume and a professor of Scots law. Faithfully, the pupil Walter Scott frequented Hume's lectures, later copying them over in his own hand. Taken by the brilliant lecturer's historical approach, Scott recapitulated his mentor's views thus:

> . . . the fabric of the law, formed originally under the strictest influence of feudal principles, and innovated, altered, and broken in upon by the change of times, of habits, and of manners, until it resembles some ancient castle, partly entire, partly ruinous, partly dilapidated, patched and altered during the succession of ages by a thousand additions and combinations, yet still exhibiting, with the marks of its antiquity, symptoms of the skill and wisdom of its founders, and capable of being ana-

lysed and made the subject of a methodical plan by an architect who can understand the various styles of the different ages in which it was subjected to alteration. Such an architect has Mr. Hume been to the law of Scotland, neither wandering into fanciful and abstruse disquisitions, which are the more proper subject of the antiquary, nor satisfied with a dry and undigested detail of the laws in their present state, but combining the past state of our legal enactments with the present and tracing clearly and judiciously the changes which took place and the causes which led to them.[31]

Scott's critical awareness of the development of society as a generalized process owed much to the conjectural history practiced by his two instructors. Dugald Stewart taught and wrote the history of civil society. Since evidence of change from primitive to advanced commercial society was sparse—especially for the beginnings and the medieval world—it was judged legitimate to make certain speculations concerning bygone ages based on comparisons between one early civilization dimly known and another virtually unknown. Philosophic or conjectural history remained confident that there were definite stages through which society must pass, with one mimicking the other. In 1791 the young Scott read a paper to the Speculative Society in Edinburgh, entitled, "On the Origins of the Feudal System." That Scott adopted a strict theory of causation is evident in a summary of the paper the proud nephew sent to his uncle, Captain Robert Scott of Kelso:

> You will see that the intention and attempt of the essay is principally to controvert two propositions laid down by the writers on the subject;—1st., That the system was invented by the Lombards; and, 2dly, that its foundation depended on the king's being acknowledged the sole lord of all the lands in the country, which he afterwards distributed to be held by military tenures. I have endeavoured to assign it a more general origin, and to prove that it proceeds upon principles common to all nations when placed in a certain situation.

Dugald Stewart, influential teacher and robust popularizer, helped spark Scott's enthusiasm for the study of how society as a whole had been transformed over time. Stewart argued that the laws emerged from the relationship between the intricate circumstances of society on the one side and its institutions on the other. Attempts to account for changes in the condition of humankind taking place in different stages over time required careful analysis of mutations in human institutions. Dugald had a gift for simplifying intricate questions of social development:

> When, in such a period of society as that in which we live, we compare our intellectual acquirements, our opinions, manners, and institutions, with those which prevail among rude tribes, it cannot fail to occur to us as an interesting question, by what gradual steps the transition has been made from the first simple efforts of uncultivated nature, to a state of things so wonderfully artificial and complicated.[32]

VI

Perhaps nowhere in Europe does a single author's oeuvre provide a more textured and detailed account of the movement of a "backward society" to one housing certain marked features of "modernity." From the first of Scott's Waverley novels to *Redgauntlet,* a portrait of an archaic and heroic world is presented based upon the best available accounts of customs, habits, households, clan rivalry, bards, and feasts. A wealth of accounts such as Edward Burt's *Letters from the North of Scotland* and a library of other texts, coupled with memories of survivors, folklore, archaic poetry and family tradition, allowed Scott to make his fictional re-creation. He situated himself at the "sociological museum" at Edinburgh's back door, surveying the ups and downs of Scotland's rocky historical landscape. Scott himself became increasingly anxious about the relationship between the individual and an emerging civil society as he plotted the historical vectors of the past two centuries. Tonal shifts and mood shifts were evident in the sequence of the six novels carrying the narrative almost to the present (*Redgauntlet,* the 1760s). What Scott referred to in celebratory accents as "the bonds of society" were perceived by him as fraying over time. Often characters, heroic and otherwise, lost social place and were in the end compelled to depend upon meager psychological resources in order to survive. Sometimes desperate, sometimes anxious, Scott worked to redefine ethical values as well as to discover those new virtues seeming to have staying power.

When Adam Smith referred to advanced civil society as "the great school of social command," he was voicing a painful but necessary injunction that Scott himself would reluctantly come to appreciate. The novelist's narrative skills allowed him to chart a rough and troubled passage from *rude* to *polished* in the Uplands and Lowlands of his native country. Investigating the relevance of "glamorous heroism" in the dull but historically necessary "world of commerce," his fiction explored the question of how honor might be transformed into honesty, and martial courage into civil courage. (The term "civil courage" was mentioned earlier and we shall return to it when reviewing *Redgauntlet.*) Never does Scott belittle the psychic price paid by his characters for the loss of golden ideals and comforting illusions. The young romantic Waverley in the novel of the same name (the first in the series) has his spirit tamed in the harsh school of experience. At the close he will stand at the side of Windermere, acknowledging that the "romance" of his life has ended with stern reality and disciplined habit now ingrained. His ordeal concludes with an ascent to property and taking the role of landed gentry. His marriage to the domesticated daughter of the eccentric and harmless Baron of Bradwardine will resolve the once destructive antagonism between the insurrectionary times of the past and the present civil order. At the crucial moment, Waverley recognizes the devastating consequences of his allegiance to the Jacobites and their cause. Reflecting over his brash but strangely satisfying loyalty to the Pretender, Charles Edward Stuart, "he felt himself entitled to say firmly, though perhaps with a sigh, that the romance of his life was ended, and that the real history had now commenced."[33]

Waverley distanced himself from the golden land of military valor and romantic adventures of the heart. In renouncing this glamorous life he was also putting behind a primitive social world of rural poverty—the depressed economy of the decaying Upland hamlet. There one did indeed find elegance of custom and "symmetry of shape." So much was admirable among the denizens of the villages, but

Waverley found himself chastened by the stark reality of "the dirt and misery." He had the eye of an economic improver cognizant of the need for agricultural reform:

> The broken ground on which the village was built had never been levelled; so that the inclosures presented declivities of every degree, here rising like terraces, there sinking like tanpits. The dry-stone walls which fenced, or seemed to fence, (for they were sorely breached) these hanging gardens of Tully-Veolan, were intersected by a narrow lane leading to the common field, where the joint labour of the villagers cultivated alternate ridges and patches of rye, oats, barley, and pease, each of such minute extent, that at a little distance, the unprofitable variety of the surface resembled a tailor's book of patterns.

On one side Scott induced his reader to share the attractions of archaic custom and manners, whereas on the other he presented an unblinkered view of impoverished villages and rock-poor farms doomed to extinction in the romantic landscape of a backward and misery-wracked world. Unimproved agriculture had neither an economic future nor even an economic present. This was a judgment Scott repeatedly made in articles and diary notations. Furthermore, in *Waverley,* the glamour of the tartan was often to camouflage the play of petty and vicious politics and meanness of cattle rustling. Regularly, Scott was to invoke the figure of Don Quixote to give the flavor of mad comedy to the narrative. Characters deeply involved in the action such as Fergus MacIvor treated the "barbarous ritual of our forefathers" mockingly. It was precisely this devotion to a lost cause that rendered Fergus's death at Carlisle a tragic one. Waverley's compromises correspond quite well with Scott's own convictions: coming to terms with historical inevitability allows for the prospect of a civilized life.[34]

Scott was to return to the undeniable fact of the loss of values of old Scotland. The unequal impact of historical change is well illustrated in such a novel as *Rob Roy.* Bailie Nicol Jarvie, Glasgow merchant and kinsman of the freebooter Rob Roy, like many a man of business and property, could anticipate a bright future. This single speech epitomized the advantages gained by the Union with England (1707):

> 'Whisht, sir!—Whisht!' he cried to Andrew Fairservice when the latter complained of the Union. 'It's ill-scraped tongues like yours that make mischief between neighbourhoods and nations. There's naething sae gude on this side o'time but it might have been better, and that may be said O' the Union. Nane were Keener against it than the Glasgow folk, wi' their rabblings and their risings, and their mobs, as they ca' them nowadays. But it's an ill wind that blaws naebody gude—lit ilka ane roose the ford as they find it.—I say, let Glasgow flourish! whilk is judiciously and elegantly putten round the town's arms by way of by word. Now, since St. Mungo catched herrings in the Clyde, what was ever like to gar us flourish like the sugar and tobacco trade? Will anybody tell me that, and grumble at a treaty that opened us a road west-awa' yonder?'

That the life of a Rob Roy in the new world had become increasingly improbable did not render it unheroic. The clash between the values of the Glasgow commercial men and Edinburgh lawyers on the one side, and proud Highland independence that would not "bide the coercion of gude braid-claith about [the] hinderlans, let a be breaks o'freestone, and garters o'iron" on the other, was a fact of recent history. Clan morality and the code of chivalry still exerted a fatal fascination. They will be obeyed by Roderick Dhu (in *The Lady of the Lake*) while in the service of the East India Company and when fighting in the Peninsular War. Yet new styles of leadership will be dramatized in Scott's *The Lord of the Isles*. In *Redgauntlet* there was no prospect that the citizens and legal profession of Edinburgh will chance their lives and fortunes for a doomed ideal.

In this series of novels Scott narrated the losses and gains of an ethical odyssey from a traditional civilization to an advanced civil society marked by a commitment to economic improvement and commerce. In his most contemporary of fiction—the epistolary novel *Redgauntlet*—set as we have noted in the 1760s, he dramatized two worlds: modern Scotland and the way of life of the young men of the bustling city of Edinburgh on the one side, and the older world of the Border on the other. Just below the extravagant surface of this melodramatic novel are a series of telling observations rendered by the author concerning a changing society. Perhaps none is more pertinent than the redefinition of the hero and of heroism. In an exchange of letters with his friend Darsie, Alan Fairford, junior, castigates his friend for making light of Alan's father by mocking his undistinguished service as a volunteer on the Hanoverian side at the time of the Jacobite insurgence (1745–46). Alan stoutly avers that his father displayed a "civil courage," for he would defend "a righteous cause with hand and purse." The proud son concludes the letter with the following perspicacious observation:

> And you impeach my father's courage, I tell you he has courage enough to do what is right and to spurn what is wrong—courage enough to defend a righteous cause with hand and purse, and to take the part of a poor man against his oppressor without fear of consequence to himself. This is civil courage, Darsie; and it is of little consequence to most men in this age and country whether they possess military courage or no.[35]

The younger Alan's own brand of heroism derived in the first instance from the law, not from the battlefield. His spurs were earned from judicial combat in the case of Peebles versus Plainstanes. His father, Alan Fairford, senior, would have "shuddered" at his son's "acquiring the renown of a hero"; instead the laurels of the law were the prize he sought for his progeny. Like "Alpheus preceding Hercules, he himself encountered the Augean mass of Peter Peebles's law matters." This was a labor of love to the old man, and his patient concern for detail would bring victory to his son in court and justice to poor Peter Peebles. The novel casts the heroic resistance of the Jacobite Highlanders of 1745 in doubt; so, too, the commercial aptitude of the later-day Lowlanders remains ethically suspect. Neither bravado nor business cunning are adequate when placed on the scales of morality. Not so with civil courage, however. Here Scott stands firm.

An overview of his five Waverley novels and *Redgauntlet* suggests that he was attracted to middling characters who were able to accommodate themselves to an advanced civil society yet were not entirely distanced from the values of an older world. Bailie Nicol Jarvie, Jonathan Oldbuck, and counselor Pleydell exhibit competent professional zeal or high generosity or a good sense of humanity. Jarvie is emblematic of the prized virtues: a man of commercial interests and a lover of peace, yet one who can cross the Border and comport himself with honor in the violent Uplands. Only in a single novel of Scott's, *Old Morality,* a narrative of the fanatical seventeenth-century Covenanters and their cruel fate, are there no moderate and middling characters who might point a path to the future. *Old Morality* portrays a society of extremists having no place for the humane and sensible Henry Morton.

To discover relevance for glamorous heroism in the necessary but monotonous, numbing world of modern civilization was a daunting task. Were old values and virtues available to the new society? Could the arrogance of a traditional code be scaled down? Is it necessary to make a stern equation between mercantile credit and the exacting claims of honor (pride of name, blood, and loyalty to a cause)? How distanced was the outlaw adventurer from the venturing merchant? Must commercial prudence be carried to the point of inhumanity? Is it possible through some form of literary alchemy to make the transformation from martial bravery to civil courage rationally persuasive as well as emotionally appealing? Could the extravagant demands of honor become simple honesty? Can display and largess be converted into simple generosity or anonymous philanthropy? Must ruinous hospitality be overcome only through stinting and avarice? Must intolerance for beggars, gypsies, and marginal folk prevail over old-fashioned kindliness? Must these fringe folk be degraded instead of being licensed and allowed? What of the "kinder" or customary tenants who gave military service in return for their holdings? Does the state owe no paternal regard to clansmen? Are they mere caterpillars eating the green leaves of the commonwealth? Might not these brave men be the best support of the nation in time of war? Scott himself would write, "If the hour of need should come—and it may not perhaps be far distant—the pibroch will remain unanswered." Of course the tone of a Montesquieu, a Hume, an Adam Ferguson, or an Adam Smith differed from that of the novelist Scott, but each in his own way was attempting to understand the nature of modernity. They would guarantee that their country, although experiencing the bitter side of a new and expansive age, was also bound to enjoy the numerous fruits and advantages.[36]

In April, 1818, an article appeared in *Blackwoods,* entitled "Effects of Farm Overseers on Farm Labourers." Nominally, it was written by William Laidlaw, but most probably the author was Sir Walter Scott himself. He notes that improvement in agriculture led to what was termed "high farming" with its discipline of labor, and this caused demoralization and alienation among tenants and rural workers:

> [In the old days] the whole household also constituted one family which looked to the gudeman as their natural and patriarchal head, and considered his interest as in some degree connected with their own. The words *our har'st* and *our crops* were commonly used to express those of their masters. . . . All this kindly communication is cut off.

In Scott's *Guy Mannering,* that fair-minded, frugal, honest good neighbor, Dandie Dinmont, is asked to take up another farmstead as an investment for his excess capital. His reply dramatizes an ethical dilemma:

> I dinna ken, the Deuke's no that fond o' led farms, and he canna bide to put away the auld tenantry; and then I wadna like, mysell, to gang about whistling and raising the rent on my neighbours.

Symptomatic of this malaise, as we have observed, was the troubled attention given to the decline of old-fashioned tolerance for beggars, the homeless, and all manner of itinerants and idle parasites. It was not easy to dismiss their plight in the name of advanced economic thinking. In Scott's *The Antiquary,* the scoundrel beggar, Edie Ochiltree, cannot adjust to the new work ethic: "I downa be bound to hours o' eating and sleeping." Treatment accorded the old-fashioned beggar was a true measure of the benevolence of a country community. Furthermore, that he had a role in society was a measure of its kindliness:

> And then what wad a' the country about for want o' auld Edie Ochiltree, that brings news and country cracks frae ae farm steading to anither, and gingerbread to the lasses, and helps the lads to mend their fiddles, and the gudewives to clout their pans, and plaits rush-swords and gredadier caps for the weans.

Scott approaches Wordsworth's King Lear vision of homeless poverty. The reprisal that society visited on homeless gypsies constituted a tragic moment for the human community. In an essay also written by Scott for *Blackwoods,* "The Gypsies of Hesse-Darmstadt" (Germany), his voice rang clear:

> I have dwelt longer on these dreadful scenes than you or your readers may approve; yet they contain an important illustration of the great doctrine, that cruel and sanguinary laws usually overshoot their own purpose, drive to desperation these [sic] against whom they are levelled, and, by making man an object of chase, convert him into a savage beast of prey . . . [this] may serve to stimulate the exertions of those humane persons who have formed the project of reserving this degraded portion of society from mendicity, ignorance and guilt.[37]

What did country society lose by the unroofing of gypsy cottages and the pulling down of their wretched doors and windows? Scott wrote about the costs in his *Guy Mannering:*

> These things did not pass without notice and censure. We are not made of wood or stone, and the things which connect themselves with out hearts and habits cannot, like bark or lichen, be rent away without our missing them. The farmer's dame lacked her usual share of intelligence, perhaps also the self applause which she had felt while distributing the *awmous* (alms) in the shape of a *gowpen* (handful) of oatmeal to the mendicant who brought the news. The cottage felt inconvenience from interruption of the petty trade carried on by these itinerant dealers.

Were gypsies surrogates for "customary" or "kindly tenants" of the Highland Straths who paid for their holdings with military duty? How deep were Scott's regrets for the loss of a traditional world of rural ritual and routine! How keen was his regard for social solidarity! But was the passage from a clan and traditional civilization to a modern society ineluctable? Were they at the end of a long revolution? The intellectual power of Scott's fiction, like that of Adam Smith's moral theory, rested in his refusal to accept an easy equation or comforting determinism between the rise of commerce (inevitable as it might be) on the one side and virtue on the other.[38]

VII

Scott's admiration for his friend, the Irish novelist Maria Edgeworth, was unstinting; he freely acknowledged his literary debt to her. Edgeworth's narrative of extravagant and long-negligent landlords, suffering peasants, and general rural decline in Ireland was adumbrated in her early novels *Castle Rackrent* and *The Absentee*. These works strengthened Scott's resolve to fix his own characters' destiny in the web of social and economic circumstance woven by the moving and indifferent finger of history. He recognized that her Ireland could serve as a dark mirror image of the very wrenching changes disturbing the rural life of his native Scotland. Scott also appreciated the movement toward improvement which had been initiated in Ireland a generation before it had taken hold in Scotland. Jonathan Swift and the philosopher George Berkeley found Dublin society dedicated to the economic development of Ireland. Both showed regret that gentry of old were unable to adapt time-honored loyalties to modern circumstance. But Edgeworth held the improving landlord as exemplary and was confident concerning his role in civilizing the Irish rustic. The enlightened landlord was pitted against his profligate absentee kin with a degree of moral fervor. Landlord as hero gained acceptance from the people because he had been raised by a peasant family in keeping with Gaelic tradition. Scott seldom permitted himself any such easy out: in his work the pace of economic history and social change is virtually inexorable. When his art was most mature and his narrative most cohesive and intense, as in *The Bride of Lammermoor*, tragedy was the likely outcome. The defeat of Edgar's idealism signified the loss of the "old way." But for the villagers of Wolf's Crag, the eclipse of feudal lordship was amply compensated for by the opportunity offered these once-impoverished folk to pursue the profit motive without inhibition. True to character, Scott created a feudal nobility who perceived the decline of their order not as a consequence of a struggle for material advantage, but as the result of an inexplicable decline. The tragic contest in *The Bride of Lammermoor* which kills the ill-fated lovers Lucy and Ravenswood is joined by an ancient aristocracy and the new men of power. The struggle is between equity and law, proprietary rights and opposition to the fact of possession:

> As a lawyer Scott saw the Ashton's Whig case for property and order, but his Tory sympathies and his imaginative grasp of tradition through folklore and folk language

led him to write with extra *brio* of the old order, even when standing on the side of the new.[39]

Scott's heroes were ordinary individuals whose interests brought them into conflict with both historical necessity and needs of the greater society. In novels such as *Old Morality,* social obligation asked so much of the hero that he barely escaped with his life. Scott's message in *The Antiquary* is against the odds:

> It is . . . incumbent on you to move steadily in the path of duty, for your active exertions are due not only to society—but in humble gratitude to the Being who made you a member of it, with powers to serve yourself and others.

He is neither partisan nor optimistic about his hero's fate. *Waverley* shows the rotting away of the old Highland order by the forces of progress set in play by the Union of 1707. The ancient Lowland aristocracy was in eclipse: even if the Baron of Bradwardine survives, his traditional status will be gone. In *Guy Mannering,* the Ellangowan lands of old gentry inheritance will be acquired through purchase by the corrupt upstart lawyer Glosin. He, in turn, will achieve neither stature nor reputation. With the *Black Dwarf* we have a sequence of work that reflects the many ways in which society victimizes its members. In *Old Morality,* Scott views the isolation of the Covenanters, not their fanaticism, as rendering them ever more dangerous:

> The government . . . drove them altogether from human society. In danger, want and necessity . . . expelled from civil intercourse it is no wonder that we find many of them wanderers avowing principles and doctrines hostile to the government that oppresses them.

Humans cannot exist as solitaries divorced from society. Scott's message was urgent: retain faith in community despite the fragility of justice. On the law, Edgar Ravenswood's position was near to Scott's own:

> I hope to see the day when justice shall be open to Whig and Tory . . . men will not start at these nicknames as at a trumpet sound. As social life is better protected, its comforts will become too dear to be hazarded without some better reason than speculative politics.

In his finest poetry Scott will do justice to the irreversible and fated changes of contemporary society. His elegaic tone will pay tribute to the losses stemming from dissolution of community and the dismissal of a rural population with its deeprooted traditions. In the *Marmion,* the poet hears a Highland tune and this prods melancholy recollections of Scottish migration across the sea to North America. Regretfully, he chants:

> . . . the lament of men
> Who languish'd for their native glen . . .
> Where heart-sick exiles, in the strain,
> Recall'd fair Scotland's hills again!

An appreciation of the rich and complex anomalies of the recent past did not blinker Scott's gaze. His responses to these wrenching transformations could, on occasion, go far beyond pessimistic antiquarianism or devotion to the ruling Hanoverians and "fat George." In the article in *Blackwoods*, "Effects of Farm Overseers on Farm Labourers," Scott contended that the present age was one of adjustment between two stages in social development. Not without perils but fated to pass:

> The evil, like all other evils, will work its own cure, or it will be productive of good in some way or other, that we had not yet foreseen—perhaps we may be assisted in our conjecture by attending to an analogy. The old feudal state of society has been compared to a tree; the old connexions of master and servant, that we have seen broken assunder before our eyes, were the terminating branches; they had ceased to shoot and grow, but they still continue to bear leaves and sometimes a little fruit. The filial affection, generosity and self-devotion of the clans are no more; but neither is their individual helplessness, ignorance and servility. Men value themselves more as individuals . . . the rural labourers will learn to disdain to be compelled to work and to be over looked like slaves. . . . Those who have most industry will begin to prefer piece work.

Just such a view elevated self-interest and rational planning while investing diminished trust in the power of social affection. The pill was to be at best bittersweet. What was the cost of embracing the present? How were "the poor to be restored to that relative place in society from which they had been [forcibly] displaced"? Scott called for "a gallant or generous resolution on the part of the nation at large . . . lest all should destroy all." However, this moral exhortation did not dispel the dilemma of the landlord. Two entries in Scott's lighthouse-yacht diary lay bare ethical ambiguities:

> To have good farming you must have a considerable farm, upon which capital may be laid out to advantage. But to introduce this change would turn adrift perhaps twenty families, who now occupy small farms *pro indiviso*, cultivating by patches, or *rundale* and *runrig*, what part of the property is arable, and stocking the pasture as common upon which each family turns out such stock as they can rear, without observing any proportion as to the number which it can support.

> On Lord Armadale's estate, the number of tenantry amounts to 300, and the average rent is seven pounds each. What can be expected from such a distribution, without the greatest immediate distress and hardship to these poor creatures? It is the hardest chapter in Economicks; and if I were an Orcadian lord, I feel I should shuffle on with the useless old creatures, in contradiction to my better judgement.[40]

VIII

As we have already remarked, in the ultimate chapter of *Waverley*, Scott pays tribute to the rich texture of his country's history. For this novelist the dynamics of social change fueled his imagination and peopled his fiction:

There is no European nation which, within the course of half a century, or little more, has undergone so complete a change as this kingdom of Scotland. The effects of the insurrection of 1745,—the destruction of the patriarchal power of the Highland chiefs,—the abolition of the heritable jurisdictions of the Lowland nobility and barons,—the total eradication of the Jacobite party, which, averse to intermingle with the English, or adopt their customs, long continue to pride themselves upon maintaining ancient Scottish manners and customs, commenced this innovation. The gradual influx of wealth, and extension of commerce, have since united to render the present people of Scotland a class of beings as different from their grandfathers, as the existing English are from those of Queen Elizabeth's time.

So quick and dramatic a transformation, and it was deemed inevitable to boot! With the exception of the eccentric Earl of Buchan, most Scottish moralists acknowledged the need for commercial development. What did remain at issue among Lowland literati of the generation of Hume and the next was the effect on Scotland of the unequal rates of change between Highland and Lowland. Opposing ways of life prompted an appetite for comparison that extended even to England. Lowland society and economy altered markedly in the generation after 1740. Crowded in these three decades or so were developments which in England had taken more than two centuries to unfold. An eighteenth-century historian of Glasgow writing in 1777, and taking a backward glance over events of the past generation, concluded that "luxury advanced with hasty strides everyday, and yet from this area we may date all improvements which have taken place." In 1741 Glasgow's tobacco imports totalled 8,000,000 pounds, and by 1745 the figure had reached 13,000,000 pounds. The Ship Bank and Arms Bank financed much of the trade, and in 1761 Thistle Bank was founded. The peak was reached in the 1770s with tobacco reckoned at a little less than 50 percent of all Scottish imports from beyond Britain. The wealthy importers of Glasgow controlled the ports on the lower Clyde, therefore ensuring themselves a 98 percent share in this lucrative trade.

Close ties with England and its empire benefited Glasgow in particular and the rest of Lowland Scotland as well. Commerce metamorphosed Lowland intellectual, social, and economic life. In the Highlands agricultural improvement was in evidence before the Uprising of 1745, but the insurrection and its subsequent failure worked to facilitate the transformation. Two acts of 1747, one abolishing heritable jurisdiction (legal, fiscal, and administrative rights essential for magnate independence), and the other appropriating to the Crown confiscated estates, created a temporary vacuum. Ancient juridical rights and the pseudo-military authority of the chiefs were terminated but replacements were not yet effective. The Disarming Acts of 1746 and 1748 prohibited traditional clan dress, and this struck a melancholy chord in the heart of Lowland sympathizers—a chord to echo amongst the Romantics for the better part of three-quarters of a century. The domination of the chiefs lingered briefly even as the pathos surrounding their fall endured in the next generation's prose and poetry. Over the following decades attitudes toward clan lands, rituals, and ceremonies were altered no matter how the Romantics resisted in novel or verse.[41]

An intellectual and literary interest in the Highlands and its culture had been promoted by the Jacobite uprising of 1745. Among Lowland literati this fascination was nourished by a steady stream of information pertaining to the civilizations of primitive peoples. Recognizing that Highland culture was widely perceived as patriarchal, clan-dominated and economically impoverished, with a shaky agricultural base and a pastoral economy too dependent on the export of cattle, Scottish political men and literary people alike argued that a second "Scottish Reformation" was in order. The Highlands should not stand remote from the English language, the English crown, and English economic advantage. Vernacular Scots was viewed by the more elegant as a dialect, and uncouth at that. Jacobite loyalties, though in themselves often admirable, had led to brief struggles against English authority in 1708 and 1719, and uprisings in 1715 and 1745, each more futile than the last. Efforts to resurrect an order of society suppressed in the Lowlands during the mid-seventeenth century, calling for Lowland magnates to dispatch their followers equipped to do battle for political and personal interests, had proved an abject failure. Furthermore, military considerations did not always outweigh economic interests even in the traditional pastoral regions of the Highlands. The clan chief was responsible to his followers, and they in turn were obligated to him for military service. This proved too costly for some—both materially and emotionally. Justice administered in private courts, determined on occasion by local allegiances, weighed heavily on the scales of justice. All of this was perceived as being done at the behest of eccentric magnates. Finally, the Jacobite program of abandoning the war with France and the Protestant succession was judged no political program at all. The historical clock could not be turned back to 1688, but must continue to tick. Alliance with France in the face of fierce international competition in trade and authority over colonial territory in the midst of a third war, yet undecided, was unrealistic policy. The Jacobites offered no practical remedy for this relentless economic rivalry.

After 1745–46, with the final defeat of the Jacobites and the passage of the Disarming Acts (1746 and 1748), the warlike cohesion of the Highland clans was fractured. Nostalgia and sentiment endured for the "brave times," but the will to action was stilled. The north was no longer a safe haven for the disaffected, the fugitive, and the outlawed. Even before the Uprising, clan chiefs, like Lowland lairds, had been thinking in economic terms. Since the late seventeenth century they had regarded themselves as landowners; now they simply became owners. The social, financial, and political claims that clan and kin might make upon them were much diminished. A new pattern of society was emerging wherein traditional obligations of lordship and landlordship were substantially reduced. The push for economic improvement evident in the Lowlands had surfaced in the North, though its success was much in doubt. Indeed, its practical achievements were limited for the time being, yet challenges toward betterment worked against traditional ideals of good lordship and peasant cooperation in matters agricultural. The first was countered on the ground of economic wastefulness (feeding useless mouths), and the second for its inefficiency and low productivity (grazing in common and cultivating scattered plots). The thrust for economic change from a world of "wasteful" lordship and peasant mutuality aimed to raise the economic base of Highland life. Early attempts on the Argyll Estates failed to produce a higher return, even threatening social cohesion. Sheep, it was argued, would be more profitable; displaced tenants would then be resettled in new villages. Relocated Highlanders were to fish, gather kelp, or work in linen manufacture. Clan chiefs were to be absorbed in Lowland society. Ideas from the South designed to improve this archaic, tribal and pastoral world were imported first from England to the Lowlands of Scotland, then mediated through native Scots who, for the most part, were recruited from landlords, cultivated gentlemen and middling folk. Often their ambitions for improvement were stymied but this did not prevent them from espousing a program of new work habits, a sense of enterprise, and a ready disposition to thrift. Village life, modeled on the English example, was to be the base of domestic industry as well as a market for manufacture. A hundred planned villages were constructed by enlightened landlords during the century after 1730. Certain of these nucleated settlements failed while others flourished. Improvement cannot legitimately be separated from the risk-taking—even gambling instinct—of an aristocracy. Their lifestyle was not tarnished by failure nor did they hanker after respectability and approval as their progeny were to do in Victorian times. The numerous banking and financial failures did not deplete a pervasive sense of aggressive optimism. Between the mid-eighteenth and early nineteenth centuries more than 3,000 miles of new turnpikes were constructed, though many proved financially disastrous.

Mineral surveys were undertaken by governmental commissions at considerable expense in order to locate commercially viable mining properties. That they failed, especially in the Highlands, did not diminish the ideology of improvement. A preoccupation with social reform in the Highlands transcended the politics of punishment for the rebellion of 1745. Andrew Fletcher, Lord Milton (1692–1766) was the Duke of Argyll's man in Scotland. A member of the Board of Trustees, he had worked hard and successfully for the expansion of linen production. Perceiving clearly the linkage between commercial progress and the political stability of the Highlands, his recommendation for the inhabitants was "civilising them by introducing Agriculture, Fisherys, and Manufactures, and thereby by degrees extirpateing their barbarity, with their chief marks of distinction, their language and dress, preventing their idleness, the present source of their poverty, Theift and Rebellion."

The improvers formed societies in the Lowlands dedicated to the rescue of their "rude and unpolished" brethren of the North. The Annexed Estates Commissioners struggled to improve the productivity of lands in their care. Officials appointed to this end were given the by-now familiar charge by government of "civilising the Highlands by instructing and training up their youth in the early knowledge and practice of the several branches of husbandry, manufactures and other necessary arts." Logically enough the improving movement first carried to Highland areas bordering the Lowlands. General economic conditions in the south of Scotland were favorable and, as we have noted, town population turned up in the 1740s and 50s; urban demand for foodstuffs was thus on the rise. The price of grain increased, making farming more profitable. Improvement did not begin at this historic moment, but it certainly accelerated between the 1740s and 70s. In agriculture the rate of specialization and extent of rationalization of practices and techniques was dramatically augmented in keeping with increased urban demand for food.

For the first time in Scottish history the cycle of feast and famine was broken: few now starved as a result of harvest failure; money could be raised at short notice to bring in needed grain. Church administrators and landlords made food available, and Midlothian gentry were eager to claim credit for the large sums they donated for relief. Poor relief, grain imports, and accumulated wealth mitigated the ancient and grim remedy of starvation and disease for overpopulation. Coastal and inland transport was now in place; imported grain saved the Highlands and Western Isles from disaster in 1782–83.

Between the 1740s and 1770s, Scotland developed a complex and advanced system of private banks. During these three decades bank assets rose some 800 percent. Adam Smith remarked that by 1760 Scotland had new banking companies in virtually every medium-sized town, and indeed in "some country villages." This growth advantaged Scottish overseas trade; their percentage of re-exports in relation to the total of exports was almost twice as high as that of England. Credit was eased and insurance readily available, clearing houses were at work and postal service and news regular. Legal and commercial education expanded, if not geometrically, at least arithmetically. Water works, docks, canals, roads, and a myriad of physical improvements provided an infrastructure for the industrialization soon to follow. The "improvers" were at work encouraging dissemination of the latest agrarian science in order to increase profitability of agriculture. An improver such as Thomas Guthrie recalled how difficult it had been between the glorious revolution of 1688 and the Jacobite insurrection of 1745 to induce landed folk "in those precarious times to invest money in the cultivation of soil." Leases were long and rents too low. The success of agricultural enterprise was now apparent with ready capital available for investment. By the end of the eighteenth and beginning of the nineteenth century, land rents were increasing by some £100,000 to £200,000 per year, and the 8,000 or so individual landlords had the wherewithal to invest in improvements and an infrastructure designed to increase productivity. These same landlord improvers became missionaries of the doctrine of progress, taking their message north. The backward and turbulent Highlands, when secured from raids and cattle thefts, proved profitable. The price of grasslands rose about 1,000 percent over the second half of the eighteenth century. At first, pacification of the North did not take: whereas traditional authority had been broken, cattle thieving and blackmail appeared on the increase. But over the decades the stationing of small garrisons, regular patrols, and military roads reduced the levels of thievery and violence. New cultivation of turnips and artificial grasses may have done even more than troops and roads to facilitate the cattle trade.[42]

When Dr. Samuel Johnson and James Boswell arrived at the Isle of Skye in 1773 in quest of a primitive community and patriarchal culture, they were astonished to discover that tenants paid rent to their lairds in bills of exchange which they had received from drovers who came north with credit instruments and went south with black cattle. One does not want to put too high a gloss on the inroads of economic improvement in place in the Highlands at this time, but then neither did Dr. Johnson and his companion, who found much evidence of an archaic civilization. Such a perspicacious observer as Adam Smith remained cautious—even skeptical—concerning prospects for commercial improvement in the North. He was right: Highlanders were not self-sufficient. Their economy called for subventions whether from cattle raids, kindly landlords, Christian charity, or the public treasury. In summation, however, we will finally witness a spectacular transformation as ancient antipathies between Highlander and Lowlander develop into a relationship far beyond mere toleration.

The historical novel is a unique creation of the Scottish Enlightenment and it served to dramatize a vision of movement and change, one at least partly unpredictable. It also highlighted the contrast between one age and another, one society and another, and one people and another. Unpredictability (the unforeseen consequences of historical change) undermined the role of omniscient narrator. Characters were baffled and frustrated by historical forces they misunderstood. The contrast between past and present sharpened the reader's sense that the latter was as much a creation of history as the former. The individuality of characters was derived from the singular features of their times. This distinguished the Scottish novel from the great contemporary English novel which accepted the present as something given. For Walter Scott, John Galt, and James Hogg the problem at center was whence and how had present times come to be?

IX

The rapidity with which the effacement of "auld" country ways, personal loyalty, and fealty occurred was matched by the recognition by contemporaries of its ineluctability. Geographic mobility and economic expansion had severed traditional social bonds at an alarming rate. A more martial society than that of its neighbor to the south, it still experienced pronounced differences in social organization and language. Over the eighteenth century, however, these were to diminish considerably. Scotland had endured more extensive poverty and had a lower standard of living, but with the onset of the eighteenth century the threat of famine was no longer endemic, and as in England the political waters were relatively calm. They were to remain so in the Lowlands, and except for the Highland uprisings, civil peace was the order of the day. Indeed, the uprisings along the Highland border gained little support from Lowland townsmen. Unlike in Ireland, for example, political events of the later eighteenth century such as the American Revolution had only minimal repercussions. It was not until the time of the French Revolution that political turbulence was in evidence; even then it was mild when compared with outbreaks on other shores. As in England the stormy history of the seventeenth century served to teach a keen lesson. Also like England, there were in Lowland Scotland among literati and clergy strong intellectual impulses working toward consensus. *The Old Statistical Account*, which offered a profile of Scottish economic and social activity, had been drawn up from regional reports largely by clergy and it breathed a smug complacency. A recent historian of Scotland has suggested that the country was "the most undemanding and subservient of British provinces." Scottish rural society was marked by a comparative absence of popular unrest. Popular protest, when it did occur, tended to be spontaneous and ephemeral. This disaffection was not a regular means by which the rural population expressed and orchestrated its relation to authority. Only in the late eighteenth century would this change, with meal riots and anti-clearance disturbances affecting town and country.[43]

Materially advantaged by its inclusion under the English commercial umbrella, this backward country had at the beginning of the eighteenth century a fifth the population of the mother country. Her wealth, however, as measured by contemporaries in terms of yield from the land tax and from customs and excise revenue, was hardly one-fortieth that of England. By the end of the century, however, a very different measure would be in place.

In the four major towns of Scotland population growth between 1755 and 1775 was three times the national average. Glasgow's population increased by more than 500 percent between 1755 and 1821 (from 27,451 to 147,043). Edinburgh increased from 52,720 to 138,235 over the same time period. Aberdeen had a population of almost 16,000 in 1755 and this expanded to just under 45,000 in 1821. Population growth in Dundee matched that of Aberdeen, whereas the smaller town of Paisley, starting with just under 7,000 in 1755, reached just above 47,000 in 1821. Fortunate newcomers found employment in the burgeoning linen industry whose growth has been termed "preindustrial." Flax grew well in Ireland but not in Scotland; therefore, production was separated from farming. Total production of linen for sale was 2,000,000 yards and valued at just over £103,000 in 1728; by 1815, linen produced for sale totaled 36,000,000 yards and was valued at just above £1,400,000. The first signs of property constructed on a scale that might legitimately be characterized as factories were near port cities engaged in the linen trade. In these structures groups of looms were now being assembled under one roof. We observe peasants divorced from land searching for work in the cities. Guilds were no longer able to restrict competition by excluding outsiders from local markets. In Edinburgh society was volatile; the Merchant Company was compelled to relinquish its ancient system of controls and complaints mounted against the too numerous hawkers and peddlers crowding the streets.

The migration of people from the Highlands to the South created an overabundance of unskilled workers displaced from their rural world and livings come to crowded Lowland cities. The total population of Scotland in 1755 has been reckoned at 1,263,380. The Highlands and Western Isles covered 70 percent of the land surface and had 652,000 or 51 percent of the total population in that year. In 1801 the population of Scotland stood at 1,608,000—an increase of 0.52 percent per annum since 1755. The increase continued, and by 1821 the population totalled 2,100,000; this figure reflected a 1.42 annual percentage increase over the previous decade. Highland population remained stagnant at best, and, as a percentage of the total population of the country fell from one-half to one-quarter during the years from 1755 to 1821. The Central Lowlands with only 14 percent of the country's land area served as a magnet for immigrants.

Scotland lost many of its social ties and ligaments once so binding. Patronage and dependency were no longer the rule. Scottish literati of the Enlightenment were much beguiled by the view that society was itself the unintended consequence of a host of disparate acts and gestures. Adam Ferguson, the first to write a history of civil society in English, formulated the law of "unintended outcomes." The ability of man to direct his own affairs was woefully limited and indeed "men stumble upon establishments." Social institutions were shaped by the circumstances and "inheritance of particular societies." Most vital was an understanding of the economic base of a society. Civil society itself has a life of its own and within it conflict may be as useful as concord. Twice in the writings of Adam Smith he refers to the workings of an "invisible hand" which operates to regulate human transactions in ways unforeseen by historical agents. The idea of the state as independent of the ruler was matched by the conception of society as functioning according to its own laws. Clearly, insight into the latter development required the conditions of a vigorous commercial society.[44]

David Hume ceased doing philosophy at a relatively early age in order to write history and analyze contemporary commercial society. His most popular writings reveal a deep historical reflection on that dual necessity imposed on humankind: the need for "peace and order" and for "liberty." The following observation, voiced in his "Essay on the Origin of Government," illuminates the genesis not only of his views of society in general but of civil society in particular:

> In all governments there is a perpetual intestine struggle, open or secret, between Authority and Liberty, and neither of them can absolutely prevail in the contest. . . . In this sense it must be owned that liberty is the perfection of civil society, but still authority must be acknowledged essential to its very existence. . . .

Here Hume rendered explicit the guiding motif of his multi-volume *History of England*. This work would illustrate the truth that neither liberty nor authority must prevail in any extreme form. Both are required in institutions and forms working together under the rule of law "and with the support of the opinion of the nation." This he seeks to demonstrate in his history, starting with the accession of James I (1603) and concluding with the Revolution of 1688 and its aftermath. Hume reviews the bitter strife, emphasizing not the personal ambition or moral intervention of the individual but the inevitable march of events. Again proof is offered by an appeal to history: when liberty itself becomes unlimited, it leads to new authority also unlimited. Yet we must strike a cautionary note: the historical outcome of 1688–89 was most felicitous and thus highly exceptional. England was to benefit from the mechanism of civil rights allowing men to maintain and exercise their natural rights within a given social and political order, a consequence of efforts to reduce the threat of despotic authority. This settlement was singular, based as it was on public opinion and the popular voice. It was during those years of bitter struggle

(1603–1688) that the English constitution took shape in the minds of the people. Hume, like numerous other literary contemporaries, appreciated the fact that social and political institutions should be understood as developing in response to the exigencies of the human condition. Theories with a rationalist bias—for example, those of natural law and the social contract—he viewed as consoling fictions without any historical grounding. Furthermore, he emphasized, the very origins of political authority were themselves entirely historical. When Alexander Hamilton was composing his last contribution to the Federalist papers (a work he was engaged in with James Madison and John Jay to secure acceptance of the newly framed constitution), he closed with a quotation from the "judicious reflections" of David Hume's essay, "The Rise of the Arts and Sciences":

> To balance a large state or society (says he) whether monarchical or republican, on general laws, is a work of so great difficulty, that no human genius, however comprehensive, is able by the mere dint of reason and reflection, to effect it. The judgments of many must unite in the work; experience must guide their labour; time must bring it to perfection, and the feeling of inconveniences must correct the mistakes which they *inevitably* fall into in their first trials and experiments.[45]

Civilization implied the widespread use of mechanical arts and observance of legal norms. For historians such as Hume, the totality of human customs and interactions was the proper object of historical study. Clearly, good manners were no trivial pursuit; the varied forms of social intercourse served to secure social peace, which was anchored in subscription to the rule of law. The latter were conventional rules concerning the stability of possession and keeping of contracts. These had emerged spontaneously and therefore by definition unplanned. Hume entertained a vision of society in which there was a balance between the commercial order and the landowners: the former encouraged social mobility, whereas the latter promoted stability. Hume like other Scottish literati regarded men and women as creatures of limited benevolence situated in an environment where resources were limited relative to inexhaustible human desires. In these circumstances the virtues required were not extravagant; indeed, one could suggest that they were extremely modest. Wit and elegance, and above all, civil prudence, served to cushion the individual from a too strenuous conflict. But one should note that although the qualities of citizens were mostly prosaic rather than flamboyant, in the long run they might even save the state at a moment of crisis. When Alexander Hamilton spoke at the Constitutional Convention in Philadelphia in 1787 against a proposal to enact legal measures *contra* venality and corruption in office, he again quoted the Scottish philosopher: "Hume's opinion of the British Constitution confirms the remark that there is always a body of firm patriots who often shake a corrupt administration."[46]

In general, Hume had faith in the capability of men and women but was reluctant to give them much scope. The hero in his highly successful and widely read *History of Britain* was George Monck, who represented a broad consensus but did not himself harbor personal ambition. The historian Edward Gibbon, who produced the most compelling, imaginative picture of the individual caught in a dizzying spiral of social change, was quick to acknowledge his debt to Scottish historiography and sociology. For Gibbon it was the tragically fated fifth-century philosopher Boethius who elicited unstinting admiration. Boethius's intellectual independence showed that the philosopher had served civilization best, rather than those strutting heroes whose bellicose virtues proved so costly to humanity. The moral intervention of the Antonines, grand as it was, had proved unable to arrest Rome's decline. The literary personae of Gibbon and Hume were rather like that of the person of "sensibility" in the popular contemporary English and Scottish novels. Neither Gibbon nor Hume had admiration for pretensions of the religious to sublime experience or claims of the worldly to higher knowledge. Civil prudence and propriety outscored holy martyrdom and heroic grandeur. Unforgivable was the ruin of classical Roman civilization, and the historical lesson was clear—the Church must never again enjoy hegemony. Compared to religious fanatics, the barbarians of the early Middle Ages were to be admired for they did indeed love liberty. Above all, religion must be kept in its civil place.[47]

X

In the eighteenth century the general vocabulary of the virtues reflected the quest for ethical modesty. *Moeurs* were now frequently limited to manners and bearing rather than morals. *Honnêteté* was likewise often reduced to a matter of breeding. *Belles lettres* polished the young, and learning in general was cast in a polite mode. Civility, which had nudged courtesy aside in the sixteenth-century manuals of conduct, was itself now to be challenged by a broader and more ambitious conception. By the early eighteenth century discourses on *civilité* were frequently reduced to rules about good table manners and appropriate forms of address. Ethical rules were perceived as manifestations of the ethos of a particular society or, better still, of a particular type of society. These rules or conventions could best be understood by reference to historical accounts of the various stages of social and economic development. Sir Walter Scott expressed his intellectual debt to John Bruce (1745–1820), teacher of logic at the University of Edinburgh and illustrious scion of the Scottish house of Bruce. His mentor's *Elements of the Science of Ethics, or the Principles of Natural Philosophy* explicated in detail the by-now familiar account formulated by the Scottish school of the ways in which obligations and rights came to be installed in the four stages of human history: hunting, pastoral, agricultural, and commercial. By giving a history to ethical phenomena, the generations of an Adam Smith or a Walter Scott could self-consciously revise the moral vocabulary to render it more appropriate to the given structure of a particular society. For example, we notice that between the first and last editions of *The Theory of Moral Sentiments* (1759–90), Adam Smith was able to enhance notions of prudence and self-reliance so that they became ideal contemporary manifestations of the moral order.[48]

The idea of law as originating in the circumstances of society had been formulated by Montesquieu in his *The Spirit of Laws*. His views were revolutionary for

Scotland and had an instant impact. The jurist Lord Kames in his *Historical Law Tracts* argued that law itself became a rational study "when it was traced historically, from its first rudiments concerning savages, through successive changes, to its higher improvement in a civilized society." (Of course the Scottish lawyer and historian of morals had fastened on to Montesquieu's comparative study an alien notion–that of progress.) Kames made an analogy between the Nile River and the law:

> When we enter upon the municipal law of any country in its present state, we resemble a traveller, who crossing the Delta, loses his way among the numberless branches of the Egyptian river. But when we begin at the source and follow the current of law . . . all its relations and dependencies are traced with no greater difficulty, than are the many streams into which that magnificent river is divided before it is lost in the sea.

Kames aspired to make a comparative study of law and morals and then draw general conclusions. In a letter of 1759 to Adam Smith, the practical-minded David Hume observed that Kames's method was too philosophical for the lawyer and too complex for young students of civil society.[49]

Eighteenth-century academies, provincial societies, and a host of intermediate institutions characteristic of civil society cast learning—economic, political, and scientific—into a polite mold. In the *lingua franca* of the day, public preference was recorded for *le naturel, négligence, badinage* and *caprice* over a sterner classical idiom. Words such as *politesse* were to become synonymous with the grander term *civilization*. The British experience and French sensibility prompted a vision of progress in which humanity as a whole was converted from rude to barbaric to the polish and refinement of an advanced commercial society. The concept of polishing the individual was now deemed appropriate for entire nations. For a backward land such as Scotland *politesse* became a political program. In England, France, and Scotland the novel, grown increasingly popular, was to provide a model for agreeable talk and behavior. The epistolary novel in particular permitted different voices to be heard and different views ventilated. This form was also used as a vehicle for social criticism. The brilliant success of Montesquieu's *Persian Letters* (10 editions in the first year of its publication in 1727) attests to its popularity and impact. The essay form worked to create the literary illusion of informality, projecting as it did a conversational tone. The letter, too, documents the striving for intimacy. The accent was on a type of sociability less hierarchical and more egalitarian: greater weight was to be placed on ideas instead of rank.

Gradually, as we have noted, and with many blips and slidebacks, civility became synonymous with elementary etiquette. The lessons could be learned by children and, miracle of miracles, even by lowly peasants. By the end of the eighteenth century this once-proud word was somewhat faded and old-fashioned. In the previous two centuries civility had been celebrated as essential for tempering the obstreperous behavior of an arrogant nobility. The *vita civile* had been a school for teaching urbanity and one of its prime lessons was to release the individual from the extreme claims of an honor community. No longer did the ethos of civility serve these grand purposes. The drama of the resolution of the conflict between passion and duty through invocation of its agency was not at center stage. In an earlier monograph I suggested that civility betokened the psychic capacity of a resolute individual to endure the tension between the lure of the pleasure principle and the harsh demands of the reality principle. Certainly the term carried no such heroic cargo over the waves of the eighteenth-century Enlightenment.[50]

Now heroes were to be made of more malleable qualities. Their characters were shaped by experience and they had less inclination to impose their own convictions and values on the world. If indeed the inclination was there, it would be best to camouflage it under a polished social veneer. (The beguiling figure of the Scot James Boswell, caught between a world of heroic impulse and the consciousness of his own triviality and lack of worth, comes to mind.) Eighteenth-century manuals of conduct warned against the social risk of being right too often when engaged in conversation: one was presumably dealing with people on an equal footing and therefore must temper claims for attention and respect; also one must demonstrate sensibility in order to gain the sympathy of others. The very idiom of public opinion and its force was being minted at this moment.

Just as the term "civility" was being generalized almost beyond recognition into the concept of "civilization," so too the notion of society was being transformed from one small-scale and face-to-face into an entity distant and abstract with a life of its own. Increasingly and often anxiously, writers portrayed it as bereft of active fellowship and traditional sociability. Social bonds, mutuality, and time-honored obligations were backgrounded: a minimalist ethic subverted neighborliness, good works, good lordship, hospitality, and the vulgar need to make friends. Ironically, this scaling down of the claims of a small community and of an honor community did not hamper economic "improvement"; in the eyes of some it even fostered it. However, society as distant and competitive made many literati nostalgic for the past and anxious for the future. Some were eager to slow down the rate of "improvement," whereas others decried the brutal fact that commercial civil society of the present did not allow for individuals to fulfill their moral potential. Specialization and division of labor were deemed psychologically costly by Adam Smith and many others. Remedies for this were sought in education and religion. Adam Ferguson's regretful commentary on the triumph of advanced civilization must stand for a legion of other similar judgments:

> We may, with good reason, congratulate our species on their having escaped from a state of barbarous disorder and violence, into a state of domestic peace and regular policy; when they have sheathed the dagger, and disarmed the animosities of civil contention; when the weapons with which they contend are the reasonings of the wise, and the tongue of the eloquent. But we cannot, mean-time, help to regret, that they should ever proceed, in search of perfection, to place every branch of administration behind the counter, and come to employ, instead of the statesman and warrior, the mere clerk and accountant.[51]

Misgivings were widespread and few doubted that commercial civil society required different talents or more muted virtues. Whatever position they assumed on these vexing questions, thoughtful Scots concurred in general about the direction of historical change. Minor writers from Sir John Dalrymple to James Dunbar and Gilbert Stuart joined major figures such as Smith, Lord Kames, William Robertson, and John Millar, as well as a succession of leading jurists, in holding particular assumptions concerning the social nature of humankind and the trajectory of economic progress. Unlike Montesquieu, to whom many owed so much, the Scottish disciples employed evidence to chart a progressive view of the different stages of human society. (An English translation of *The Spirit of the Laws* was published in 1756 in Aberdeen, Scotland.) For them the theory of progress became a sturdy tactic in sociological investigation. John Millar, pupil of Adam Smith, numbered among Lord Kames's circle, and teacher of law at the University of Glasgow, was not too extravagant when he remarked in his *An Historical View of English Government:*

> The great Montesquieu pointed out the road. He was the Lord Bacon in this branch of philosophy. Dr. Smith is the Newton.[52]

Modes of production and ownership of property were the principal markers on the road to transition from barbarian times to the present. Rights and obligations prevailing in a given society were situated in property relations. They, like the government and legal institutions, were placed within a historical context that was virtually synonymous with the framework of changing economic structures. Whether these developments occurred in three or four stages (hunters, shepherds, agriculture, and commerce) was hardly relevant; the fact was that Scottish literati tended to follow the same pathway when explaining the emergence of modern society. They emphasized the economic base of an advanced commercial civilization and its faithful partnership with civil society. Samuel Johnson's complex reactions toward the displacement of an archaic Highland code by economic advances may stand for a legion of other troubled commentators. First he expressed bitterness at the decline of the heroic Highland ethic:

> It affords a generous and manly pleasure to conceive a little nation gathering its fruits and tending its herds with fearless confidence, though it lies open on every side to invasion, where, in contempt of walls and trenches, every man sleeps securely with his sword beside him.[. . .]This was, in the beginning of the present century, the state of the Highlands. Every man was a soldier, who partook of national confidence, and interested himself in national honour. To lose this spirit, is to lose what no small advantage will compensate.

Yet there is no indication that Johnson would favor preserving the ancient life of the Highlands for himself. The advantages of civilization and the commercial spirit are apparent, he argued, especially if one recognizes the addiction of a primitive people to ''wild justice'' and revenge: ''To make a country plentiful by diminishing the people, is an expeditious mode of husbandry; but that abundance, which there is nobody to enjoy, contributes little to human happiness."[53]

Like David Hume, Adam Smith, and a score of other literary figures, Johnson valued the consummate benefits the commercial spirit afforded the citizenry; and like them he argued that its felicitous condition must be anchored in a civil society, with its high regard for law and the security of property. One can readily score Johnson as a stern critic of the pace of improvement: he and many of his contemporaries were well aware of the tragic consequences of the destruction of a way of life grounded in martial valor and heroic obligation. For Adam Smith there was much drama in this, but it was one replete with the ironic rather than the tragic. He would offer a deep-textured account of the gradual displacement of an archaic and traditional world over centuries of time: ". . . order and good government, and along with them the liberty and securities" were first obtained in the Europe of the Middle Ages. It was then "in cities, at a time when the occupiers of land in the country were exposed to every sort of violence." Townsmen advantaged by kingly protection had the needed security "to better their condition and to secure not only the necessaries, but the conveniences and elegancies of life." As a consequence of the "increase and riches of commercial manufacturing towns . . . order and good government [were gradually introduced], and with them, the liberty and security of individuals, among the inhabitants of the country." The traditional landlord had exercised boundless hospitality and maintained legions of "idle men" since spoilage of the earth's bounty was sure. Without a market economy there was little advantage in husbanding agrarian production. But now the towns promoted an appetite for luxury among the lordly; moreover, they offered markets for sale of the fruits of the great landowners' estates. Tenants were now perceived as a source of revenue from rents rather than as a pool of soldierly manpower.

> . . . the great proprietors were no longer capable of interrupting the regular execution of justice or of disturbing the peace of the country. Having sold their birthright . . . in the wantonness of plenty, for trinkets and baubles, they became as insignificant as any substantial burgher in a city.

Smith closes with his usual tribute to the effectiveness of the law of unforeseen and unintended consequences. With this he couples his familiar denigration of merchant judgment. Nothing less than "a revolution" was "brought about by two different orders of people who had not the slightest intention to serve the public. . . ." The first were the great landowners motivated by "the most childish vanity" and the second were merchants and artisans following slavishly "their own pedlar principle of turning a penny whenever a penny was to be got."[54]

XI

Popular protests against change and the "commercial spirit" by everyday English and Scots have recently been judged by historical researchers to be "small beer." These actions were principally defensive and, in the words of a recent reviewer, "the bulk of the commonality were instinctive conservatives." Popular discontent had the support of tradition and even a certain sympathy from government. The purposes of mob violence were restricted to the righting of wrongs and preservation of ancient liberties. Plebeian protest was local and in fact "piecemeal," drawing upon "ideals of community within the validating framework of custom, common law and Constitution." Popular rituals and festivities, occasioned by public executions, did not necessarily signify plebeian dissent from the workings of the law. Not only were humble folk the most frequent victims of crime and violence but they also served as jurors and prosecutors. Cases of forceful rebellion such as the Gordon riots in London in 1780 were exceptional, and even there the results were broken bones, not broken heads. (Even during the Jacobite invasions there were few corpses.) Despite the Licencing Act armed troops rarely took aim against the mob. Although the Riot Act was enacted in 1715, the conviction was widely held that calling out the troops to put down popular unrest was no part of the English Constitution.[55]

The ruling order cancelled traditional customs and time-honored work practices in the name of greater profit and the free play of market forces. Technological innovation was introduced in the manufacture of textiles, and agricultural improvement increased productivity of land by undoing ancient arrangements between tenant and landlord. Mounting numbers of bills were introduced in parliament over the century for the purpose of enclosing common land. While there were still many riots, the violence was often symbolic. Protests were designed to restore common norms such as a just price of necessities or traditional work rules. It is indeed an irony that whereas popular protest was in the main limited, the ferocity of English statutes against crime seemed to be boundless. Furthermore, the strengthening of the Game Laws was a vicious exercise in upper-class repression. At a time when legal reform on the Continent aimed at the dismantling of barbaric codes and punitive statutes, the English political class sometimes appeared shameless in their defense of privilege. Yet this was only one piece of a tangled historical narrative. As we have noted, middling folk (farmers, tradesmen, craftsmen, and artisans) were beneficiaries of the legal system, and the lion's share of prosecutions of property offenses were initiated by people of humble origin. At quarter sessions, perhaps as many as a fifth of the *prosecutors* of property offenses were humble folk (laborers, agricultural workers, sailors, and servants). Their number went even so far down the scale as to the laboring poor. Furthermore, jurors of modest status served repeatedly. Not only did the law defend the estates and property of the well-born and well-to-do but it has also been characterized as a "limited multiple-use right available to most Englishmen."[56]

The times and historical circumstances were propitious, one might say even singularly so, for the unfolding of civil society and the acceleration of commercial capitalism. A consensus held at the upper and middling reaches of the nation until the late eighteenth century. In a later day, workers and the poor would not be so docile in an England first experiencing the early impact of industrialization. A third of the total number of strikes over the eighteenth century occurred in the 1790s. An older order anchored in land, title, and church was not to be undermined. The contradiction between dedication to the free market in labor, land, and commodities on the one side, and devotion to deference, traditionalism, and "ordered ranks" did not sap their confidence. Adam Smith, writing on the other side of the divide—that is, just after the mid-eighteenth century, and before the challenge to settled times— voiced suspicion of modern philosophy's heavy reliance on reason when analyzing the social response to authority:

> That kings are servants of the people, to be obeyed, resisted, deposed, or punished, as the public conveniency may require, is the doctrine of reason and philosophy; but it is not the doctrine of nature.

The conduct of men and women in society often baffles rational expectation. Moreover, any effort to deny human free agency and explain human institutions by invoking a mechanical model is to be distrusted:

> The man of system . . . seems to imagine that he can arrange the different members of a great society with as much ease as the hand arranges the different pieces upon a chess-board. He does not consider that the pieces upon the chess-board have no other principle of motion besides that which the hand impresses upon them; but that, in a great chess-board of human society, every single piece has a principle of motion of its own, altogether different from that which the legislature might chuse to impress upon it. If these two principles coincide and act in the same direction, the game of human society will go on easily and harmoniously, and is very likely to be happy and successful. If they are opposite or different, the game will go on miserably.[57]

In general Smith was optimistic about "the game," and his world, like that of the lawyer Blackstone, was much more composed than that of Hobbes and Locke of an earlier time. Fears of royal absolutism and popery were light years removed from their seventeenth-century flashpoints. Religious faith now found expression in pamphlets rather than on the battlefield. The spiritual fervor that had sown dragon's teeth was sublimated into the harmless by-ways of introspection. The language and accent of seventeenth-century parliamentary debate may at first blush appear entirely familiar, but upon further examination it becomes clear that the values and assumptions of the discourse are alien to those of later centuries. A recent commentator on Stuart politics observes that what was at issue was "not merely truth and error, still less the play of free expression, but good and evil." Views were harsh and exclusionary, with popery seen as the purveyor of antiChrist and his dread minions. A hundred years later, anti-Catholicism still had strong popular appeal, but the will to maintain penal laws against the followers of the Prince of Darkness had grown slack. Estimates of Catholic population suggest that it declined from 115,000 in 1720 to 70,00 by 1770. Great landholding Catholic families whose patronage was vital for subsidizing chapels and priests numbered perhaps only 200, many having turned to Anglicanism.

Perhaps Voltaire had it right when he opined in the 1730s that there was safety in the very "multitude" of religions:

> If one religion only were allowed in England, the government would very possibly become arbitrary; if there were but two, the people would cut one another's throats, but as there are such a multitude, they live happily and in peace.[58]

It is not easy to determine the size of the English electorate. Recently, the figure for the eighteenth century has been put at about 14 percent of the adult population (though it varied over time). The figure of course depended on demographic growth and voter turnout. Also, it was necessary to take into account the still nebulous but emergent "public opinion." The need to hold parliamentary majorities and the requirement that they justify themselves compelled ministers to follow policies in line with national interests. A comparison of the courses followed by Walpole Pelham and the elder Pitt with those of the earlier Stuart ministers is particularly illuminating on this matter. Petitions, addresses to members of parliament, newspapers, and political pamphlets tied Westminster and Whitehall to the provincial towns of England. Men might go to parliament for a variety of personal reasons, but what they accomplished there certainly had bearing on whether they remained at Westminster. Much legislation was sponsored that benefited regions thoroughly unrepresented. For example, the outlands of London, Birmingham, and Manchester were served by members of parliament and peers responding to the interests of friends, neighbors, or tenants. Elections might indeed be corrupt but the landlord representatives could not afford to ignore the views of the wider society. The term "politician" was losing something of its earlier meaning of expertness in the art of politics and beginning to signify an individual simply engaged in political activity. Parliamentary debates at the mid-eighteenth century produced division and disagreements which more exactly mirrored the relative balance between property and interests; this in the stead of reflecting contest between court and country. The use of statutory intervention to secure the passage of minor bills declined, as did the strong party identity of a former time. Political discourse was increasingly conducted in the public domain, principally through newspapers. This was an age of information and the ill-informed were being read out of the political nation. Pamphlets and treatises replete with statistics and facts stimulated debate in clubs and literary societies. Extra-parliamentary politics were tailored to serve the needs of a propertied society. In an age of information the lower orders were being squeezed out.[59]

Civil society not only worked to secure contractual obligation, property, trade, and profit but also facilitated the politics of interests. These interests were varied and manifold; they could not be subsumed under the older dichotomy of land versus money. Instead, a political consensus for "improvement" took precedence over the intolerable division of sharply defined interests. One thinks of William Pitt the younger as a hero of the "improving middle class," recalling the stunning tribute in his toast to Adam Smith as teacher of us all. Parties remained but they stayed within borders deemed legitimate where prospects for improvement overmatched sectarian and partisan strife. Change was perceived as ineluctable, even providential, whatever the misgivings. This assessment appeared to be confirmed by improvement in English economic life, hesitant at first, but after 1740 sustained and vigorous. Techniques of exchange grew cheaper and more reliable. Real national output increased at a rate of one percent per year until the mid-eighteenth century, and after that at just below two percent. The measure of innovation may be judged by the number of patents granted: between 1760 and 1789 almost five times the number of patents were conferred as in the period from 1660 to 1760. The pace of economic change quickened, with traditional sharp distinctions between real and personal property becoming blurred.[60]

As we have noted, contradictions did hold between commercial advance and agricultural improvement on the one hand and traditional ways on the other. Important elements of political society disagreed not so much about the inevitability of change as about its rapid pace. Yet, while we have featured here the potent thrust toward transformation, it might be well to remember that it was not only in the Highlands of Scotland but also in the English villages and countryside that quotidian life remained encadred in that thick social matrix of a small-scale society. Only one in five lived in towns of 20,000 or more. A large sector of the population stayed fixed in face-to-face communities where terms of work, village boundaries, rights of way, and the thousand mutualities and obligations were sustained. Proverbial wisdom and the manly virtues, including a sturdy defense of communal norms, evoked admiration, loyalty, and even reverence. Overall community wisdom continued to sanction informal settlement of village disputes, and popular feeling against transgression of collective norms was greeted with ancient rituals of shaming. But no politics or political programs emerged to maintain these primitive simplicities, heroic ideals, and communal customs. The political nation listened to these traditional voices, mourned their passing, and was perhaps rendered a bit more humane by their nagging persistence. Their presence did, however, bestow on conservative argument a certain cogency. The Burkean version of society was extremely solicitous of the many ways in which archaic custom wove networks of community. True, as Burke maintained, property was the necessary precondition for human society, and with this proposition poets such as William Wordsworth did agree. But for him and a widening circle of literati, property was not to be viewed in narrow Lockean legal terms. Instead it was to be conceptualized in the various ways by which individuals were "imaginatively, emotionally and psychologically rooted in land."[61]

The political nation of eighteenth-century England and Scotland was surely not unfamiliar with or unresponsive to the imperatives of society written with a small "s". In fact one might suggest that sometimes the better part of themselves dwelled in it. Their politics and economic interests, however, favored a civil society—a society less intimate, more abstract, and written with a capital "S": one which discouraged government intervention and regulation of economic life. These limitations would be extended so that a plethora of intermediate institutions and voluntary societies were shielded from government interference. Meanwhile, employer responsibility for workers could be minimized. In this environment workers were subject to more exacting discipline. In an earlier time the putting-out system and subcontracting, as well as the collection and distribution of materials, had freed workers from rigid routine. But in 1749 acts of "embezzlement" by workers in industry were subject to the summary jurisdiction of the Justices of the Peace. "Chips" customarily kept by dockyard workers and "wastages" retained by framework knitters were declared property of the employer. What had been traditional practice was now criminalized. Individual discipline was stiffened and wages defined in cash terms. Yet a cautionary note must be entered: in the matter of gleaning, the Chief Justice of Common Pleas (1784) characterized it as "inconsistent with the nature of property which imports exclusive enjoyment." Here, as elsewhere, there was a gap between law and practice, and the custom of gleaning persisted into the nineteenth century.[62]

Recently, a careful historical study has followed the migration from West Inverness to Canada (1770–1820), charting the eroding ties of a traditional society. The effects of sheep farming and clearing on archaic norms and practices suggest that *auld ways* were already unraveling before the Rebellion and 1745. Payment in goods and military service to the great landlords was in decline. In the Hebrides the transformation from joint tenancy to single crofts was well advanced and familiar mutualities undermined. Of course the Scottish Highland example was dramatic and not to be compared to the English experience; south of the border the time-frame ran in centuries instead of decades. But here too the imperatives of a cohesive community had once been satisfied by enforcing time-honored customs and economic arrangements such as fixing the price of necessities. The tillers of open fields had to concur as to planting of crops, their rotation, and the details of harvesting. Villagers shared wells and pumps, ploughs and oxen teams; it was essential to reconcile claims and counter-claims for running water by farmers, millers, and barge owners. Cooperation was fundamental for performing many types of physical labor. The folk culture of proverbial wisdom had grown over the centuries in response to the accommodation of competitive interests: "The warp of self-preservation had to be interwoven with the weft of neighborliness."[63]

In an intermediate stage it was hoped that civility would reconcile something of the ethos of the past with the exigencies of an advanced commercial society. It would be an antidote of self-interest and might serve as a basis for an amicable and benevolent society. But an emerging devotion to the idea of a civil society placed a premium upon the proposition that self-interest and the social good were not opposites. The pursuit of the former might well redound to the benefit of society writ large. Moreover, the best impulses of humankind were realized not so much in the quotidian world of acts of civility but in that grander abstraction—civilization itself. There general refinement and the progress of the arts and learning would be the choice fruits of commercial advance. Of course there were portents of rough seas, but it was not until the last decade of the eighteenth century and the French Revolution that these amounted to much more than storm warnings. This had been a privileged age for England and Scotland.

EPILOGUE

Goethe in later life spoke with envy of the literary magic of Sir Walter Scott. The inexhaustible variety of the history of Scotland and England, and the splendors of the British kingdoms were in his mind set against the barren spaces of German politics and society. There was nothing the German novelist could fruitfully use between the Thurgian forests and the sandy wastes of Mecklenberg. In the British Isles the social classes (nobles, bourgeoisie, peasants) could be brought into focus and confrontation. The absence of a specific and textured social environment made the writing of Goethe's novel, *Wilhelm Meister's Apprenticeship* (1795–96) a difficult literary chore. The very fissures in the work remained unhealed, baffling the utopian energies intended to close them. Instead of being able to resort to a stable society, Goethe was forced to people his work with strolling players and pitiful squires in order to move the plot forward. It is worth noting that in one of his last works, *Wilhelm Meister's Journeyman Year,* Goethe depicted a world light years away from that of the earlier novel—a world far less poetic and far less humane. The later novel portrayed the coming of a commercial age in which the development of the individual character and his moral education was of much less moment than formerly. What was significant was practicality, prudence, and specialization: above all, the prosperity of society in general.[1]

A recent biographer of Goethe has convincingly argued that his German literary genius rested in large part on his talent for responding to shifts in the bedrock of European cultural history. The trajectory of his intellectual development from the early days of *Wilhelm Meister's Apprenticeship* to the last years of *Wilhelm Meister's Journeyman Year* spanned almost a generation. During that time Goethe observed a transformation of the possibilities of the novelist's art and of Germany's place in modern literature. In the 1770s he characterized the relationship between civil and literary culture as a great divide. On the one side was the theatrical troupe, who aspired to nothing higher than the country fair and art of puppetry, whereas on the other stood the court with its princely patronage of French tragedies and operas in Italian. The chasm between popular and princely literature was marked by mass-produced and ill-printed trash romances for barely literate readers, as opposed to the elegant fashioned folio anthologies of flattering verse and fictional handbooks of statecraft for princes. Middling folk remained dutiful and cowed, fed on a steady diet of devotional literature and morally edifying weeklies. The latter were pale imitations of Addison's *Spectator* but without the wit and charm: earnestness stood in place of stylistic achievement.

In Goethe's youth, then, there had been no middling range of middlebrow literature. In his judgment this was because there was no general society to chronicle. Thus he envied a Walter Scott who could find both a "bourgeois" audience for his readership as well as a highly textured society for character and plot. The stable civil society of the British Isles generated by an advanced commercial economy had allowed Scott a firm grasp of the nature and direction of historical change. Goethe, like Scott, desired to bring unity to and make sense of fractured experience in a world undergoing wrenching social change. Like Scott he perceived the new world of advanced commerce and civil society as less human and less poetic. It was a world more concerned with society than with the individual and less preoccupied with the spiritual education (*bildung*) of the person and his moral growth.

Goethe maintained that "an artist is a part of the public and he too has been formed in the same times and events." In Germany for most of the eighteenth century artists and literati had been formed within a one-dimensional system. In large measure cultural achievement had been the work of an intellectual bureaucracy drawn principally from the universities and dependent upon princely employment. A middle class with literary interests had virtually ceased to exist. There was, in the words of a recent historian of German literature in the age of the young Goethe, no "bourgeois culture secure in its own public self-image" as was to be found in the England and Scotland of Sir Walter Scott and Jane Austen. Recent efforts by modern social historians to argue in favor of an eighteenth-century German Bürgertum, bourgeoisie, or middle class have come to grief. Instead of a middle class there was a spate of middle classes sharply separated by regional loyalty, religious faith, economic role, and even their very language. The term "bourgeois" has been judged appropriate enough for eighteenth-century Britain: journals, periodicals and newspapers had a wide reading public of artisans, shopkeepers, merchants, clergy, professionals, and gentlemen farmers. In France and the German states the profile was quite different; in the latter a "service elite" predominated. In the time of Goethe and Schiller enlightened men probably spent little time reading literary criticism or fiction. There was nothing comparable to the British print market.

Scott had recognized that as an author he was advantaged by his times and geography; thus he paid tribute to the rich texture of his society as well as to the heightened historical consciousness of his age. He reminded his readers of the radical discontinuity between the commercial present and a recent archaic past. As we noted in the ultimate chapter of his novel *Waverley,* he explained how the dynamics of social change fueled his imagination and peopled his fiction:

> There is no European nation which, within the course of half a century, or little more, has undergone so complete a change as this kingdom of Scotland. The effects of the insurrection of 1745,—the destruction of the patriarchal power of the Highland chiefs,—the abolition of the heritable jurisdictions of the Lowland nobility and barons,—the total eradication of the Jacobite party, which, averse to intermingle with the English, or adopt their customs, long continue to pride themselves upon maintaining ancient Scottish manners and customs, commenced this innovation. The

gradual influx of wealth, the extension of commerce, have since united to render the present people of Scotland a class of beings as different from their grandfathers, as the existing English are from those of Queen Elizabeth's time.[2]

How, in Scott's view, had this transformation been achieved? Had the new order been reconciled with the old? If so, at what cost? How many false starts and stops were there along the way? A recent literary critic explicates Scott's interpretation thus:

> In *The Bride of Lammermoor*, Scott once again locates his central thematic opposition in the figure of a hero-like character. Edgar Ravenswood combines the residual loyalty of a feudal aristocrat to the memory of his family's ascendancy with the rational and moderate disposition of his family's bourgeois nemesis. The fascinating twist of *The Bride* is that Scott provides the possibility of resolving the novel's central social conflict through the affair of Ravenswood and Lucy Ashton, but then describes the historical and psychological processes by which the projected marriage is thwarted.[3]

Scott chronicled in detail the rough moral passage of his society into the world of modern, commercial civilization. Of course his novels were situated before the great divide marked by the French Revolution. Therefore, it was easier for him to maintain distance from the recent past, thus allowing for a chart in bold relief. The Waverley novels offer guidance by featuring prominent landmarks permitting simpler navigation through the turbulent waters of moral anxiety. It should be noted that the two major novelists of the Scottish Enlightenment, Tobias Smollett and Scott himself, paid ample tribute to the literati of Edinburgh (denizens of that "Athens of the North") for their thorough mapping of this ethical landscape. Smollett, in his *Humphrey Clinker*, has his fictional character Matthew Bramble praise the city as a "hot-bed of genius," when recalling his meetings with "many authors of the first distinction such as the two Humes, Robertson, Adam Smith, Wallace, Hugh Blair, Ferguson, Wilkie, and others." Scott, in *Guy Mannering*, speaks of this eminent company and a "circle never closed against strangers of sense and information, and which has perhaps at no period been equal, considering the depth and variety of talent which it embraced and concentrated."

This talent attempted to found a science of morals. The tradition worked in was that of Shaftesbury, Mandeville, Bishop Butler, and Hutcheson. Here the passions were the grounding for moral sentiment, moral rules, and moral judgment. The formulation of ethical rules was a consequence of social sensibility and sympathy generated by the diurnal interaction of individuals. It was as if these sentiments were to serve as surrogate for the empathetic responses allegedly prevalent in a more intimate and closely knit society of days gone by. This oft-referred to "naïve anthropology" was fortified by the persistent and pervasive idea that the question most pressing in these times was to explain the origin and division of labor. It was this radical fragmentation that gave scope for market forces and regional specialization. For Adam Ferguson, Adam Smith, and others, an explanation for structural change was not to be found in mechanization or population growth: for them the key was the organization of labor. The greater the atomization of society and allowance for the play of market forces and self-interest, the more the need for reliance on "human creature feelings" (humanitarianism), if one was to think well of oneself.

Acknowledging the inevitability of a less demanding civil society, commercial change, and radical division of labor, the question yet remained: how did the individual come to terms with the need for a more lightly shaded ethic?

Views of history, society, and human nature underwent revision. At the first part of the eighteenth century there was fear that the study of Scottish history would only stir up the "Old National Grudge, that should now be sopited and industriously forgotten." This was the anxious view of Francis Pringle, Professor of Greek at St. Andrews, in 1736. Hume, Principal Robertson, and others wrote their histories allaying these troubled thoughts. The Scots had had a long and honorable antiquarian interest in the past; now this concern was conjoined with philosophical or conjectural history. Sir Walter Scott was not alone in proclaiming that the work of Sir David Dalrymple (Lord Hailes) was a precursor of this new genre: Scott paid tribute to the author of *Annals of Scotland from the Accession of Malcolm Canmore* as "the father of national history." Lord Hailes was the recipient of fulsome praise when he was compared with Voltaire by the leading Edinburgh bookseller of the day, who published his collected works in 1797. Although these volumes and the boastful comparison with Voltaire have not held up, the impulse at the root of the new history was sustaining for Scott and his contemporaries.[4]

Scott translated the historical message voiced by his teachers at Edinburgh University and his clubbable literary friends into a coherent and systematized new form of fiction. At the core was the observation that no society could claim ultimate sanction for its cultural standards. Over time cultural change favored new psychological types in successive generations. The history of Scotland demonstrated that political extremists and religious enthusiasts were relegated to convents, monasteries, or social death. Emancipation from the high road of neo-classicism with its secure and fixed standards, so attentive to Augustan Rome, was now rivaled by the projection of a less scenic and less lofty historical route. Furthermore, conceptions of human nature and society were no longer so likely to be viewed as unchanging. The latter, except for technology, was judged virtually timeless in most aspects. One recalls Hume's confident assertion in his *Enquiry Concerning Human Understanding:* "The same motives produce the same actions, the same events follow from the same causes." This static and assured view did not hold so firmly for the next generation of men of letters. For them society changed as did the types destined to prosper in it. The past was recorded as receding with a hitherto unmatched velocity. In fact, Scott and his contemporaries—novelists, poets and painters—avidly and lovingly chronicled the vanishing archaic manners and ways, the loss of village and peasant culture, and the failed allegiances of Jacobite lairds. From the novelist John Galt to the painter David Wilkie, the memorialization of a vanishing past was to be a growth industry.[5]

Historical writing became the record of those virtues—however reluctantly acknowledged—favoring survival in a more prosaic world. Honor, constancy, and loyalty may have served Quentin Durward of Scott's novel against the Spider King Louis XI, but not Rob Roy or the Jacobites of the eighteenth century. A recent critic assessed Scott's achievement in this way:

> . . . he made it possible to describe any society in its temporal dimensions. Before Scott the novel had been restricted to portraying social organization as static, as seen only in its contemporary aspect. . . . Scott presents society as the product of past experiences and traditions which are in the process of becoming different.[6]

In his own fragmentary "Ashestiel Autobiography," Scott expresses his intellectual delight at being introduced to philosophical or conjectural history under the tutelage of Dugald Stewart and Baron David Hume. He voices his regret that upon leaving the Highschool, "the philosophy of history, a much more important subject [than the technicalities of history] was . . . a sealed book at this period of my life." Subsequently, his intellectual modesty notwithstanding, the closed book was opened. In his novels Scott was able to narrate an ethical odyssey, from a traditional civilization to a commercial society, with remarkable philosophical poise.[7]

The young Goethe may have been envious of Scott for the rich palette of colors with which he was able to paint the history and portraits of his characters moving through the wrenching drama of historical change. By the end of his life, however, in those days when he was composing the last part of *Faust*, Part II (1831), only a few years after Scott's death, the German perceived, as had the Scot, that technological and industrial change was both brutal and inevitable. A new social and economic order had been initiated and was to bring instability at best and chaos at worst. He writes to Wilhelm von Humboldt (17 March, 1832) that in confusing times there are only confusing doctrines. Even the victory of his hero Faust in holding back the sea with monumental dikes will come at a terrible cost. Scott is no Goethe and Waverley is no Faust, but Scott's character understood well the stern demands the present was exacting from the past. He was not alone in having to relinquish dreams and even love in order to come to terms with a more prosaic contemporary world.[8]

Hegel quarried the writings of Scottish economic and moral philosophers, acquiring an extensive knowledge of British institutions, both political and fiscal. He discovered in their tracts and treatises on economic improvement and the emergence of civil society a viable alternative to the terror, turbulence, and dictatorial ambitions of the French Revolution and Napoleonic aftermath. Hegel recognized "civil society as the tremendous power which draws men into itself and claims from them that they work for it, owe everything to it, and do everything by its means." Men and women were united through a form of exchange in which each perceived the other as a means for satisfying his own need. On the one hand individuals remained free and independent in that civil society, since there was no authoritarian allocation of work and reward. On the other hand, however, the objective interdependence of individual relations was augmented when compared to an earlier archaic world of centuries past. Was this a good thing? Was this not inevitable? Who was advantaged and who disadvantaged?[9]

Kant had surely answered many of these questions in the affirmative. In his essay *The Idea of Universal History from a Cosmopolitan Point of View* (1784), he voiced his conviction that antagonism was "the means used by nature to further the development of all her dispositions. . . ." For Kant the term "antagonism" signified the individual's tendency to gain his own interests in competition with those of all others. It was this proclivity which aroused all his energies, leading him to triumph over his natural propensity to indolence while at the same time prompting him to strive for prominence among his fellows. When contrasting the antagonistic with the harmonious society from a moral as well as economic perspective, Kant opined:

> In the absence of unsociability, all human talents would remain confined to an embryonic stage within an Arcadian pastoral existence; men, like the obedient sheep under the shepherd's guidance, would ascribe no value whatsoever to their life.

He followed this radical judgment with a paean to the sagacity of creation:

> Let thanks be given to nature for the stubbornness she engenders, the invidious and vainglorious spirit of emulation, the never sated greed for wealth—and for power too! For without her, all the excellent natural human dispositions would remain forever dormant and deprived of development.[10]

In his "Was ist Aufklärung?" Kant defined the Enlightenment as predicated upon the ability of the individual to achieve his majority as a morally responsible being. For the philosopher the release of the individual from tutelage (paternalism was the grossest form of despotism) allowed one to enjoy religious, political, and economic freedom. This felicitous transaction could occur only in a public world protected from paternalistic interference by an enlightened sovereign—in other words, in a civil society. Kant's concerns were close to those of Adam Smith and the Scottish moral philosophers, featuring as they did the importance of economic freedom and material self-interest. The authority of the sovereign was limited to the defense of society against external threat, protection of the individual against injury from others, and support of public works that could not be successfully undertaken for private profit. Royal paternalistic interference was anathema:

> . . . a government founded on the principle of benevolence towards the people, like the governance of a father over his children, in other words, a paternalistic government (*imperium paternale*), in which the subjects, like minors who cannot distinguish between what is good and what is bad for them, are forced to adopt a passive role, and must look to the sovereign to determine the nature of their happiness, expecting nothing except what he chooses to bestow on them: such a government is the worst possible despotism one can imagine.[11]

Kant believed that an essential feature of this "enlightening" age (there was as yet no English word for "enlightenment") was the extension of the public use of reason. This was yet another benchmark of civil society. He optimistically contended that "men naturally extricate themselves from the state of rudeness and barbarity when intervention is not purposely plied to keep them in it.'' Man is a moral creature, having passed through a long phase of moral evolution starting as an amoral animal (human only in the biological sense) and developing into a being more or less capable of sublimating his animal appetites to the requirements of membership in a genuine society.[12]

When Hegel spoke of "bürgerliche Gesellschaft" (civil society), he positioned it as a historically generated sphere of "ethical life" located between the simple world of the patriarchal household and universal state. In taking this position he was much beholden, as he generously acknowledged, to a legion of intellectual forebears, principally English and Scottish Enlightenment thinkers—especially the latter. Leaving aside the term "bürgerliche," and holding on to the word "Gesellschaft," we can feature the conception of society itself as being perceived as historically producing an extended domain of ethical life. (The Hegelian individual discovered the criteria for his maxims in a free and rational society.) If Hegel was near, could Marx be far behind? What Hegel termed "civil society," Marx was to call "bourgeois society."[13]

For Hegel the creation of civil society "is the achievement of the modern world." (We might here underscore the point that civil society had its modern origins in eighteenth-century England and Scotland.) He would make a distinction between society as a sphere of "universal egoism" omnipresent and characteristic of every society and that of civil society in present times. In modern societies individual self-interest is sanctioned and then emancipated from "religious and ethico-political considerations." Until recent times these traditional constraints had hampered the free play and full extension of individual interests. As we have noted, his debt to the Scots was great. There is evidence to indicate that he had read Adam Ferguson, and Hegel's definition of civil society is much beholden to the free-market model of Adam Smith and Sir James Steuart:

> Civil society—an association of members as self-subsistent individuals in a universality which, because of their self-subsistence, is only abstract. Their association is brought about by their needs, by the legal system—the means to security of person and property—and by an external organization for attaining their particular and common interests.[14]

Hegel was intent upon not confusing civil society and the state as had many a less rigorous commentator:

> If the state is represented as a unity of different persons, as a unity which is only a partnership, then what is really meant is only civil society. Many modern constitutional lawyers have been able to bring within their purview no theory of state but this. In civil society, each member is his own end, everything else is nothing to him.

In this assessment he closely replicates the views of Adam Ferguson who, as we have seen, emphasized the fact that members of civil society had no substantial concern for society as a whole. Hegel goes beyond this, however, to propose that civil society is predicated on needs and a lower kind of knowledge. This lower kind of knowledge or understanding (*Verstand*) is contrasted with the higher level of reason (*Vernunft*), which is to be discerned in the state. *Verstand* signifies in this context "cognitivability grasping only the external necessity binding people together, not realizing the inherent reason for it." Civil society, although it precedes "the state in the logical order, is ultimately dependent upon the state for its very existence and preservation." With finality, Hegel concludes:

> Civil society is the stage of difference which intervenes between the family and the state, even if its formation follows later in time than that of the state, because as the stage of difference, it presupposes the state: to subsist itself, it must have the state before its eyes as something self-subsistent.

Hegel's epistemological differentiation between state and civil society prompts him to designate political economy as the theory of civil society. He places this science in a specific context and in his treatment elicits its dialectical nature. On the one side he celebrates its theoretical accomplishments, whereas on the other he is not hesitant to single out its limitations. The latter he will attribute to the fact that it involves a lower form of understanding—*Verstand* instead of *Vernunft:*

> Political economy is the science which starts from the view of needs and labour but then has the task of explaining mass-relationships and mass-movements in their complexity and their qualitative and quantitative character. This is one of the sciences which have arisen out of the conditions of the modern world. Its development affords the interesting spectacle (as in Smith, Say and Ricardo) of thought working upon the mass of details which confront it at the outset and extracting therefrom the simple principles of the thing, the understanding effective in the thing and directing it. . . .
> But if we look at it from the opposite point of view, this is the field in which the understanding with its subjective aims and moral fancies vents its discontent and moral frustration.

Thus the universality of civil society is in Hegel's view purely instrumental—not an end in itself as is the state. In his capacity as an individual, a burgher in the state is a private person whose chief end is the realization of self-interest.

The basis of civil society is a system of needs with human labor mediating between man and nature. These needs are neither purely physical nor materialistic, therefore one must speak of the mediation of consciousness. There is a conjunction of natural needs with mental needs. Unlike animal needs, human needs have no ultimate limits. Here Hegel takes a stand against Rousseau and the Frenchman's romantic view of the state of nature and the nature of civilization:

> The idea has been advanced that in respect of his needs man lived in freedom in the so-called 'state of nature' when his needs were supposed to be confined to what are known as the simple necessities of nature. . . . This view takes no account of the moment of liberation intrinsic to work. . . . Apart from this, it is false, because to be confined to mere physical needs as such and their direct satisfaction would simply be the condition in which the mental is plunged in the natural and so should be one

of savagery and unfreedom, while freedom itself is to be found only in the reflection of mind into itself, in mind's distinction from nature, and in the reflex of mind in nature.

Human beings are liberated by not being limited in their needs. This freedom serves as an engine to propel human society to pursue the production of commodities. Here is the locus of the restlessness and turbulence of civil society. Where moral philosophers of an earlier time such as Hume and Adam Smith saw the production of goods and craftsmanship as part of a civilizing process, Hegel took a bleaker view. Hume and Smith judged human beings to be beneficiaries both esthetically and morally of the increased variety of commodities. This expansion amplified the range of their sensibilities as well as opening up new possibilities for development. Hume was among the first to appreciate craftsmanship apart from its inherent value. Hegel assumed a very different stance concluding that individuals deceived themselves if they imagined that consciousness was expanded by owning new commodities. In fact, by indulging in acquisitive practice, they were only satisfying the desire of the producer for greater profit. Civil society for Hegel was the mechanism not only through which "felt needs are satisfied," but through which additional demand was created consciously by producers. "Hence the need for greater comfort does not exactly arise within you directly; it is suggested to you by those who hope to make a profit from its creation." Like Tocqueville and John Stuart Mill, Hegel concluded that the rush toward equality—so prominent a characteristic of modernity—propelled civil society to ever higher levels of productivity and the attendant products. Equality itself augments pressures for greater consumption. Unlimited human cravings for goods will generate its antithesis, that is, deprivation and poverty. Society creates new desires without end but also "want and destitution" which are boundless. Poverty and alienation are no innocent or accidental by-products of civil society. Moreover, the dialectic at work in civil society calling for greater productivity creates "a universal dependence of man on man." This universal dependence is further intensified by an increase in radical specialization and division of labor. It in turn leads to the introduction of machinery in order to enhance profit and production. Machinery and industry are perforce the necessary results of an advanced civil society. Here Adam Smith's free market, self-interest, and self-assertion model is appropriated by Hegel. But with the German this model leads to greater social polarization, poverty, and alienation. Hegel will not allow the market free rein, and here the state must intervene to restore economic equity and social equilibrium.[15]

Smith and his confreres were of course located at a very different historical moment and therefore could be generally optimistic concerning economic prospects for societies adhering to their free-market model. Moreover, felicitous conclusions could be drawn by invoking the operation of the invisible hand working to convert private selfishness into public good. The unintended consequences of human egoism could indeed redound to the benefit of society in mysterious ways. Hegel did not have any such *deus ex machina*. For him it was a zero-sum game: as surely as the night follows day, the quest for riches breeds poverty. "In these contrasts and their complexity, civil society affords a spectacle of extravagance and want as well as of the physical and ethical degeneration common to them both.''

Of course neither Adam Smith nor his fellow Scottish economic and moral philosophers could possibly imagine the beginnings of an industrial revolution with its large-scale manufacturing. These *gens de lettres* recognized a host of new problems, particularly moral and psychological ones resulting from radical specialization of labor and the displacement of rural folk into crowded cities. Further, there were attendant matters such as the erosion of the martial spirit. But the very essence of the benefit of the commercial advance remained for them the marginalization of poverty. Economic improvement would also serve to reduce polarization among social classes. For at least a century before the publication of Smith's *Wealth of Nations* (1776), British moral philosophers and legists, as well as their confreres on the Continent, had contended that a less regulated and therefore less encumbered economy would allow all boats to rise. As the mosaic of a civil society was put in place with its full acknowledgment of property rights, the right of voluntary association, the sacredness of contracts and its many other tesserae, it was being viewed in a favorable light. Was it not a check against despotism? The best guarantee of religious toleration? The sphere for the play of critical reason? To this list could be added a legion of benefits from civil liberties to the freedom from censorship of speech and press. For Hegel civil society indeed provided substantial advantages, but in the end, as we have stated, it was a zero-sum game. Therefore civil society must be transcended dialectically. In common parlance this means that Hegel would subordinate it to the higher universality of the state.

In defining the limits of civil society Hegel launched a very modern exegesis on the culture of poverty:

> When the standard of living of a large mass of people falls below a certain subsistence level—a level regulated automatically as the one necessary for a member of the society—and when there is a consequent loss of the sense of right and wrong, of honesty and the self-respect which makes a man insist on maintaining himself by his own work and effort, the result is the creation of a rabble of paupers.

Pauperization was a structural component of civil society and therefore controls must be placed on industry and the price of commodities. The state's intervention, however, if excessive, would conflate the distance between it and civil society—the latter would simply disappear. This posed an exasperating dilemma for Hegel: he appreciated the value of civil society and its manifold benefits of moral and economic freedom and thus was reluctant to call for the invoking of state power which in the end would certainly crush it. This remained an insoluble problem for the philosopher—perhaps the only major one the great systematizer had failed to accommodate:

> Against nature man can claim no right, but once society is established, poverty immediately takes the form of a wrong done to one class by another. The important question of how poverty is to be abolished is one of the most disturbing problems which agitate modern society.

One cannot write history using the pluperfect subjunctive, but a bit of speculation may be in order. Were Adam Smith and his fellow economists and moral philosophers of the Scottish Enlightenment writing in the 1830s rather than in the 1750s and 60s, their observations would have had a very different historical coloration. Scottish cities of the first part of the nineteenth century were beset with problems of poverty, sanitation, and the terrible incidence of cholera. Society had more need of sanitation engineers than of "conjectural or philosophical" historians. A different perspective—a gloomier and starker one—on civil society with its endemic problems of public health and private wretchedness might well have emerged. They might even have agreed with Karl Marx's exposure of its ideological distortions. But of course they wrote and thought in a different age when a burgeoning civil society was nurtured by gentle rains and not yet tested by battering winds. It was much easier to come to terms with historical change in 1750 than in 1850.

NOTES

The notes contain citations for quotations only when the works are not commonplace or editions not readily available. Because the secondary literature is so vast, I shall, whenever possible, cite the most recent monographs and review articles. My scholarly apologies are offered to the numerous now-classic accounts which will not be consistently noted. There are particular authors to whom I am much beholden and I will acknowledge my obligation upon the first reference to their work.

Introduction

1. A. Ferguson, *An Essay on the History of Civil Society* (New Brunswick, 1980), p. 225.

2. Ibid., pp. 117–18.

3. Ibid., p. 183.

4. For the comments of Saul Bellow, see *Partisan Review* 59 (1992), 531–33, 537, 541–45, 550. See also Donald Fanger, "The Post-Heroic Let-Down," *Times Literary Supplement* (15 May 1992), 14. Charles Taylor, in *The Ethics of Authenticity* (Cambridge, Mass., 1991), pp. 17–18, considers modern political theorists who would banish discussion of what constitutes the "good life" from its once central position in political debate. Cf. Ronald Dworkin, *Taking Rights Seriously* (London, 1977).

5. Peter Berger, in "On the Obsolescence of the Concept of Honor," *Revisions: Changing Perspectives in Moral Philosophy*, ed. A. MacIntyre and S. Hauerwas (South Bend, Indiana, 1983), 172–81, provides a trenchant analysis of the shift away from traditional conceptions of honor. Also see J. G. A. Pocock, *The Machiavellian Moment: Florentine Political Thought and the Atlantic Republican Tradition* (Princeton, 1975).

6. For a useful explication of the changing vocabulary of the social orders once rooted in a tripartite division of society, see Peter Burke, "The Language of Orders in Early Modern Europe," *Social Orders & Social Classes in Europe Since 1500: Studies in Social Stratification*, ed., M. L. Bush (London, 1992), 1–12.

7. Ibid., p. 7.

8. H. Grotius, *On the Law of War and Peace*, trans. F. Kelsey (Oxford, 1925), *Prolegomena*. Carneades was selected by Grotius as the very model of a skeptical philosopher. On the complex literary history of this philosopher of the Academy, see Richard Tuck, "Grotius, Carneades and Hobbes," *Grotiana* 4 (1983), 43–62. Here I should like to express my scholarly debt to Stephen Buckle, whose magisterial *Natural Law and the Theory of Property: Grotius to Hume* (Oxford, 1991), has been an indispensable guide in working through the tangle of seventeenth- and eighteenth-century legal thought.

9. S. Buckle, ibid., pp. 11–12, 22, 25, 30, 66–73, 214–15, 263–68.

10. The traditional discourse on *amour propre* (self-love) was of course both Christian and Stoic. The recommendation was that the individual overcome his or her preoccupation with "the good opinion of others." He or she was asked "to step outside this dimension of human life, in which reputations are sought, gained, and unmade." It was this moral stance that was challenged by numerous men of letters in the seventeenth and eighteenth centuries

as being contrary to the essence of human psychology. *Amour propre* was seen as an ineradicable element of the human personality. Rousseau was undoubtedly influenced by the Stoics when embracing their identification of pride in self as a source of evil, but he ended up on different ground.

11. R. Chartier's "From Text to Manners. A Concept and Its Books: Civilité between Aristocratic Distinction and Popular Approbation," *Cultural Uses of Print in Early Modern France*, trans. L. Cochrane (Princeton, 1987), 71–109, illuminates the transition from a culture of "preferences" to one more responsive to public opinion.

12. The origins of modern European civil society have been fixed in eighteenth-century England and Scotland–a privileged time. John Gray, a contemporary scholar of liberalism, argues cogently that both in the eighteenth century and in modern times, democracy was and is not essential for its genesis. He points to present-day examples of civil society such as Singapore, Korea, and Japan. Perhaps a bit harshly, he suggests that the republican-democratic tradition "typified in our time by Hannah Arendt" is irrelevant for post-communist countries aiming to establish the lineaments of a civil society. John Gray, "Post-Totalitarianism, Civil Society, and the Limits of the Western Model," *The Reemergence of Civil Society in Eastern Europe and the Soviet Union*, ed. Z. Rau (Boulder, 1991), 145–60.

13. The designation *"ancien régime"* is of course something of an anachronism, since it was employed retrospectively by Tocqueville and others. Despite present-day unease concerning this term, it yet remains a valuable sign-post. I wish to thank my former student Jay Smith for allowing me to read his unpublished paper, "Restoring Personal Monarchy."

14. I wish to thank my colleague Geoff Eley for allowing me to read his incisive paper, "Nations, Publics, and Political Cultures: Placing Habermas in the Nineteenth Century."

15. R. Pipes, "In the Russian Intellectual Tradition," *Solzhenitsyn at Harvard*, ed. R. Berman (Washington, D.C., 1980), p. 171.

1. Toward an Understanding of Civil Society

1. Jürgen Habermas's *The Structural Transformation of the Public Sphere: An Inquiry into a Category of Bourgeois Society,* trans. Thomas Burger, with the assistance of Frederick Lawrence (1962; reprint, Cambridge, Mass., 1989) is a work that has promoted a veritable growth industry of research and scholarship. For an incisive appraisal of its strengths and limitations, see A. La Vopa, "Conceiving a Public: Ideas and Society in Eighteenth-Century Europe," *Journal of Modern History* 64 (1992), 79–116. Cf. Also P. Hohendahl, *The Institution of Criticism* (Ithaca, New York, 1987), pp. 247–60; T. Eagleton, *The Function of Criticism: From the "Spectator" to Post-Structuralism* (London, 1984). Martin Whyte, in his "Urban China: A Civil Society in the Making?" *State and Society: The Consequences of Reform,* ed. A. Rosenbaum (Boulder, Colorado, 1992), 77–102, provides ample bibliography and discussion of work being done in Chinese studies, Eastern Europe, and Russia on the topic of the emergence of civil societies. (I have used different editions of the same texts because I worked in various libraries.)

2. For a discussion of changing meanings of the term "society," and its implications for the study of civility and civil society, see R. Williams, *Key Words: A Vocabulary of Culture and Society,* expanded ed. (London, 1985), pp. 291–93; L. Febvre, *A New Kind of History,* ed. P. Burke (New York, 1973), pp. 219–57; M. Becker, *Civility and Society in Western Europe, 1300–1600* (Bloomington, 1988), pp. 1–2. Very useful is T. Finkenstaedt, E. Leisi, and D. Wolff, *A Chronological English Dictionary* (Heidelberg, 1970). New words from the *Oxford English Dictionary* (hereafter, *OED*) are listed alphabetically, year by year. For further discussion of the terminology of "society" and "civil society," see M. Waltzer, "The Idea of Civil Society," *Dissent* (Spring 1991), 293–304; Charles Taylor, "Modes of Civil Society," *Public Culture* 3 (1990), 95–118; two articles by Edward Shils are most useful: "The Virtues of Civil Society," *Government and Opposition* 26 (1991), 3–20; "Was ist eine Civil Society?" *Europe und die Civil Society,* ed. K. Michelski (Stuttgart, 1991), 13–52.

3. John Brewer, in his *The Sinews of Power: War, Money and the English State, 1688–1783* (Cambridge, 1990), pp. 69ff., presents a balanced perspective on the persistence of

ancient custom and archaic practice in English political life, emphasizing their gradual displacement by stronger government over the centuries. Still, patronage and the "civil list" remained as firm reminders of the durability of older political forms predicated upon gifts and exchange of favors. See also Linda Peck, *Court, Patronage and Corruption in Early Stuart England, 1603–1640* (New York, 1990). Catherine Bates's *The Rhetoric of Courtship in Elizabethan Language and Literature* (Cambridge, 1991) suggests that the English experience closely replicates that of France, as evidenced in the linguistic transformation of their respective courtly vocabularies. For the sale of offices in France, see the classic account of R. Mousnier, *La vénalité des offices en France sous Henri IV et Louis XIII* (Rouen, 1945), pp. 365–86. Because it was impossible to live on fees or salaries, great office-holders were expected to receive emoliments and gifts from petitioners, constituents, etc. For the decline of the nexus of obligation (abolition of feudal tenure and Court of Ward) in England, see Christopher Hill, *Reformation to Industrial Revolution, 1530–1780* (Harmondsworth, 1971), p. 135.

4. For a survey of recent literature on changes in family structure in England, see Leonora Davidoff, "The Family in Britain," *The Cambridge Social History of Britain 1750–1950*, ed. F. M. I. Thompson (Cambridge, 1990), Vol. II, 71–129. P. Langford's recent survey *A Polite and Commercial People, 1727–1783* (Oxford, 1989) is deeply saturated with contemporary reactions and observations on social and economic change. This work will be drawn upon regularly in my monograph. Langford notes that turnpikes were blamed for the flight of nobles and gentry from their patriarchal responsibilities. See also F. M. I. Thompson, "Town and City," *Cambridge Social History of Britain*, p. 17. Lawrence Stone's enthusiasm for the modern family (origins eighteenth century) and "affective individualism" might be balanced against the growing isolation of individual and family from broader social bonds. At the upper reaches of society, privacy, inwardness, and the pursuit of self-interest were invested with higher values than hitherto. Publicity, familiarity, and solidarity were, on the other hand, less prized; cf. Stone's *Family, Sex and Marriage in England, 1500–1800* (London, 1977), passim.

5. P. Borsay's *The English Urban Renaissance of Culture and Society in the Provincial Town, 1660–1770* (Oxford, 1989) provides an admirable account of the diffusion of ideas, manners, and polite culture throughout England. Not only is the townscape etched deftly but examples from literature are drawn upon to flesh out the historical record. H. Payne, "Elite versus Popular Mentality in the Eighteenth Century," *Studies in Eighteenth-Century Culture*, VIII (1979), 3–32, offers an analysis of the distancing of the well-to-do from the enthusiasms and recreation of the plebeians. A. Kernan, *Samuel Johnson and the Impact of Print* (Princeton, 1989) emphasizes the importance of print for projecting "authorial dignity." Print technology prompted critics and scholarly editors to legitimately lay claim to independent authority. See also A. La Vopa, p. 108.

6. On the question of corporate or constituted bodies as distinguished from voluntary forms of association, see N. Henshall, *The Myth of Absolutism: Change and Continuity in Early Modern European Monarchy* (London, 1992). In these bodies individuals sharing the same interests were constituted "as a collective legal personality with corresponding rights in law. . . . They were endowed with organs for expressing their collective will, discharging their functions and defending their powers and privileges. Specimens are *parlements*, provincial Estates, town councils, village assemblies, noble assemblies and assemblies of the clergy." To this list might be added such corporate bodies as the guilds. See especially "decentralized corporations," pp. 8–16. For a classic discussion of the formation and proliferation of secondary groups and associations (voluntary) from differing backgrounds, and their contribution to modern public life in the West, see Emile Durkheim, *The Division of Labor in Society* (New York, 1964); Alexis de Tocqueville, *Democracy in America* (New York, 1954). A Laumann's *Bonds of Pluralism: The Form and Substance of Urban Social Networks* (New York, 1973) is a very useful account of the proliferation and complexities of the associative impulse in the modern city. For France in the Age of the Enlightenment, see D. Roche, "Die 'sociétés de pensée' und die aufgeglarten Eliten des 18 Jahrhunderts in

Frankreich,'' *Socialgeschichte der Aufklärung in Frankreich*, ed. H. Gumbrecht (Munich, 1981) Vol. I, 77–115. On the reduction of the obligation of clergy in the eighteenth century in England, see J. Obelkevich, ''Clergy and Religion,'' *Cambridge Social History of Britain*, Vol. III, 370–74.

7. On philosophical societies and lodges, and their differences in France, England, and the German states, see François Furet, *Interpreting the French Revolution* (Cambridge, 1981). The chapters on Tocqueville and Cochin, pp. 132–204, are especially illuminating. A recent work by Margaret Jacob, *Living the Enlightenment: Freemasonry in Eighteenth-Century Europe* (New York, 1992), presents a thorough review of the debates on and the historical literature pertaining to the proliferating forms of associative life throughout Europe. Cochin's *Les sociétés de pensée et la révolution en Bretagne* (Paris, 1925) remains a classic in this field. His study of the Breton countryside and the shift from personal government to more impersonal forms has stimulated much fruitful debate, as Furet and Jacob's work prove. See also N. Heinrich, ''Arts et sciences à l'age classique professions et institutions culturelles,'' *Actes de la recherche en sciences sociales* 67 (1987), 47–78.

8. On Smollett, see D. Daiches's ''Smollett Reconsidered,'' *Smollet: Author of Distinction*, ed. A. Bold (London, 1982), 13–46. J. Cropsey's *Politics and Economics: An Interpretation of the Principles of Adam Smith* (The Hague, 1957) advances the plausible thesis that the choice proffered by Hume, Adam Smith, and many another was between a social order based on principles of virtue or some substitute of virtue such as commerce.

9. For a general discussion of Adam Ferguson and his appreciation of the associative impulse, see J. Keane, ''Despotism and Democracy,'' *Civil Society and the State*, ed. J. Keane (London, 1988), 42–46. B. Lenman, in his *Integration, Enlightenment and Industrialization: Scotland, 1746–1832* (London, 1981), pp. 30–32, 63–64, gives useful background on Ferguson and his career. For the pertinent observations of Ferguson himself, see his *An Essay on the History of Civil Society*, ed. D. Forbes (Edinburgh, 1966), pp. 217–20. It should be noted that Scottish interest in the new forays into social and civil history was prompted by the Scot James Ogilvie's translation of Pietro Giannone's *The Civil History of the Kingdom of Naples* from Italian into English in 1729. A list of its subscribers is provided by H. Trevor-Roper in his ''The Scottish Enlightenment,'' *Studies in Voltaire and the Eighteenth Century* 58 (1967), 1635–58, esp. 1652–53.

10. For a review of the ideals of civil humanism, as well as the norms of good lordship and ''permiscuous sociability,'' see M. Becker, pp. 1–42 (chapter entitled, ''The Tilt toward Civility and the Winds of Change''). Very useful for a survey of the changing meaning of key terms, such as benevolence, love, self-love, and humanity employed by British moral philosophers, is the index of D. Raphael's *British Moralists, 1650–1800* (Oxford, 1969), Vol. II, pp. 361–431. Adam Seligman, in his *The Idea of Civil Society* (New York, 1992), underscores a new appreciation of the problematics of the individual's place in society evident in the writings of Adam Ferguson, Francis Hutcheson, Adam Smith and other Scottish Enlightenment moralists. The basis for a social order became, in Seligman's view, the centerpiece of an increasingly speculative (''conjectural'') historical narrative.

11. On Pufendorf, see J. Schneewind's introduction to the text, *On the Duty of Man and Citizen* in *Moral Philosophy from Montaigne to Kant: An Anthology* (Cambridge, 1990), Vol. I, 156–58; 26–30. Where distinctions between private and public were unclear, there was greater need for a single, comprehensive code. See Louis Dumont's discussion of what he classifies as ''holistic society,'' in his ''A Modified View of Our Origins,'' *Religion* 12 (1982), 1–127. On conduct manuals, see D. Javitch, ''Rival Arts of Conduct in Elizabethan England,'' *Yearbook of Italian Studies* 1 (1971), 178–98, and his ''Poetry and Court Conduct,'' *Modern Language Notes* 87 (1972), 865–82. Julia Briggs's assessment of tension and ambivalence in this literature is cautionary, reminding one of the intricacies of courtesy and the honor code. See her *This Stage-Play World: English Literature and Its Background 1580–1625* (Oxford, 1983), pp. 119–59.

12. For a discussion of the intellectual grounds for reconceptualizing discourses on society, see A. MacIntyre, *Whose Justice? Which Rationality?* (South Bend, 1988), pp. 241–80.

A. Seligman, pp. 26ff., analyzes the effort made by moral philosophers of the late seventeenth and eighteenth centuries to think society as "something over and beyond its individual parts. . . ." Seligman follows MacIntyre in observing that these efforts evident in the writings of Descartes's French disciple Nicolas de Malebranche were to be more fully explicated in the works of the English moralist and esthetician Shaftesbury. John Bossy's *Christianity in the West 1400–1700* (Oxford, 1985) is a bold and sensitive exploration of the decline of the idea of the interdependence of communal norms and religious sanctions. On peasant family solidarity in the late Middle Ages, see B. Hanawalt, *The Ties that Bind: Peasant Families in Medieval England* (Oxford, 1986). Otto Brunner's *Adeliges Landleben und europäischer Geist* (Salzburg, 1949) discusses *Herrenschaft* and the cultural responsibilities of nobles extensively, though this order is a bit idealized. Society had been customarily conceptualized as fragile, thus norms governing relations tended to be absolute and were regarded as part of a world ruled by transcendental forces. Further, violators of obligation were threatened by strict codes of honor. For a bold extension of the discussion on the relationship between hierarchy and the representation of women's bodies, as well as models of gender differences, see Thomas Laqueur, "Orgasm, Generation and the Politics of Reproductive Biology," *Representation* 14 (1986), 1–18: in portraying the female body, "an anatomy and physiology of incommensurability replaced a metaphysics of hierarchy in the representation of women in relation to men."

13. On the theme of manners and conviviality, see F. Heal, "The Idea of Hospitality in Early Modern England," *Past & Present* 102 (1984), 16–84. On the subtleties of the exchange system and transfer of social credit, see P. Bourdieu, *Outline of the Theory of Practice,* trans. R. Nice (Cambridge, 1977). Bourdieu's ideas have a ready application to the social and economic experiences of early modern daily life. Cf. C. Klapisch-Zuber's *Women, Family and Ritual in Renaissance Italy,* trans. L. Cochrane (Chicago, 1985), pp. 77ff. G. Duby, *La Moyen Age 987–1460* (Paris, 1987), displays something of this penchant for chronological closure. N. Elias's *The Civilizing Process: Sociogenetic and Psychogenetic Investigations (The History of Manners)* (Oxford, 1978), Vol. I, merits criticism for its neglect of the Italian experience. The steady reliance of present-day scholarship on its conclusions with their excessive focus on the French court also calls for serious revision.

14. I am much indebted to my former student Jay Smith for his full discussion of the significance of a gift culture and the nobility of seventeenth-century France. See his "The Culture of Merit in Old Regime France: Royal Service and the Old Nobility, 1600–1789" (University of Michigan dissertation, 1991). Hugh Trevor-Roper's now classic piece, "The General Crisis of the Seventeenth Century," *Crisis in Europe, 1550–1600,* ed. T. Ashton (London, 1965), 59–95, offers rich evidence as to the texture of seventeenth-century political culture. Lawrence Stone, in his *The Crisis of the Aristocracy 1558–1641* (Oxford, 1965), provides an abundance of details as to the nature of ties of obligation at the upper reaches of English society from the second half of the sixteenth century through the first part of the seventeenth. For a further discussion of the political networks and social webs spun in the world of the gift and counter-gift, see M. Becker, pp. 15–19, 144–46. For a general sociological view of these ties, see A. Gouldner, "The Norm of Reciprocity: A Preliminary Statement," *American Sociological Review* 25 (1960), 161–78; cf. also G. Homans, "Social Behavior as Exchange," *American Journal of Sociology* 63 (1958), 597–608. On the vital subject of clientage, see Mack Holt, "Patterns of *Clientèle* and Economic Opportunity at Court during the Wars of Religion," *French Historical Studies* 13 (1984), 305–22. And of course the fundamental work to which all subsequent scholarship on mutuality and exchange has been indebted is Marcel Mauss's *The Gift: Forms and Function of Exchange in Archaic Societies,* trans. I. Cunnison (Glencoe, Illinois, 1954); cf. also B. Porchnev, 'Pour une histoire anthropologique: la notion de reciprocité," Symposium in *Annales,* E. S. C. 29 (1974), 1309–80.

15. For a full discussion of honor culture, see Mervyn James, *Society, Politics and Culture: Studies in Early Modern England* (Cambridge, 1986), pp. 308–413, esp. ch. 8, "English Politics and the Concept of Honor, 1485–1642." For a critical discussion of Trevor-

Roper's thesis, see *Crisis in Europe*, 97–116. N. Keohane's *Philosophy and the State in France: The Renaissance to the Enlightenment* (Princeton, 1980) provides an encyclopedic survey of moral and political philosophy in early modern France.

16. For a discussion of the history of the word "moral," see A. MacIntyre, *After Virtue* (South Bend, 1984), pp. 39ff. Gradually the concept of morality was lent a cultural space of its own separate from any legal, theoretical, or esthetic fixity. Priscilla Parkhurst Clark discusses the role of patronage in French literature in her *Literary France: The Making of a Culture* (Berkeley, 1987), pp. 39ff. She cites the epitaph the playwright Corneille composed for the mighty Richelieu: "He did too well by me for me to speak ill of him. He did too much ill for me to speak well of him." C. L. Barber, in his *The Idea of Honour in the English Drama 1591–1700* (Gothenberg, 1957), investigates an honor culture in England paralleling that of France. On Richelieu, the nobles and dueling, see William Church, *Richelieu and Reasons of State* (Princeton, 1972). For broader aspects of politics and political thought, see also Church's *Constitutional Thought in Sixteenth-Century France* (Cambridge, 1941). For a study of the literary characterization of "gloire," see O. Ranum, *Artisans of Glory: Writers and Historical Thought in Seventeenth-Century France* (Chapel Hill, North Carolina, 1980); E. Schalk, *From Valor to Pedigree: Ideas of Nobility in France in the Sixteenth and Seventeenth Centuries* (Princeton, 1986).

17. The ideal of *honnêté* involved setting norms for behavior featuring the unexceptional, inconspicuous, as against extravagant gestures and flamboyant language. For Descartes the "*honnête homme*," like the philosopher himself, "accepts his social role as a role, while remaining free of it as a mind." Cf. L. Gossman, *Men and Masks: A Study of Molière* (Baltimore, 1963), pp. 178–79. For the theme of civility, see J. Revel, "The Uses of Civility," *A History of Private Life*, ed. G. Duby and P. Ariès, trans. A. Goldhammer (Cambridge, Mass., 1989), Vol. III, 167–205. Also in the same volume, see A. Farge, "The Honor and Secrecy of Families," 571–611. For a study of the influence of French moralists on Corneille, see J. Maurens, *La tragedie sans tragique: Le néo-stoicisme dans l'oeuvre de Pierre Corneille* (Paris, 1966). One might suggest that literati of the seventeenth century were more likely to dramatize the misgivings and anxieties felt by men and women stemming from consciousness of human limitations than their confreres of a later time. The literary path to Voltaire was tortuous and tracked laboriously by French playwrights, moralists, and poets. Voltaire in his *La mort de César*, III, 4, provided a coda:

> Change the way you feel, I implore you
> Do not force your soul to overcome nature.

18. R. Mousnier, "Les concepts d'''ordres', d'''états', de 'fidélité', et de 'monarchie absolue' en France de la fin du XVe siècle à la fin du XVIIIe siècle," *Revue Historique* 247 (1972), 289–313. See also his *The Institutions of France under the Absolute Monarchy*, trans. B. Pierce (Chicago, 1978), Vol. I, pp. 107ff. It should be pointed out, and numerous critics have done so, that Mousnier's concept of fidelity did not preclude satisfying personal interest. See Jay Smith, pp. 11–37, in which he deals with the culture of obligation. For a critique of Mousnier, cf. S. Kettering, *Patrons, Brokers and Clients in Seventeenth-Century France* (Oxford, 1986) and W. Beik, *Absolutism and Society in Seventeenth-Century France: State Power and Provincial Aristocracy in Languedoc* (Cambridge, 1985), pp. 12–27. For further discussion of changing rituals and forms of clientage and fidelity, see Russell Major's articles, "Bastard Feudalism and the Kiss: Changing Social Mores in Late-Medieval and Early-Modern France," *Journal of Interdisciplinary History* 17 (1987), 509–35; "Forum: Fidelity and Clientage. The Revolt of 1620: A Study of Ties of Fidelity," *French Historical Studies* 14 (1986), 391–408.

19. A. Lovejoy, in his *Reflections on Human Nature* (Baltimore, 1961), discusses French seventeenth-century moralists in general and Pascal in particular; see esp. pp. 234–44. On the role of honor in sixteenth-century French political culture, see K. Neuschal, *Word of*

Honor: Interpreting Noble Culture in Sixteenth-Century France (Ithaca, 1989). Cf. also J. Bergin, *Cardinal Richelieu: Power and the Pursuit of Wealth* (New Haven, 1985); D. Bitton, *The French Nobility in Crisis, 1560–1640* (Stanford, 1969); R. Bonney, *Political Change under Richelieu and Mazarin, 1624–1661* (Oxford, 1978). For further discussion of the contribution of Mousnier, see B. Mettam, "Two-Dimensional History: Mousnier and the Ancien Regime," *History* 66 (1981), 229ff. For England, see J. Hurstfield, "The Profits of Fiscal Feudalism 1541–1602," *Economic History Revue*, 2nd ser. 8 (1956), 52–60. N. Keohane, pp. 283–311, in a chapter entitled, "Self-Love and Society: Jansenists and the *Honnête Homme*," offers a nuanced discussion of key ideas of Pascal, Bayle, Domat and others; see also William Church, "The Decline of French Jurists as Political Theorists," *French Historical Studies* 5 (1967), 1–40. William Strahan's excellent translation of Domat's *The Civil Law in Its Natural Order, together with the Public Law*, was published in London in 1722.

20. It is worth noting that comparable developments are described for England and its theater by Robertson Davies in his "Playwrights and Plays," *The 'Revels' History of Drama in English* (London, 1975), 145–269, esp. the conclusions. In plays such as John Home's *Douglas*, the emotions indulged in carried more self-pity than was appropriate to any tragedy. R. Chartier, Dominique Julia, and Madeleine Compère's *L'education en France du XVIᵉ au XVIIIᵉ siècle* (Paris, 1970) provides excellent background for the study of education and values.

21. P. Bénichou, *Morales du grand siècle* (Paris, 1948), provides a sensitive analysis of the volatile mix of archaic and heroic ideals contained under the canopy of a restraining political authority. Cf. also O. Nadal, *Le sentiment de l'amour dans l'oeuvre de Pierre Corneille* (Paris, 1946), esp. the conclusions, pp. 268–86. J. Starabinski, *L'oeil vivant* (Paris, 1961), discusses the psychological interdependence of the hero and his admirers. Guy de Balzac's writings and career offer an ample representation of the code of heroic glory and its limitations, with mood swings from courtier to *devot* in the age of Louis XIV. Cf. F. Sutcliffe, *Guy de Balzac et son temps* (Paris, 1959).

22. My interpretation of Corneille owes much to I. Nagel's *Autonomy and Mercy: Reflections on Mozart's Operas*, trans. M. Faber (Cambridge, Mass., 1991). See also Pierre Corneille, *Oeuvres complètes* (Paris, 1963), pp. 268–88.

23. Nowhere was an analysis of the passions more subtle than in Baroque music, especially the opera and madrigal. See S. Leopold, *Monteverdi: Music in Transition* (Oxford, 1991). We observe music becoming "process"; the quest was for "aural synonyms" for the re-enactment of "the ways in which people, here and now, feel, think and act." Cf. W. Mellers, "Out of Arcadia," *Times Literary Supplement* (17 Jan. 1992), 21. Also see the several relevant articles in *Conscience and Casuistry in Early Modern Europe*, ed. E. Lettes (Cambridge, 1988). The word "emulation" underwent a semantic revolution extending its range of meaning. In the seventeenth century it implied imitation of hereditary virtues. The genealogist of the La Rochefoucauld family, Pierre Hutin, in the seventeenth century, boldly asserted that everyone in that family "had the same emulation to surpass everyone else so much are excellent courage and virtue hereditary in this illustrious house." In the eighteenth century this archaic usage of the word "emulation" was still in vogue but was rivaled by a more democratic concept. An army lieutenant of the eighteenth century wrote: "Emulation is the desire to achieve what someone else has achieved using the same method." Further, one must model oneself on an individual "whose talent or merit, have elevated and sustained him in the rank which he occupies. Emulation is shown only by our exactitude in filling with distinction the grade which fate has placed us in. . . . It is in this manner that we obtain a higher grade." See Jay Smith, pp. 217–18.

24. L. Gossman, pp. 163–252, compares Molière with Corneille and Racine. See also the incomparable E. Auerbach's *Mimesis: The Representation of Reality in Western Literature*, trans. W. Trask (Princeton, 1953), pp. 359–94. In Molière's plays the dominant metaphor of social cohesion is one of exchange. Social relations are conceived of as commerce, with trafficking not merely in goods but in conversation, friendship, love, and all manner of obli-

gation. Out of human interaction networks of exchange were generated. The opening lines of *Don Juan* portray an ideal world from which the hero/villain withdraws by breaking all contracts with kin, merchants, and, of course, women. Relations with females are represented not as sexual but as generating sacred ties upon which the well-being of society depends. The offended Don Carlos recognized that it was only these bonds that could sustain and lend coherence to social arrangements. Furthermore, this fragile social world was endowed with spiritual force essential for visiting retribution on violators.

I wish to thank my student Jacob Melish whose ideas on Molière stimulated my thoughts.

25. For a discussion of the psychology of Descartes's *Traité des Passions,* see P. Yarrow, *The Seventeenth Century, 1600–1715,* in *A Literary History of France* (London, 1967), Vol. II, 108–12. See also L. Gossman, pp. 190–93; R. Cumming, "Descartes' Provisional Morality," *Review of Metaphysics* 9 (1955), 208–35. The portrait of the "generous man" is found in the last section of *Traité des Passions.* For a translation see *Philosophical Works of Descartes,* ed. E. Haldane and G. Ross (Cambridge, 1931), pp. 201–4. Further comments on this topic are found in Descartes's *Discourse on Method;* here he allows for the psychological power of *la gloire* (the desire to be esteemed) as a legitimate route to virtue. See Descartes's *Philosophical Writings,* ed. E. Anscombe and P. Geach (Edinburgh and London, 1954), pp. 24–28. Descartes's vision of society in the *Traité des Passions* was grounded in the principle of *natural* obligation; thus advantages, favors, and benefits flowed freely between king and subject, neither to be insisted upon by the ruler nor claimed by the ruled.

26. A. Levi's *French Moralists and the Theory of the Passions 1585–1659* (Oxford, 1964) contains a general discussion of the passions and moral philosophy at a time of bracing intellectual change. For an appreciation of subsequent views on the passions, see Arthur Wilson, "Sensibility in France in the Eighteenth Century," *French Quarterly* 13 (1931), 38–48; see N. Keohane, pp. 309–11 for a discussion of the leading ideas of Nicolas de Malebranche, optimistic follower of Descartes, who demonstrated exquisite ethical refinement in discoursing on *amour propre* and the value of human love and generosity.

27. Basil Willey's *The Eighteenth-Century Background: Studies on the Idea of Nature in the Thought of the Period* (London, 1950) offers a discussion of Shaftesbury's "natural morality" as well as his reactions to Hobbes's psychology of selfishness. A Seligman's *The Idea of Civil Society,* p. 6, discusses the development of a theory of personality incorporating contradictions in human nature and human motivation. The challenge to develop such a theory was met by seventeenth-century moralists who positioned altruism at one pole and egoism at the other. Neither could entirely displace the other and so one lived with the mix. This led to the problematizing of relations between private and public. In turn, these tensions prompted exploration into the ability of individuals to endure stresses between benevolence and selfishness. Investigation into these tangled connections encouraged the naturalizing of the claims of egoism as well as the lightening of the requirements of benevolence. In this way moralists of the seventeenth century were to reduce the distance between fulfillment of the public good and satisfaction of private interests. A. MacIntyre's *After Virtue* is a classic account of the development of the new ethics. The influence of Shaftesbury's defense of the passions remained pervasive over the eighteenth century. Diderot translated his *Inquiry Concerning Virtue or Merit* (1699). The Frenchman's views of religious toleration were informed by Shaftesbury's major work *Characteristics of Men, Manners, Opinions, Times* (1711): toleration should be withdrawn only from those who advocate intolerance. For details of Shaftesbury's influence on European thought, see Louis Bredvold, *The Natural History of Sensibility* (Detroit, 1962), pp. 1–16; Janet Todd, *Sensibility: an Introduction* (London, 1986), pp. 24–36.

28. Francis Bacon's distinction between the false sense of honor of the vainglorious and the magnanimity of the man of wisdom is considered by Mervyn James, p. 410. Bacon is concerned with reducing private violence and the feuding of an honor community: blood must be spilled only in just and public causes, not in personal vendettas. See also J. Weinberger, *Science, Faith and Politics: Francis Bacon and the Utopian Roots of the Modern Age* (Ithaca, 1985), pp. 302–21.

29. D. Pennington, "Political Debate and Thomas Hobbes," *The New Pelican Guide to English Literature*, ed. B. Ford (Harmondsworth, 1982), Vol. III, 303–17. For background, see J. Marston, "Gentry Honor and Royalism in Early Stuart England," *Journal of British Studies* 13 (1973), 21–43. Account should also be taken of the Puritan reliance on "disciplined" solidarity in battle rather than individual heroism as a formula for bringing victory. See Mervyn James, p. 411.

30. Keith Thomas provides a deft analysis of Hobbes's social thought, placing it effectively within the context of the ethical concerns of his times. See his "Social Origins of Hobbes' Political Thought," *Hobbes Studies*, ed. K. Brown (Oxford, 1965), 185–236. Cf. also Hobbes's *Leviathan*, ed. M. Oakeshott (Oxford, 1947), pp. 87–92, as well as Oakeshott's *Rationalism in Politics* (New York, 1974), pp. 290–97. For criticism of Hobbes, see John Bowle, *Hobbes and His Critics: A Study in Seventeenth-Century Constitutionalism* (London, 1951); S. Mintz, *The Hunting of Leviathan: Seventeenth-Century Reactions to the Materialism and Moral Philosophy of Thomas Hobbes* (Cambridge, 1962).

31. J. Wallace, in his "John Dryden's Plays and the Conception of a Heroic Culture," *Politics from Puritanism to the Enlightenment*, ed. P. Zagorin (Berkeley, 1980), 115–34, provides a succinct and effective discussion of the importation of French ideas pertaining to honor and generosity. L. Brevold, in his *The Intellectual Milieu of John Dryden* (Ann Arbor, 1934), gives much detail on the French influence.

32. For an appraisal of Dryden's tragedies, see R. J. Kaufman, "On the Poetics of Terminal Tragedy," *A Collection of Essays on Dryden*, ed. B. Schilling (Englewood Cliffs, New Jersey, 1963), 83–111. On English tragedies in general, see *The Revels History of Drama*, Vol. V, pp. 256–87. On the general question of problem solving, see M. Peckham, *Man's Rage for Chaos* (Philadelphia, 1960).

33. See L. Teeter, "The Dramatists' Use of Hobbes' Political Ideas," *English Literary History* 3 (1936), 140–65, for a discussion of Dryden's drama and the Hobbesian villain. For background, see S. Zebouni, *A Study in Heroic Characterization* (Baton Rouge, 1965). See also W. Birthoff, *Literature and the Continuation of Virtue* (Princeton, 1986); P. Harth, *Contexts of Dryden's Thought* (Chicago, 1968).

34. Cf. *The Critical Opinion of Johnson*, ed. J. E. Brown (Princeton, 1926), pp. 72ff.; Samuel Johnson, *Prose and Poetry*, ed. M. Wilson (London, 1957), pp. 489–529.

35. Alisdair MacIntyre gives the most textured and provocative discussion of these changes in his chapter "The Augustinian and Aristotelian Background to the Scottish Enlightenment," in *Whose Justice? Which Rationality?*, pp. 209–40. See also the chapter in his *After Virtue*, "The Virtues, the Unity of Human Life and the Concept of Tradition," pp. 200–25. The author acknowledges his debt to Karl Polanyi's classic work, *The Great Transformation*.

36. For a discussion of the career and works of Saint-Evremond, see *La litterature Français*, eds. A. Legarde and L. Michard (Paris, 1970), Vol. II, pp. 77–83. Saint-Evremond went into exile for criticizing the Treaty of the Pyrenees and spent the last forty years of his life in England, where he was a great literary favorite. He is buried in Westminster Abbey. See A. Yarrow, pp. 330–36. Also Charles de Saint-Evremond, *Oeuvres en prose*, ed. R. Ternois (Paris, 1962–69), 4 vols.; esp. Vol. 2, pp. 12–22, Vol. 3, pp. 6–20, 149–53. Saint-Evremond characterizes the *honnête homme* as an individual who exercises "true honor that governs the behavior of reasonable individuals." His counsel of moderation for the *honnête homme* resembles that of Descartes for his *homme généreux*. Neither the strict pursuit of self-interest nor individuals "exclusively occupied with their own affairs" bereft of compassion are admirable. Similarly objectionable are those "moved by passion and the search for pleasure. . . ." While the latter are amenable to appeals of human feeling, they are ineffective, since their behavior is entirely inconstant. Saint-Evremond espouses the doctrine of moderation over and against naked self-interest and sterile moralism. His strength as a literary man stems from his appreciation of the fact that it was not possible to preach virtue to the corrupt members of his generation. For them it was necessary to demonstrate the advantages of virtue so that the individual would seek to purify his conception

of interest. Society was not possible if "rigid virtue" and narrow self-interest prevailed. See
N. Keohane, 231–32; E. Caramaschi, "Un honnête homme libertin: Saint-Evremond," *Il
pensiero politico* 8 (1975), 160–70.

37. A. La Vopa, 106, provides extensive bibliography on cultural differences between the
reading publics of France and England. See S. Botein, J. Censer, and H. Ritvo, "The Periodical Press in Eighteenth-Century England and French Society: A Cross-Cultural Approach," *Comparative Studies in Society and History* 23 (1981), 464–90; J. Brewer,
"Commercialization and Politics," *The Birth of a Consumer Society,* ed. N. McKendrick
(Bloomington, Indiana, 1982), 197–262. For a bold series of comparisons between elite culture in France and that of England, see P. France, *Politeness and Its Discontents: Problems
in French Classical Culture* (Cambridge, 1992), pp. 65ff.; also, the very useful monograph
by Philip Knachel, *England and the Fronde* (Ithaca, 1967).

38. Bacon's essays on private topics such as children and marriage take the view that
these are obstacles to "worldly advancement." Hospitality, friendship, and the multiple ex-
penses incurred thereby, often do not work to the generous man's advantage. Friends are
useful as "receptacles for one's emotional overflow." In fact there is little friendship in the
world, and least of all between equals that is "wont to be imagined." For a summary of
Bacon's ideas on these themes, see A. Quinton, *Francis Bacon* (New York, 1980), pp. 70–
78. For recent scholarship on the Fronde, see N. Henshall, *The Myth of Absolutism: Change
and Continuity in Early Modern European Monarchy* (New York, 1992), pp. 30–31.

39. See Q. Skinner, "Hobbes's Leviathan," *Historical Journal* 7 (1964), 321–32, and his
"The Ideological Context of Hobbes's Political Thought," ibid., 9 (1966), 296–317. See
also J. Habermas's *Theory and Practice,* trans. J. Vertel (Boston, 1973), pp. 47–81; J. G. A.
Pocock, "Time, History and Eschatology in the Thought of Thomas Hobbes," *Politics, Language and Time: Essays in Political Thought and History* (New York, 1971), 148–201.

40. J. Hampson, *Hobbes and the Social Contract Tradition* (Cambridge, 1985) offers an
intellectual context for the present discussion. Leo Strauss, in his *The Political Philosophy
of Hobbes,* trans. E. Sinclair (Chicago, 1952), pp. 129–70, explores the salient features of
the "new political science."

41. For background on Hobbes, see M. Oakeshott, *Hobbes on Civil Association* (Berkeley, 1975). Also see J. Habermas for a discussion of Hobbes's *De cive,* in *Theory and Practice,* pp. 70–78; J. Plamenatz, *Man and Society: A Critical Examination of Some Important
Social and Political Theories from Machiavelli to Marx* (London, 1963), pp. 119–42. For a
recent account of Hobbes's political philosophy, see Noel Malcolm, "Hobbes and Spinoza,"
The Cambridge History of Political Thought 1450–1700, ed. J. H. Burns (Cambridge,
1991), 530–45.

42. See especially H. Warrender, *The Political Philosophy of Thomas Hobbes* (Oxford,
1957). C. Macpherson's "Hobbes Bourgeois Man," *Hobbes Studies,* ed. K. Brown (Oxford,
1965), 109–83, is a controversial study that has sparked extensive debate and is effectively
challenged by Keith Thomas's article in the same volume, pp. 185–236, already cited in n.
30. The bitter critique of Hobbes by Ralph Cudworth, the Cambridge Platonist, is one that
might stand for many: the dangerous Hobbes aimed "to shake the foundations of all things,
and to deny that there was any immutable nature . . . of anything, and by consequence any
absolute certainty of truth or knowledge; maintaining this strange paradox, that both all being and knowledge was fantastical and relative only, and therefore that nothing was good or
evil, just or unjust, true or false, white or black, absolutely and immutably, but relatively to
every private person's humour or opinion." R. Cudworth, *The True Intellectual System of
the Universe* (London, 1845), pp. 540–41.

43. J. G. A. Pocock, in his *The Machiavellian Moment* (Princeton, 1975), discusses Hobbes's redefinition of the conventional definition of pride, as well as his "trashing" of the
Greco-Roman heritage of virtues. In Pocock's view, Hobbes substitutes private for public
and active virtue.

44. A. Lovejoy, in his *Reflections on Human Nature* (Baltimore, 1961), pp. 230–39,
gives an apposite discussion of Pascal's leading ideas pertaining to the nature of the individual.

45. An interest in social psychology was a key feature of the thought of moralists of the seventeenth and eighteenth centuries. The question beggaring an answer might be framed thus: How can one explain the good order of society so far as it exists if it is attributable to neither reason nor virtue? See A. Lovejoy, p. 21. See also B. Pascal, *Pensées*, trans. W. F. Trotter (New York, 1941), pp. 128–30.

46. In addition to Arthur Lovejoy's discussion of Pascal's ideas, see the telling comments of A. Hirschman in his elegant essay *The Passions and the Interests* (Princeton, 1979), pp. 12–13; 402–403. Very useful for appropriate quotations and explication from Pascal's writings is A. Béguin, *Pascal par lui-même* (Paris, 1957). L. Goldmann's *Le Dieu caché* (Paris, 1955) is a controversial but very worth reading interpretation of Pascal and his times. For background on La Mothe le Vayer, see Ira Wade, *Intellectual Origins of the French Enlightenment* (Princeton, 1973), pp. 179–87; R. Pintard, *Libertinage érudit dans la première moitié du XVIIe siècle* (Paris, 1943), pp. 127–47. La Rochefoucauld and La Bruyère explicated the psychology of *amour propre* without asserting the superiority of *caritas* or need for divine grace. Cf. N. Keohane, p. 307.

47. For a general discussion of the French moralists, see C. De Mourgeus, *The French Moralists La Rochefoucauld and La Bruyère* (Cambridge, 1978); cf. also A. Adam, *Les Libertins au XVIIe siècle. Textes choisis* (Paris, 1964). The classic account is by Paul Hazard, *La crise de la conscience européenne, 1680–1715* (Paris, 1935).

48. W. G. Moore's "The World of La Rochefoucauld's *Maximes*," *French Studies* 7 (1953), 335–45, summarizes scholarly views. Also see his "Le premier état des Maximes," *Revue d'histoire littéraire* 52 (1952), 417–24. On Descartes, see F. Alquié, *Descartes l'homme et l'oeuvre* (Paris, 1956).

49. A. Krailsheimer's *Studies in Self-Interest from Descartes to La Bruyère* (London, 1962) presents a thoughtful synthesis of literary evidence pertaining to the pursuit of self-interest. P. Bénichou's work has been cited in the English edition, but the French edition should be consulted, *Morales du grand siècle* (Paris, 1948).

50. J. Passmore, in his "The Malleability of Man in Eighteenth-Century Thought," *Aspects of the Eighteenth Century*, ed. E. Wasserman (Baltimore, 1965), 29ff., provides citations from Nicole's *Essai de morale* (1675–78). See also D. Raphael, *British Moralists 1650–1800* (Oxford, 1960), 2 vols., for references to the troubled engagement of British moralists with the writings of La Rochefoucauld; cf. Vol. I, p. 357 (Francis Hutcheson); ibid., p. 382 (Bishop Butler); Vol. II, p. 618 (David Hume); ibid., p. 994 (Bentham). Dale Van Kley's "Pierre Nicole, Jansenism, and the Morality of Enlightened Self-Interest," *Anticipations of the Enlightenment in England, France and Germany*, ed. A. Kors (Philadelphia, 1987), 69–86, makes a strong case for the view that the secularized enlightenment may have had other than secular origins. He challenges Trevor-Roper's argument that seventeenth-century heterodoxies such as Arminianism, Socinianism and extreme Molinism were mere manifestations of Erasmianism, taking the form of religious heresies. Kley couples Nicole's defense of self-interest with his Augustinan reading of human frailty. The later-day proximity between Jesuit or Molinistic theology worked to rehabilitate human nature and freedom of the will. Simultaneously, the role of divine grace was minimized and sin restricted to conscious violations of divine commands. These views allowed Jesuits and French philosophes to meet at least halfway. Cf. also Carl Becker, *The Heavenly City of the Eighteenth-Century Philosophers* (New Haven, 1932); Robert Palmer, *Catholics and Unbelievers in Eighteenth-Century France* (Princeton, 1939), pp. 23–58.

51. For the text of Nicole, see *Moral Philosophy from Montaigne to Kant*, ed. J. Schneewind (Cambridge, 1990), Vol. II, pp. 369–87. Cf. also E. D. James, *Pierre Nicole: Jansenist and Humanist* (The Hague, 1972); N. Abercrombie, *Origins of Jansenism* (Oxford, 1936). On the *Port Royal Logic*, a work which Nicole composed with Antoine Arnauld, see *The Art of Thinking*, trans. J. Dickoff and P. James (Indianapolis, 1964). For background on Pascal's intellectual development, see A. Baird, *Studies in Pascal's Ethics* (The Hague, 1975).

52. For the quote from Nicole's *Of Charity and Self-Love*, see J. Schneewind, p. 372. Cf. also L. Strauss, "On the Spirit of Hobbes' Political Philosophy," *Hobbes Studies*, ed.

K. Brown (Oxford, 1965), 1–29. Definitions of *honnêteté* and *honnête homme* can signify the Latin *honestas* (decency). This is turn may denote either a superficial decency bereft of inner-moral worth or it may imply a more genuine and deeper quality.

53. For the quote ˈfrom La Rochefoucauld and a discussion of its significance, see A. Hirschman, pp. 38ff. Cf. also H. Grubbs, "La genèse des 'Maximes' de La Rochefoucauld," *Revue d'Histoire Littéraire* 39 (1932), 481–99, and his "The Originality of La Rochefoucauld's Maxims," loc. cit., 36 (1929), 18–59. Cf. also Michael Oakeshott's incisive introduction to Hobbes's *Leviathan* (Oxford, 1947).

54. For comments on Montaigne, see J. Schneewind, Vol. I, p. 17. Pascal, of course, charged Montaigne with "nonchalance of the soul." Pascal appreciated the spiritual price paid for civility. His bitter notation: "Christian piety annihilates the human self, and Christian civility conceals and suppresses it," is itself worthy of a special chapter. Cf. Pascal's *Pensées*, trans. A. Krailsheimer (London, 1966), p. 356. For an excellent discussion of the legal background of seventeenth-century moral thinking, see Stephen Buckle's *Natural Law and the Theory of Property: Grotius to Hume* (Oxford, 1991), esp. ch. 1, pp. 1–35. I am much indebted to this work and believe that it will rank as an indispensable guide to legal thought and legal thinkers of the seventeenth and eighteenth centuries.

55. Stephen Buckle, p. 31. David Hume paid special tribute to the Dutch lawyer Grotius; Hume also believed in the human trait of sociability, but for him men and women acquired it and it was not a natural trait sufficient to itself. Cf. also J. Schneewind, Vol. I, p. 109 for a discussion of perfect and imperfect moral qualities as explicated in Grotius's *De Jure Belli ac Pacis libri tres* (1625), trans. F. Kelsey (New York, 1964). For background, see Charles Edwards, *Hugo Grotius* (Chicago, 1981), and especially K. Haakonssen, "Hugo Grotius and the History of Political Thought," *Political Theory* 13 (1985), 239–65. Jean Barbeyrac, historian and legal theorist, was the foremost continental explicator of natural rights and natural law; see R. Derathé, *Jean-Jacques Rousseau et la science politique de son temps* (Paris, 1970), pp. 88–93. One should note Adam Smith's debt to Grotius and natural law legists of the seventeenth century; see Peter Stein, "From Pufendorf to Adam Smith: the Natural Law tradition in Scotland," *Europäisches Rechtsdenken in Geschichte und Gegenwart: Festschrift für Helmut Coing* (Munich, 1982), 667–79.

56. We observe a movement from moral treatises formed as a collection of aphorisms to a comprehensive ordered survey; see M. Delgarno, "Reid's Natural Jurisprudence," *Philosophers of the Scottish Enlightenment*, ed. V. Hope (Edinburgh, 1989), 13–31. Among Scottish jurists we observe a shedding of prolix style and the scaling down of catalogues of duties formerly listed by illustrious predecessors. Cf. J. Moore and M. Silverthorne, "The Moral Philosophy of Carmichael," *Philosophers of the Scottish Enlightenment*, p. 2. A. MacIntyre, in his *Whose Justice? Which Rationality?*, p. 227–34, makes the same point when noting key changes in an understanding of property from the late seventeenth century (Sir James Dalrymple of Stair) to Blackstone's *Commentaries on the Laws of England* (1765), wherein obligations of the property holder diminished and the right became absolute. In a word, former constraints dissipate and "definite restrictions in the public interest" recede. Grotius maintained that the natural sense of society did not entail any obligation to help others, merely to refrain from doing harm to them. He will quote Horace, as will numerous other legists and moral philosophers, to the effect that expediency is called the mother of justice and equity. Finally, he rejects Aristotle's record of social life featuring the power of friendship and the fostering of virtue. I am much indebted to the writings of Richard Tuck, especially his recent "Grotius and Selden," *The Cambridge History of Political Thought 1450–1700*, ed. J. Burns (Cambridge, 1991), 499–522. See R. F. Teichgraeber III, *'Free Trade' and Moral Philosophy: Rethinking the Sources of Adam Smith's Wealth of Nations* (Durham, 1986), pp. 62–64, for a discussion of the influence on Scottish moral philosophers of Grotius's rejection of any attempt to found a polity on the ideal of distributive justice. Joyce Appleby's *Economic Thought and Ideology in Seventeenth-Century England* reminds the reader of the vitality of economic thinking in this period.

57. James Tully, *A Discourse on Property: John Locke and His Adversaries* (Cambridge, 1980), pp. 43ff. For further discussion of the status of obligation and its decline in the writings of Scottish jurists, see Peter Stein, "Law and Society in Eighteenth-Century Scottish Thought," *Scotland in the Age of Improvement,* ed. A. Phillipson and R. Mitchison (Edinburgh, 1970), 149–52. On Samuel Pufendorf's legal and moral thought, see S. Buckle, pp. 53–124. Also see S. Pufendorf, *De Jure Naturae et Gentium Libri Octo* (Lund, 1672); republished facsimile of Amsterdam edition of 1688, with the English trans. by C. H. and W. A. Oldfather (Oxford, 1934), II.iii.15, pp. 207–208, for the relevant quotation. Duncan Kennedy, "The Structure of Blackstone's Commentaries," *Buffalo Law Review* 28 (1979), 203–332, offers an incisive discussion of his subject's legal philosophy. (I owe this reference to my esteemed colleague, Thomas Green.) Blackstone ratified the scaling back of the purview of law. It was not to be preoccupied with morality or right conduct. In regard to "absolute duties," which individuals were bound to perform as mere individuals, it was not to be expected that "any human municipal law was required to explain or enforce them. . . . Let a man therefore be ever so abandoned in his principles or vicious in his practice, provided he keeps his wickedness to himself and does not offend against the rules of public decency, he is out of reach of human laws." Also see D. Kennedy, ibid., 203–204.

58. For a discussion of the influence of Locke on Carmichael, see S. Buckle, pp. 194–95. Cf. also J. Moore and M. Silverthorne, "Gershom Carmichael and the Natural Jurisprudence Tradition in Eighteenth-Century Scotland," *Wealth and Virtue: The Shaping of Political Economy in the Scottish Enlightenment,* eds. I. Hont and M. Ignatieff (Cambridge, 1983), 68–74. Also see J. McCosh's *The Scottish Philosophers* (London, 1875), pp. 35–37, for an evaluation of Gershom Carmichael as a bridge figure in the construct of Scottish ethical thought. For a translation of Pufendorf's *De officio hominis et civis* (1673), see *The Duty of Man and Citizen,* trans. F. G. Moore (Oxford, 1972). For our purposes, chapter 8, "On the Common Duties of Humanity," is essential. Here Pufendorf deals with the theme of gifts, counter-gifts and gratitude as bonding society and creating obligation. This is a minor note in his work but not an insignificant one, and suggests the archaic yet persistent strands continuing to provide a matrix for community. Barbeyrac and Carmichael contested over Pufendorf's legal legacy and his absolutism. Carmichael incorporated leading ideas from Locke's theory of resistance to tyranny as stated in the *Second Treatise.* The French continental scholar assumed a thoroughly conservative stance, whereas Carmichael advanced Locke's arguments as a counter to the absolutist legal tradition. For pertinent passages from Locke's *Two Treatises of Government,* ed. P. Laslett (Cambridge, 1960), see pp. 309–18, 327.

59. Quotations from Locke are taken from his *Two Treatises of Government,* ed. P. Laslett (Cambridge, 1960), p. 326 (II, 90); p. 334 (II, 101). For an incisive study of Hutcheson, see T. Campbell, "Francis Hutcheson, 'Father of the Scottish Enlightenment,' " *The Origins and Nature of the Scottish Enlightenment,* ed. R. Campbell and A. Skinner (Edinburgh, 1982), 167–85. Hutcheson was matriculated at Glasgow University from 1711–17, and it was during those years that strict Calvinist views were moderated by two of his instructors, Gershom Carmichael and John Simson. The latter was professor of divinity and his moderate stance on theological questions brought him into contest with the Presbyterians of the city. Later, Hutcheson also was to have his conflicts with the orthodox Presbyterians.

60. Writings on Locke are legion, but see in particular S. Buckle, pp. 125–90; J. Dunn, "Justice and the Interpretation of Locke's Political Theory," *Political Studies* 16 (1968), 68–87, and his recent *Locke* (Oxford, 1984). For recent scholarship on Locke's religious views and his "liberalism," see W. Spellman, *John Locke and the Problem of Depravity* (Oxford, 1988) and Ruth Grant's *John Locke's Liberalism* (Chicago, 1987).

61. S. Buckle, pp. 169–73, renders a full discussion of the scholarly debate concerning Locke's views on property. For a consideration of the conflict between John Locke's theory of property and his views on slavery, see R. Grant, pp. 68–83.

62. A. Ryan, in "Locke and the Dictatorship of the Bourgeoisie," *Political Studies* 13 (1965), 210–30, treats the significance of property for Locke's theory of politics. See also

J. Plamenatz, Vol. I, pp. 209–52; John Locke, *Two Treatises of Government*, pp. 296–97 (II, 41); K. Olivecrona, "Appropriation in the State of Nature: Locke on the Origin of Property," *Journal of the History of Ideas* 35 (1974), 221–30, also his "Locke's Theory of Appropriation," *Philosophical Quarterly* 24 (1974), 220–34.

63. Basil Willey's account of Shaftesbury's esthetic and elegant mind should be consulted in his *The Eighteenth-Century Background: Studies in the Idea of Nature in the Thought of the Period* (London, 1950), pp. 57–75. For Shaftesbury's attack on John Locke's denial of moral virtue, see S. Buckle, pp. 144–46. See also John Locke's *Essay Concerning Human Understanding* (1690), ed. P. Nidditch (Oxford, 1975), p. 149. David Norton's "Shaftesbury and Two Scepticisms," *Filosofia* 46 (1968), 1–12, is very useful.

64. See the introduction by J. M. Robertson to Shaftesbury's *Characteristics of Men, Manners, Opinions, Times* (Indianapolis, 1969); also J. Tully, *A Discourse on Property: John Locke and His Adversaries* (Cambridge, 1980). For critics of Locke, see C. Broad, "Berkeley's Denial of Material Substance," *Locke and Berkeley, a Collection of Critical Essays*, ed. C. D.Martin (London, 1968), 255–83. For Bolingbroke's criticism of Locke, see I. Kramnick, *Bolingbroke and His Circle: The Politics of Nostalgia in the Age of Walpole* (Cambridge, Mass., 1965), pp. 54–63, 84–89, 95–110, 116–19.

65. On John Locke's critics (Thomas Burnet, among others), see J. Coleman, *John Locke's Moral Philosophy* (Edinburgh, 1983), p. 55. For Thomas Burnet himself, see B. Willey, pp. 27–33. Burnet was a scientifically minded Anglican theologian; see his *The Sacred Theory of the Earth*, reprinted from the 2nd edition of 1691 (Carbondale, Illinois, 1965), pp. 88–90, 280–83, 298–301.

66. For the anonymous critic of John Locke and the *Dialogue Concerning Innate Principles*, see J. Coleman's chapter "Against Innate Morality," pp. 71–75 and the bibliographical references, pp. 248–52. Since, in the eyes of many of Locke's critics, the innatist doctrine was inseparable from belief in an objective moral law, the Lockean menace to Christian ethics was certain and deadly.

67. David Norton, *David Hume: Common-Sense Moralist, Skeptical Metaphysician* (Princeton, 1982), p. 54; also see S. Buckle, pp. 197ff. Shaftesbury, the practical moralist, accented the worth of good humor, raillery, and, above all, common sense. These were reckoned as antidotes for the distemper generated by enthusiasm and the spirit of factionalism. He reviewed the history of the Jews, suggesting that had they treated the early Christians with humor and contempt instead of persecuting them, the history of religion in our time might be different. The power of cheerfulness recommended by Shaftesbury, Addison, and many another was advocated as a felicitous remedy for grander and more dangerous emotional responses to provocation. Cf. B. Willey, pp. 74–75.

68. D. Norton, p. 35; S. Buckle, pp. 309–11; A. MacIntyre, *A Short History of Ethics* (New York, 1966), pp. 160–63.

69. On Sir John Hawkins, see *Dictionary of National Biography*, ed. L. Stephen and S. Lee (Oxford, 1949–50), Vol. IX, pp. 220–21; Hawkins was the unreliable biographer of Samuel Johnson. See also Dorothy George, *England in Transition* (London, 1931), p. 10.

70. Locke and the formal causes of obligation are discussed by J. Tully, *A Discourse on Property: John Locke and His Adversaries* (Cambridge, 1980), pp. 43ff; also S. Buckle, p. 147. For further examination of Locke's religious views, see Richard Tuck, *Natural Rights Theories* (Cambridge, 1979), pp. 3–5, 79, 172–73; John Dunn, *The Political Thought of John Locke* (Cambridge, 1960).

71. For the *Prolegomena* of Grotius, see J. Schneewind, Vol. I, p. 92, also Schneewind's comments on Shaftesbury in Vol. II, pp. 483–84. Elizabeth Labrousse's *Bayle* (Oxford, 1983) is a penetrating discussion of the Huguenot's skeptical thought. Cf. also Pierre Bayle, *Philosophical Commentary*, trans. A. Goodman (Bern, 1987). On Edmund Burke, see *Thoughts on French Affairs* in *Works* (Bohn Standard Library, London, 1853), Vol. III, pp. 377ff.

72. On Pierre Bayle, see H. Mason, "Pierre Bayle's Religious Views," *French Studies* 17 (1963), 205–17. I wish to thank Lawrence Klein for permitting me to read his unpub-

lished paper, "Coffee Clashes: The Politics of Discourse in Seventeenth- and Eighteenth-Century England."

73. Ernest Tuveson's two articles on Shaftesbury are very useful: "The Origin of the Moral Sense," *Huntington Library Quarterly* 11 (1947), 241–59; "The Importance of Shaftesbury," *Journal of English Literary History* 20 (1953), 267–79. Cf. also John Bernstein, *Shaftesbury, Rousseau, and Kant* (London, 1990), ch. 1. For the tie between the intuitive, esthetic, and moral senses, see Shaftesbury's *A System of Moral Philosophy, in three books* (London, 1755), Vol. 1, pp. 58–61.

74. See S. Buckle, p. 146, for an evaluation of Hume's tribute to Shaftesbury. See also Hume's *A Treatise of Human Nature*, ed. L. Selby-Bigge, rev. by P. Nidditch (Oxford, 1978), p. xvii; A. Seligman, *The Idea of Civil Society*, pp. 24–27.

75. The theme of *sensus communis* is examined from several different vantage points in a collection of essays in *Common Sense: The Foundation for Social Science*, ed. F. van Holthoon and D. Olsen (Lantham, Maryland, 1987). See also J. Schneewind, Vol. II, p. 485; S. Buckle, pp. 304, 308.

76. For the quote from Shaftesbury, see J. Schneewind, Vol. II, p. 486; F. van Holthoon, "Common Sense and Natural Law," *Common Sense*, 103–106.

77. See especially T. Mautner, "Pufendorf and Eighteenth-Century Scottish Philosophy," *Samuel von Pufendorf 1632–1982: En rättshistoriskt i Lund* (Lund, 1986), 128–40; also L. Krieger, *The Politics of Discretion* (Chicago, 1965), ch. 1. On the eclipse of the "right of necessity," see D. Winch, *Adam Smith's Politics* (Cambridge, 1978), pp. 72–120. S. Buckle, pp. 42–47, discusses the quotations from Grotius and Pufendorf. For appropriate selections from their writings, see J. Schneewind, Vol. I, pp. 88–110, 156–82. Grotius's account of justice as "explicative" rather than distributive has been termed "modern" (that is, eighteenth-century) in recent scholarship. His was a serious challenge to the preoccupation of natural law jurisprudence with the seemingly intractable problem of how a society might ensure the absolute property rights of the wealthy without denying the poor and propertyless the wherewithal to meet their pressing needs; cf. R. Teichgraeber, pp. 189–90.

78. See Adam Smith's *Lectures on Jurisprudence*, ed. R. Meek, D. Raphael, and P. Stein (Oxford, 1978), i, 27–35, 63–67; ii, 87–93; iv, 3–9. Montesquieu's *Spirit of the Laws* is the most probable source for Smith's four-stages theory; Ronald Meek, *Social Science and the Ignoble Savage* (Cambridge, 1976), pp. 31–36.

79. See James Tully, pp. 81, 170–71.

80. See N. MacCormack, "Law, Obligation and Consent: Reflections on Stair and Locke," *Archiv für Rechts-und Socialphilosophie* 20 (1979), 387–411. For a discussion of the quotations from Locke, see S. Buckle, pp. 160, 175, 225.

81. See J. Tully, pp. 171, 213–14; also see S. Buckle, pp. 225ff. for a consideration of Locke's theory of labor value.

82. Peter Stein, "Law and Society in Eighteenth-Century Scottish Thought," *Scotland in the Age of Improvement*, ed. R. Mitchison and A. Phillipson (Edinburgh, 1970), 148–68, esp. 153; also see T. Horne, "Moral and Economic Improvement: Francis Hutcheson on Property," *History of Political Thought* 7 (1986), 115–30. Ian Ross's *Lord Kames and the Scotland of His Day* (Oxford, 1972) provides the background for Kames's legal thought. It is well to remember that although the phrase, "the greatest Happiness for the greatest Numbers," is Hutcheson's, he had no notion of the pursuit of happiness as an inalienable right. He was much too dedicated to ideas of social harmony to affirm the pursuit of happiness as an individual right. The pursuit of happiness in the eighteenth century denoted a common quest for creating a political order approaching the natural eternal one. See F. L. van Holthoon, "Natural Jurisprudence and Republicanism," *La Revue Tocqueville* 13 (1992), 43–60 for an incisive discussion of this problem; cf. also R. Manzi, *L'idée du bonheur dans la litterature et pensée français au XVIIIᵉ siècle* (Paris, 1960).

83. For a discussion of the two quotations from Francis Hutcheson's *An Inquiry into the Origins of Our Ideas of Beauty and Virtue* (London, 1726), 2nd ed., republished in facsimile ed. (Olms, 1969), pp. 284, 257, see S. Buckle, pp. 212–25. For discussion of Shaftesbury's

influence on Hutcheson, see N. Fierino, "Shaftesbury-Hutcheson Gospel," *Jonathan Edward's Moral Thought in Its British Context* (Chapel Hill, North Carolina, 1983), 353–63. For Shaftesbury's relationship with Cambridge Platonists and their denial that minds could be blank tablets lacking "innate furniture and activity," see David F. Norton, "Hume," *Ethics in the History of Western Philosophy* (London, 1989), 162–65. See F. Hutcheson, *A System of Moral Philosophy* (London, 1775), republished in facsimile ed. (Olms, 1969), pp. 271ff. for an explication of property as a right derived from natural law. The laws of nature comprehend "not merely the original determination of the mind, but likeways the practical conclusions made by reasoning and reflection of men upon the conditions of nature." Cf. F. L. van Holthoon, 53–55.

84. See David Norton's "Hutcheson's Moral Realism," *Journal of the History of Moral Philosophy* 23 (1985), 397–419. Still useful is William Scott's biography *Francis Hutcheson*, reprint (New York, 1966) [originally published Cambridge, 1900]. For a discussion of Hutcheson's life and opinions, see W. Leechman's "Some Account of the Life, Writings and Character of the Author," in the preface to Hutcheson's *A System of Moral Philosophy*. For intellectual background, see W. T. Blackstone, *Francis Hutcheson and Contemporary Ethical Theory* (Atlanta, 1965); H. Jensen, *Motivation and the Moral Sense in Francis Hutcheson's Ethical Theory* (The Hague, 1971). For his views on slavery, see the very useful article by W. Sypher, "Hutcheson and the Classical Theory of Slavery," *Journal of Negro History* 24 (1939), 263–80.

85. On Hutcheson, see A. Chitnis, *The Scottish Enlightenment: A Social History* (London, 1976), pp. 58–59. Shaftesbury's influence was paramount, with Hutcheson sharing the belief that human capacity was bereft of meaning outside the social context. Hutcheson's inaugural lecture was entitled, "The Natural Sociability of Man." See A. Chitnis, p. 94. A telling quote from Mandeville (preface to *The Fable of the Bees*) runs as follows:

> Laws and government are to the political bodies of civil societies what the vital spirits and life itself are to the natural bodies of animated creatures; and as those that study the anatomy of dead carcasses may see that the chief organs and nicest springs more immediately required to continue the motion of our machine are not hard bones, strong muscles and nerves, nor the smooth white skin that so beautifully covers them, but small trifling films and little pipes that are either overlooked, or else seem inconsiderable to vulgar eyes; so they that examine into the nature of man, abstract from art and education, may observe that what renders him a sociable animal consists not in his desire of company, good nature, pity, affability, and other graces of a fair outside; but that his vilest and most hateful qualities are the most necessary accomplishments to fit him for the largest, and, according to the world, the happiest and most flourishing societies. . . .

See J. Schneewind, Vol. II, p. 390; also B. Mandeville, *The Fable of the Bees: or, Private Vices, Publick Benefits*, ed. F. Kayne (Oxford, 1924), Vol. I. pp. 62–83. M. Goldsmith's *Private Vices, Public Benefits: Bernard Mandeville's Social and Political Thought* (Cambridge, 1985), provides an in-depth analysis of his subject's times and thinking.

86. See A. Hirschman, pp. 64–65, for a discussion of "calm desires and passions." See also J. Cropsey, *Polity and Economy: An Interpretation of the Principles of Adam Smith* (The Hague, 1957), pp. 37–43; S. Buckle, p. 310.

87. For a discussion of the science of man joined in society and highly interdependent, see the classic work of Gladys Bryson, *Man and Society: The Scottish Enquiry of the Eighteenth Century* (Princeton, 1945); also A. Swingswood, "The Origins of Sociology: The Case of the Scottish Enlightenment," *British Journal of Sociology* 21 (1970), 164–80; S. Buckle, p. 250. For a consideration of the politics of men of letters close to the time of the Glorious Revolution, see Duncan Forbes, *Philosophical Politics* (Cambridge, 1978).

88. John Keane, Introduction to *Civil Society and the State* (London, 1988), p. 16. Cf. also E. West, "The Political Economy of Alienation," *Oxford Economic Papers* 21 (1969), 1–23. Perhaps it might be fair to suggest that a more empathetic psychology, once norma-

tive, was challenged by one featuring sympathy and sensibility. This new eighteenth-century psychology may well have served to fill the "passionless void" that Keane charts. For changing definitions of the word "talent," see *Oxford English Dictionary*. Jay Smith, in his "The Culture of Merit," pp. 210–16, provides a wealth of contemporary usages prevalent in the early eighteenth century with citations and ample bibliography. One important instance is the amplification of the semantic range of the word "ambition." Once a pejorative in the lexicon of the nobility, it assumes a positive value in the discourse of the early eighteenth century. Formerly it denoted an immoderate desire for something; now it could carry a positive charge featuring "the energy one devoted to one's profession."

89. On the changing definitions of "society," see M. Becker, *Civility and Society*, pp. 1–3. A. Seligman, pp. 61–62, reviews Hume's critique of the moral basis of the social order as set forth in his *A Treatise of Human Nature*. The political philosopher Michael Oakeshott, in his *On Human Conduct* (Oxford, 1975), pp. 194–207, makes a useful distinction between *societas* and *universitas*. In the latter, members acknowledge a common goal and consider themselves an integral part of a single whole, whereas in the former, individuals assemble in loyalty to one another and in obedience to general rules governing each person's actions. However, each person follows his own interest and does not share a sense of common purpose. Oakeshott offers value judgments as to the moral strength of those frightened individuals preferring *universitas;* he sets them against the first-raters who can endure the aloneness and responsibility incumbent upon free individuals in a *societas*. Perhaps this view is not unconnected with Adam Smith's "society of strangers." We might note that Scottish patriotism declined over the eighteenth century, no longer sustained by hostility toward the English. Also, Westminster's policies directed against the formation of a Scottish militia contributed to an ebbing of the civic spirit. See John Robertson, *The Scottish Enlightenment and the Militia Issue* (Edinburgh, 1985), pp. 159–85. Adam Smith does not dispense with faith in a beneficent Diety:

> . . . the very suspicion of a fatherless world must be the most melancholy of all reflections: from the thought that all the unknown regions of infinite and incomprehensible space may be filled with nothing but endless misery and wretchedness. All the splendor of the highest prosperity can never enlighten the gloom with which so dreadful an idea must overshadow the imagination. [Spelling modernized]

See his *Theory of Moral Sentiments*, VI, ii, 3, 6th and enlarged edition (London, 1790).

90. For Hume's views as to the claims of men and women to know or even to believe, with rational justification, that objects exist independent and external of our imagination, see Lynd Ferguson, *Common Sense* (London, 1989), p. 104. Hume was to argue that there is, and indeed he would offer, a psychological explanation as to how we came to hold such convictions—convictions we are unable to justify rationally. See also A. J. Ayer, *Hume* (Oxford, 1980), pp. 13–34; Isaiah Berlin, *The Age of Enlightenment* (New York, 1984), pp. 30–35. One quote must stand for many; see Hannah More's observation: "Most worth and virtue are to be found in the middle stations. . . ."; cf. *Strictures on the Modern System of Female Education* (London, 1797), p. 62. A classic account on the subject of enthusiasm is Ronald Knox's *Enthusiasm: A Chapter in the History of Religion with Special Reference to the Seventeenth and Eighteenth Centuries* (Oxford, 1950). In Hume's writings, as well as those of his historically minded contemporaries, we observe that the term "philosophical" was freighted with a heavy anthropological charge; cf R. F. Teichgraeber III, p. 196. Nicholas Phillipson, in his "Hume as Civic Moralist: A Social Historian's Perspective," *Philosophers of the Enlightenment*, ed. S. C. Brown (Sussex, 1979), 140–61, provides important background for the intensification of anthropological sensibility.

91. See Paul Langford, *A Polite and Commercial People: England 1727–1783* (Oxford, 1989), ch. 10, "The Birth of Sensibility," pp. 461–518. The author provides an explication of the extension of the semantic range of key words pertaining to sentiment and sensibility. See also the various selections included in *A History of Private Life: Passions of the Re-*

naissance, eds. P. Ariès and G. Duby (Cambridge, Mass., 1989), Vol. III, esp. pp. 161–264. Conor Cruise O'Brien's recent *The Great Melody: A Thematic Biography and Commented Anthology* (Chicago, 1992) is a celebratory work on Burke treating his rhetoric with exquisite sensitivity. See also *The Encyclopedia of Philosophy* (New York, 1967), Vol. II, for the article "Common Sense," p. 155; Ian Maclean's review of M. Moriarity's *Taste and Ideology in Seventeenth-Century France, Times Literary Supplement* (2 June 1989), p. 616. Burke will argue, and indeed so will others, that the private stock of the ideas of an individual are not sufficient to trade on. The *senso proprio* of the individual are insufficient for resolution of problems when compared with the experience of generations and their wisdom as embodied in *sensus communis*. The latter bears that collective experience historically gained over the centuries and thus has primacy of place. See P. van Kessel, "Common Sense between Bacon and Vico," *Common Sense*, 126. On James Beattie, see D. Spadafora, *The Idea of Progress in Eighteenth-Century Britain* (New Haven, 1990), pp. 162–79, 209–10.

92. S. Copley's introduction to *Literature and the Social Order in Eighteenth-Century England* (Kent, 1984), gives an excellent survey of definitions of wealth and the various explanations and assumptions concerning productivity. See also H. Dickinson, *Liberty and Property* (London, 1977); J. Gunn, *Beyond Liberty and Property* (Kingston, Ontario, 1984); R. Ashcroft, *Locke's Two Treatises of Government* (Princeton, 1986). On the enduring attraction of English mercantilism, see Joyce Appleby, "Ideology and Theory: The Tension between Political and Economic Liberalism in Seventeenth-Century England," *American Historical Review* 81 (1976), 499–513. For background on changes in thinking, see Donald Winch, "The Emergence of Economics as a Science, 1750–1870," *The Fontana Economic History of Europe*, ed. C. Cipolla (London, 1973), Vol. 3, 511–28.

93. J. G. A. Pocock's numerous writings illuminate the theme of civic humanism and its influence on eighteenth-century English and Scottish thought. See esp. his *Virtues, Commerce and History: Essays in Political Thought and History* (Cambridge, 1985). On the connection between ideas and economic developments, see his "Early Modern Capitalism, the Augustan Perception," *Feudalism, Capitalism and Beyond*, ed. E. Kamenka (London, 1975), pp. 70ff. Michael Lynch, in his *Scotland: A New History* (London, 1991), p. 344, concludes that the replacement of Latin by English as the *lingua franca* was perhaps the major cultural shift in late seventeenth- and eighteenth-century Scotland.

94. For an evaluation of Kant's comments made in *Eternal Peace*, see L. Strauss, "The Spirit of Hobbes' Political Philosophy," *Hobbes Studies*, ed. K. Baker (Oxford, 1965), p. 23. On Adam Smith, see N. Phillipson, "Adam Smith as Civic Moralist," *Wealth and Virtue: The Shaping of Political Economy in the Scottish Enlightenment*, ed. I. Hont and M. Ignatieff (Cambridge, 1985), 179–202. On the theme of luxury, its dangers and opportunities, see John Sekora, *Luxury: The Concept in Western Thought: Eden to Smollett* (Baltimore, 1977). Also note the pertinent general comments of Q. Skinner in *The Times Literary Supplement* (23 June 1989), p. 690. It should be noted that Kant, like Hume and Adam Smith (there were philosophical differences among their views), appreciated the natural limits on human sentiments—especially of sympathy.

95. For a discussion of Hume's views on the social contract, see David Hume, *Political Essays*, ed. C. Hendel (Indianapolis, 1953), pp. xlviii–xlix, 50, 250. On Montesquieu, see I. Berlin's now classic piece, "Montesquieu," *Proceedings of the British Academy* 41 (1955), 267–96. An English translation of *The Spirit of the Laws* was published at Aberdeen in 1756. For the influence of this work on the Scots, see P. Stein, pp. 167–68. It might be useful to recall that neither Hume nor Montesquieu held a doctrine of progress. Despite the Frenchman's admiration for England and its monarchy capable of sharing sovereignty with parliament, his criticism was not stifled: "Money is highly esteemed here [England]: honor and virtue little." See R. Shackleton, *Montesquieu: A Critical Biography* (Oxford, 1961), p. 139.

96. See G. Hegel, *Philosophy of Right*, trans. T. Knox (Oxford, 1977), paragraphs 157, 251, 261, 276, and esp. 289. For a discussion of Hegel's analysis of the relationship between state and civil society, see Z. Pelczynski, "The Hegelian Conception of the State," *Hegel's*

Political Philosophy: Problems and Perspectives, ed. Z. Pelczynski (Cambridge, 1971), 1–28. The citation on Bernard Mandeville's *A Treatise of the Hypochondriack*, as well as the discussion of *A Treatise*, is found in G. Barker-Benfield, *The Culture of Sensibility*, pp. 26–27.

97. For the quotation from George Sturt, see *A History of Private Life*, Vol. III, p. 443; ibid., p. 409, for Jaucourt's discussion of friendship.

98. See A. Ryan, "Professor Hegel Goes to Washington," *New York Review of Books* (26 March 1992), 7–10; Z. Pelczynski, "The Hegelian Conception of the State," in *Hegel's Political Philosophy: Problems and Perspectives*, ed. Z. Pelczynski (Cambridge, 1971), 1–28. For a lucid discussion of politics and civil society on the world stage, see E. Kedourie, "Civil Politics in the Middle East," *American Scholar* (Winter, 1988), 107–10. See also the numerous articles in *The Reemergence of Civil Society in Eastern Europe and the Soviet Union*, ed. Z. Rau (Boulder, Colorado, 1991).

99. On Francis Place, see Dorothy George, *England in Transition* (Harmsworth, 1953), p. 10; Roy Porter, *English Society in the Eighteenth Century* (London, 1990), rev. ed., pp. 79–80, 91, 149, 263, 299–300, 359.

100. For the quotation concerning modifications in attitudes toward mortality, see John McManners, p. 463; also Roy Porter, pp. 219–20, on the decline of macabre carvings on gravestones and funeral pyres. For a general survey on recent literature pertaining to patterns of devotion, see F. Lebrun, "The Two Reformations: Communal Devotion and Personal Piety," *A History of Private Life*, Vol. 4, 69–107; also see Michael MacDonald, "The Secularization of Suicide in England 1600–1800," *Past & Present* 111 (1988), 78–88. The release from bondage to the dead hand of the past was of course a matter of concern to Adam Smith, as well as to a legion of contemporary jurists and moral philosophers. See the blistering comments made by Smith in his *Lectures on Jurisprudence* (III, 26) and *Wealth of Nations* on the subject of entails: this practice may be "agreeable to our piety to the deceased," but Smith assures the reader it was "the most absurd practice in the world." For a full discussion of the subject, see R. F. Teichgraeber III, pp. 152–54 and n. 67.

101. For a discussion of increased policing of popular culture and its entertainments, see R. Malcolmson, *Popular Recreations in English Society 1700–1850* (Cambridge, 1973); E. Bristow, *Vice and Vigilance: Purity Movements in Britain since 1700* (Dublin, 1977); W. Speck and T. Curtis, "The Societies for the Reformation of Manners," *Literature and History* 3 (1979), 45–64. On changing attitudes toward children, see the survey by I. Pinchbeck and M. Hewitt, *Children in English Society: From Tudor Times to the Eighteenth Century* (Toronto, 1970); J. H. Plumb, "The New World of Children in Eighteenth-Century England," *Past & Present* 67 (1975), 64–95. Of course deep psychic investment in the family as paramount social unit was not without its emotional price. The greater the intimacy, the more likely was the sense of suffering and loss. Threatening possibilities of incest, homoerotic attachment, and sadomasochism were fixtures in the Gothic novel. An atmosphere of random terror and demonic urge hovered over family relations like a dark angel with men and women engaged in sexual war. See Robert Kiely, *The Romantic Novel in England* (London, 1972), ch. 1.

102. For a valuable survey of changing attitudes toward death, see M. Vovelle, *La mort et l'Occident de 1300 à nos jours* (Paris, 1983). For a comparable survey on historical writing about the family, see F. Lebrun, *Le vie conjugale sous l'Ancien Régime* (Paris, 1975); also see Lawrence Stone, *Family, Sex, and Marriage in England, 1500–1800* (New York, 1977). For a more detailed and localized analysis of religious sensibility and mortality, see M. Vovelle, *Piété baroque et dechristianisation en Provence aux XVIIIᵉ siècle* (Paris, 1973). For a discussion of the theme of religion versus science in literature, see Michael McKeon, *The Origins of the English Novel 1600–1740* (Baltimore, 1987), pp. 73–78.

103. P. Borsay's *The English Urban Renaissance: Culture and Society 1660–1780* is a treasure trove of interpretation and evidence pertaining to provincial society and the arts. See also J. Barrell, *English Literature in History, 1730–80: An Equal, Wide Survey* (London, 1983); M. Foss, *The Age of Patronage: Arts in Society 1660–1770* (London, 1972). For a

study of the stresses between society and the artist, see J. Barrell, *The Dark Side of the Land-scape* (Cambridge, 1980). On music see P. Borsay, pp. 119–24; J. Black, *Eighteenth-Century Europe 1700–1789* (New York, 1990), pp. 237–40; E. Mackerness, *A Social History of English Music* (London, 1964); D. Johnson, *Music and Society in Lowland Scot-land in the Eighteenth Century* (London, 1972). Musicians will be released from liveried retinue and, from Haydn and Mozart to Beethoven, composers will brave it out, even de-termining the theme of commissioned works. In London the Royal Academy (1768) will be a market for the artist, exhibiting his wares for purchase. The mimetic purpose of art will now be rivaled by the creative or subjective function of the imagination, with the sensual and expressive highly prized. One might think on the proud comment of the English artist Constable:

> Whatever may be thought of my art, it is my own, and I would rather possess a free-hold, though but a cottage, than live in a palace belonging to another.

J. H. Plumb's "The Commercialization of Leisure in Eighteenth-Century England," in *The Birth of a Consumer Society: The Commercialization of Eighteenth-Century England,* ed. N. McKendrick and J. Brewer (Bloomington, Indiana, 1982), 271–90, investigates the broad diffusion of music listened to in new concert halls and played at home. He also notes the "rapid development and specialization of musical instrument makers" working to satisfy the ever-increasing demand.

104. On the rise of the connoisseur and decline of the virtuoso, see Iain Pears, *The Dis-covery of Painting: The Growth of Interest in the Arts in England 1680–1768* (New Haven, 1988), pp. 193–98. Cf. also B. Sprague Allen, *Tides of British Taste 1619–1800* (Cam-bridge, Mass., 1957). On Philip Skelton (1707–1787), see *The Dictionary of National Bi-ography,* ed. L. Stephen (Oxford, 1949–50), Vol. XVIII, 333–34. On the theme of politeness and esthetics, see Lawrence Klein, "The Rise of Politeness in England, 1600–1715" (Ph.D. dissertation), Johns Hopkins, 1984. Literary celebrities such as Alexander Pope were torn between the honorable role of amateur over and against the poet as profes-sional: the noble coterie of literary fellows as opposed to the mundane and soiled market-place. This tension also held in the world of fine arts as the habits of private enjoyment of art works were diffused among a wider public. The security of the commission from a prince, a courtier, or a wealthy merchant was threatened by the desire for gain from an un-certain market. This conflict is early documented in Italy; in 1633 the painters matriculated in the Academy of San Luca contended:

> It is serious, lamentable, indeed intolerable to everybody, to see works destined for the decoration of sacred temples or the splendor of noble palaces exhibited in shops or in streets like cheap goods for sale.

See Francis Haskell, *Patrons and Painters* (New York, 1967), p. 121.

105. See Raymond Williams's compelling monograph, *The Country and the City* (Lon-don, 1985).

2. Civil Society and the Case of England and Scotland

1. The stadial theories of human development propounded by eighteenth-century Scottish literati informed a host of prose and poetic works. One of a legion of these writings was Richard Payne Knight's *Progress of Civil Society* (1796). Wordsworth was reading this poem in 1798 and may have been influenced by its interpretation. The anthropological model of the genesis of humans from their origins to the present condition of civil society was divided into progressive stages. Through this "template" of the stages of the progress of humankind were read such classical accounts as Lucretius' *De rerum naturae,* esp. bk. 5. Alan Bewell presents a full account of these intellectual developments in his *Wordsworth and the Enlight-*

enment: Nature, Man and Society in the Experimental Poets (New Haven, 1989). If we compare Scottish historiography of an earlier time with that of the eighteenth century, the former, not surprisingly, featured battles, kings, and the fall of princes. These ringing events were accompanied by moral edification. At a later time writers featured society itself as the prominent player and suitable domain for research. For an effective employment of the stadial theory of the emergence of society from its "infancy" to the commercial world of her day, see Mary Wollstonecraft's *Rights of Women*. This historical strategy is discussed by G. Barker-Benfield in his *The Culture of Sensibility: Sex and Society in Eighteenth-Century Britain* (Chicago, 1992), pp. xxviii–xxx.

2. For a general discussion of the background for Smith's thoughts on social and economic development, and the changing character of obligation, see I. Hont and M. Ignatieff, "Needs and Justice in *Wealth of Nations:* An Introductory Essay," *Wealth and Virtue: The Shaping of Political Economy in the Scottish Enlightenment*, ed. I. Hont and M. Ignatieff (Cambridge, 1985), 1–44. Michael Lynch, in his *Scotland: A New Nation* (London, 1991), pp. 349–50, notes James Boswell's comments on the "comfortable answers" provided by leading preachers in Edinburgh to broad social and economic questions. In this regard he reckons the sermons of the moderate preacher Hugh Blair (1718–1800) as second only to Addison's *Spectator* in drawing consoling conclusions concerning vexing questions. See also R. Schmits, *Hugh Blair* (New York, 1948), Vol. I. pp. 53–54. The role of the moderate clergy in facilitating accommodation to social and economic change must not be neglected. On William Robertson, leader of the Moderates, a riveting figure both intellectually and physically, see D. Stewart, "Account of the Life and Writings," *The Works of William Robertson* (London, 1817), 1–204.

3. Perhaps the most decisive force for transforming the conception of civility in the late seventeenth and early eighteenth centuries was the shift from a more aristocratic ideal of distinction to one of popular approbation. Society itself begins to play a more generalized role in bringing the authority of public opinion to bear on the shaping of manners. See *A History of Private Life*, Vol. IV, for a bibliography of the numerous writings of Roger Chartier on this topic, pp. 629–30; also Y. Castan, *Honnêteté et relations sociales en Languedoc, 1750–1780* (Paris, 1974). For England, see J. Cropsey, pp. 57–60. The growing importance of society and public opinion as factors in modifying behavior is evident in Scottish writings from Hume to Smith. The need for approbation became increasingly generalized in the collectivity. The general question of improved living standards and the increased influence of town life is discussed in L. Weatherall's *Consumer Behavior and Material Culture in Britain, 1660–1760* (London, 1988), ch. 4; P. Earle, *The Making of the English Middle Class: Business, Society and Family Life in London, 1660–1730* (London, 1989); H. Perkins, *The Origins of Modern English Society, 1780–1880* (London, 1972), pp. 17–25.

4. On Beau Nash, see Iain Pears, *The Discovery of Painting: The Growth of Interest in the Arts in England, 1680–1760* (New Haven, 1988), pp. 12–14. For an overview of changes in the elaboration of manners and courtesies, see P. Langford, pp. 464ff. For further discussion of challenges to ridiculous social posturing, see *A History of Private Life*, Vol. IV, passim. The standardization of language in Britain was a major preoccupation and no meeting of the Select Society of Edinburgh was so well attended as the one in which Thomas Sheridan (father of the playwright) spoke on the elimination of "Scottisisms" from speech. It has been alleged that the only sin David Hume confessed to on his deathbed were the Scottisisms that had infected his speech; M. Lynch, p. 344. For a full discussion of the vocabulary of affective ties, see E. Erämetsä, *A Study of the Word "Sentimental" and Other Linguistic Characteristics of Eighteenth-Century Sentimentalism in England* (Helsinki, 1951); also John Mullan, *Sentiment and Sociability in the Eighteenth Century* (Oxford, 1989).

5. See Allan Ramsay, *Works*, ed. A. Kinghorn (The Scottish Text Society) (Edinburgh, 1972), Vol. V, p. 2; Jane Rendall, *The Origins of the Scottish Enlightenment* (New York, 1979), pp. 62–63, 209. For an appraisal of Lord Chesterfield and Oliver Goldsmith, see I. Pears, pp. 11–14. L. Bredvold, in his *The Literature of the Restoration and the Eighteenth Century* (New York, 1950), p. 65, underscores the fact that *The Spectator* made its "morn-

ing lectures" palpable to "easy and sociable readers." Following the relaxed conversational manner of the essays of Montaigne and his followers, Addison aimed to bring "philosophy out of closets and libraries, schools and colleges, to dwell in clubs and assemblies, at tea tables and coffee houses." On the necessity for having a bookshop and press for publication of new books in early eighteenth-century Glasgow, see *The Glasgow University Press, 1638–1931* (Glasgow, 1931), pp. 103–104. On the spread of student clubs (1723), see R. Woodrow, *Analecta* (Edinburgh, 1842), Vol. 3, p. 183. For a careful explication of the intent of periodical writings to exert a civilizing purpose, see G. Marr, *The Periodical Essayists of the Eighteenth Century* (London, 1924), pp. 21–85.

6. For the entry in the *Journal of the Easy Club*, see n. 5 in this chapter and J. Rendall, p. 63, on the taking of the names of celebrated cultural and scientific figures by members; D. McElroy, *A Century of Scottish Clubs, 1700–1800* (Edinburgh, 1969); H. Bragham, *Scottish Man of Letters in the Eighteenth Century* (London, 1901). Already in the 1690s, Edinburgh had some 40 booksellers, printers and bookbinders. An increase in a middle-class reading public has been noted. Titles published in Scotland rose from 140 or so per year at the mid-eighteenth century to 565 by 1815. See M. Lynch, p. 352.

7. On George Drummond, see J. Rendall, p. 18; he was certainly the inspiration for "Proposals for carrying on certain Public Works in the City of Edinburgh," devised by Gilbert Eliot [later Lord Minton] in 1752. See M. Lynch, p. 350.

8. P. Borsay's *The English Urban Renaissance: Culture and Society in the Provincial Town, 1660–1770* (Oxford, 1989), offers a sensitive and informed discussion of urban architecture and social life, containing a mine of information both literary and economic; see esp. pp. 80–90, 190ff. On the expansion of leisure, see P. Langford, pp. 419ff. On the quotation on "a thousand bricks" contributing to the stability of society, see G. Holmes, "The Achievement of Stability," *The Whig Ascendency*, ed. J. Cannon (New York, 1981), 1–23, esp. 21. J. H. Plumb's *The Stenton Lecture* (1972) offers an elegantly reconnoitered portrait of a significant aspect of economic and cultural change in Georgian England; see *The Commercialization of Leisure in Eighteenth-Century England* (Reading, 1973).

9. Samuel Johnson valued the *Tatler* for cooling minds overheated with political contests; P. Borsay, p. 281. I. Pears, p. 20, discusses Addison's conception of politeness as the *lingua franca*. Johnson himself identified overheated and hyperbolic language with civil unrest and social disruption. See C. Norris, *Paul De Man* (New York, 1988), p. 60. The shared nature of esthetic and literary judgments rendered taste a social rather than a private phenomenon. For a study of journal and magazine writings, see R. W. Harris, "Reason and Nature in Eighteenth-Century Thought," *A Critical History of English Literature*, ed. D. Daiches (London, 1960), Vol. 3, 766–808. See Johnson's *Lives of the Poets*, ed. G. Hill (Oxford, 1905), reprinted (New York, 1967), Vol. 2, pp. 149–50, for an analysis of Addison's use of the "middle style." So popular were the *Tatler* and the *Spectator* that, over the course of the eighteenth century, more than 600 imitations were published.

10. See *Oxford English Dictionary*, entry "culture" for literary references illustrating the changing meaning of this key word; also Raymond Williams, "The Idea of Culture," *Culture and Mass Culture*, ed. R. Davison (Cambridge, 1978), 31–38.

11. See E. Gellner's "From the Ruins of the Great Contest," *Times Literary Supplement* (13 March 1992), p. 9, for comments on the security civil society offers to economic productivity. For Montesquieu and commentary on the *Spirit of the Laws* (XX, 1–2), see J. Cropsey, pp. 86–90. For the quote of Boswell, see the entry "civilized" in the *Oxford English Dictionary*.

12. Of the numerous works of J. G. A. Pocock treating civic humanism, see esp. "Virtue and Commerce in the Eighteenth Century," *Journal of Interdisciplinary History* 3 (1972), 119–34; also his *The Machiavellian Moment* (Princeton, 1975), ch. 11–13; "The Machiavellian Moment Revisited: A Study in History and Ideology," *Journal of Modern History* 53 (1981), 60–70. R. Homowy, "Cato's Letters, John Locke, and the Republican Paradigm," *History of Political Thought* 11 (1990), 273–94. It might be well to indicate that Pocock argues that in the late 1690s in England, "the first widespread ideological perception of a

capitalist form came into being, rapidly and abruptly, in the late years of the seventeenth century and the two decades following. A financial revolution was precipitated'' and a new class of investors emerged ''who had lent government capital that vastly stabilized and enlarged it.'' War and the public debt linked the interest of the creditor order with the political regime. See his ''Early Modern Capitalism, the Augustan Perception,'' *Feudalism, Capitalism and Beyond*, eds. E. Kamenka and R. Neale (London, 1975), 70–72. On 1707 and union between Scotland and England, see T. C. Smout, ''The Road to Union,'' *Britain after the Glorious Revolution 1689–1714*, ed. G. Holmes (London, 1969), 176–96.

13. See Jane Rendall, pp. 208–209 for citations on Allan Ramsay the Younger; A. Smart, *Allan Ramsay: Painter, Essayist and Man of Letters of the Enlightenment* (New Haven, 1992). On William Robertson, see his ''A View of the Progress of Society in Europe,'' *The Works of William Robertson* (London, 1817), Vol. IV, pp. 90–91. For David Hume, see *Works of David Hume* (London, 1974–75), Vol. III, p. 303. For an excellent discussion of Scottish society in an earlier time, see J. Wormald, *Court, Kirk and Community: Scotland 1470–1625* (London, 1981) and her groundbreaking work on archaic social ties, *Lords and Men in Scotland: Bonds of Manrent, 1442–1603* (Edinburgh, 1985).

14. R. J. Morris, ''Clubs, Societies and Associations,'' *Cambridge Social History of Britain*, Vol. III, 395–447, esp. p. 394, where the author discusses the derivation of such terms as ''agenda,'' etc. Cf. also J. Strang, *Glasgow and the Clubs* (Glasgow, 1857). R. Emerson's ''The Social Composition of Enlightened Scotland: Select Society of Edinburgh,'' *Studies in Voltaire and the Eighteenth Century* 114 (1973), 291–329, is useful for providing background. See also the observations of L. Colley in her *Britons Forging the Nation 1707–1837* (New Haven, 1992), pp. 87–90. On economic differences between Scotland and England in the seventeenth and eighteenth centuries, see R. Huston and I. White's introduction to *Scottish Society 1500–1800*, eds. Huston and White (Cambridge, 1989). The novelist Tobias Smollet in *Humphrey Clinker* first graced Edinburgh with the grand appellation ''hotbed of genius,'' and he celebrated the ''advances which mankind are daily making in useful knowledge''; see D. Spadafora, *The Idea of Progress in 18th-Century Britain* (New Haven, 1990), p. 50. Hume, like his contemporaries, used the word ''club'' as a metaphor for the moral history of society; *Enquiries Concerning Human Understanding*, ed. P. Nidditch (Oxford, 1975), pp. 281–87.

15. For a review of recent work on the Masonic movement, see M. Jacob, *Living the Enlightenment* (Oxford, 1991). Contemporary evidence suggests that in cities such as Edinburgh the politics engendered by the French Revolution resonated in clubs and societies. By the late eighteenth century, splits and acrimony brought decline. When Sir Walter Scott and Francis Jeffries (founder of the *Edinburgh Review*) proposed that the Speculative Society be permitted to discuss the political topics of the day, the Society split (1794). See M. Lynch, p. 350; also Jane Rendall, pp. 224–26. For further discussion of clubs and societies, see John Timbs, *Club Life of London, with Anecdotes of the Clubs, Coffee Houses and Taverns* (London, 1866); Joan Evans, *The History of the Royal Society of Antiquaries* (Oxford, 1956); E. Bristow, *Vice and Vigilance: Purity Movement in Britain since 1700* (Dublin, 1977), ch. 1.

16. For the minutes of the Select Society, see J. Rendall, pp. 225–26. The growth of provincial culture is clear and evident, and marked by the participation of middling folk. Virtually every town of average size in the Scottish Lowlands had a printing press. The first major edition of Robert Burns's oeuvre was printed at Kilmarnock with his publisher producing Milton's *Paradise Lost;* other publications included Ansons's *Voyage around the World*, as well as innumerable sermons. The printer, John Wilson, subsequently moved to the town of Ayre which had a library society of 47 members, including lawyers, doctors, ministers, and gentry. Regularly they made purchases from the Edinburgh bookseller William Creech. The minute book of the Ayre Library Society discloses that it had acquired Vol. I of Gibbon's *Decline and Fall*, Adam Smith's *Wealth of Nations* and Lord Kames's *Gentlemen Farmer* in the year 1776. See M. Lynch, p. 352; J. Strawhorn, ''Ayrshire and the Enlightenment,'' *A Sense of Place: Studies in Scottish Local History*, ed. G. Cruickshank

(Edinburgh, 1988), 188–201. *Transactions of the Highland Society* published prize essays. For an example, see John Anderson's "Present State of the Highlands of Scotland," Vol. 8 (1827), 16–17. In this essay the author opines that "it is only by eradicating every trace of feudal dependence that the sense of individual importance which can fit him [the Highlander] to be the associate of free men can be imparted to the emancipated serf." Anderson delights in the fact that the idle men—parasites of the past—have been displaced by sheep and cattle. He hopes that many of them would migrate to Glasgow where they could work the textile looms. See G. McMaster, *Scott and Society* (Cambridge, 1981), p. 111.

17. See D. Garland's review of M. Wiener's *Reconstructing the Criminal in London* in *London Review of Books* (1 October 1991) for a discussion of the challenges to authority in nineteenth-century England. David Cannadine, in his review "Cutting Classes," *New York Review of Books* (17 Dec. 1992), 52–57, raises the question of interpretive difficulties in doing British social history of the nineteenth century, when social class no longer has the force necessary as an explanatory principle for understanding social change; also L. Colley, "Whose Nation?: Class and National Consciousness in Britain, 1750–1850," *Past & Present* 113 (1986), 97–117; P. Cornfield, "Class by Name and Number in Eighteenth-Century Britain," *Social History* 17 (1992), 43–72. J. H. Plumb's *The Growth of Political Stability in England (1675–1725)* (London, 1967) is the classic account. Especially in recent years, his views have gained substantial intellectual support. Cf. G. Holmes, "The Achievement of Stability," *The Whig Ascendency: Colloquies in Hanoverian England*, ed. J. Cannon (New York, 1981), 1–22. Note the comments of Montesquieu on his visit to England (1729–30): "I am here in a country which hardly resembles the rest of Europe . . . of all people of the world [the English have] progressed the furthest . . . in piety, in commerce, and in freedom." Roy Porter, p. 253. L. Colley, in her review of Ian Gilmour's *Riot, Rising and Revolution: Government and Violence in Eighteenth-Century England*, writes:

> For arguably, what is most striking about this society [eighteenth-century England] was not the violence its members inflicted on each other, but the limits of that violence in comparison with what was practiced elsewhere in Europe, and in comparison too with what had been common in England itself in an earlier period."

See *London Review of Books* (10 Sept. 1992), p. 13.

18. Political advances made by middling and lesser folk have been assessed not as a consequence of their opposition to the national state but rather because of their support of it. See L. Colley, *Britons: Forging the Nation 1707–1837*, pp. 371–72; Colley also notes that elites appreciated the advantages of moderating "religious strife" and exercising control of the army. After 1688, no English king leaned toward Catholicism, and virtually all forms of Protestantism were tolerated. See her first chapter, "Protestants," in volume cited above. J. C. D. Clark, *English Society 1688–1832* (London, 1985), exaggerates religious schism and dynastic division in eighteenth-century England. See J. Brewer's review of L. Colley's *Britons* in *Times Literary Supplement* (16 Oct., 1992), 5–6. Also see I. Cristie, *Wars and Revolutions* (Cambridge, Mass., 1983), pp. 204ff.; P. Thomas, "Government and Society in England and Wales," *Cambridge Social History of Britain*, Vol. III, 2–6.

19. For a recent discussion of relations between town and country, see F. Thompson, "Town and City," *Cambridge Social History of Britain 1750–1950*, 1–17. Cf. also E. A. Wrigley, "A Simple Model of London's Importance in Changing English Society, 1650–1750," *Past & Present* 37 (1967), 43–51; Mark Girouard, *Life in the English Country House* (London, 1978); On Scotland, see J. Dwyer, *Virtuous Discourse, Sensibility and Community in Late Eighteenth-Century Scotland* (Edinburgh, 1988).

20. On population, see E. A. Wrigley and R. S. Schofield, *The Population of England, 1541–1871* (London, 1991), pp. 333–35 and Appendix 3. P. Langford, p. 456, discusses real wages of London laborers. P. Deane and W. Cole's *British Economic Growth, 1689–1959: Trend and Structure* (Cambridge, 1967), 2nd ed., endpaper, treats price trends from 1720–1790. Median daily wage rates of labor in the North and West, and in London, are estimated by E. Gilboy in his *Wages in Eighteenth-Century England* (Cambridge, 1934), p. 270.

21. E. P. Thompson's "The Moral Economy of the English Crowd in the Eighteenth Century," *Past & Present* 98 (1971), 76–136 has come under increasing criticism; cf. J. Stevenson, "The 'Moral Economy' of the English Crowd: Myth and Reality," *Order and Disorder in Early Modern England,* eds. A. Fletcher and J. Stevenson (Cambridge, 1985), 218–38; D. Williams, "Morals, Markets and the English Crowd in 1766," *Past & Present* 104 (1984), 56–73. For John Brewer's review of book by E. P. Thompson (*Customs in Common*), see *Times Literary Supplement* (13 March 1992), 14–15. See also Keith Thomas's review of Peter Linebaugh's *The London Hanged: Crime and Civil Society in the Eighteenth Century, New York Review of Books* (19 Nov. 1992), 35–38. Thompson's portrayal of working-class culture over-orchestrates the scope of plebeian resistance as well as ties of class solidarity. His over-dramatic chronicle of a working class battling to preserve its identity and values against a society dominated by patricians contains no deferential, church-going, chapel-attending, nationalistic and patriotic plebes. John Brewer raises the question: Why is the reader denied an analysis of daily class relations in favor of a rich diet of heroic confrontation?

22. In comparison with the states of continental Europe, English religious toleration was entirely remarkable. Linda Colley, p. 16, writes, "No monarch after 1688 flirted with Roman Catholicism and almost all kinds of Protestant were tolerated. Whatever else they disagreed about, most Englishmen and women—and most of the Welsh and Scots as well—could agree in celebrating Protestantism and damning Catholicism." See also K. Wilson, "A Dissident Legacy: Eighteenth-Century Politics and the Glorious Revolution," *Liberty Secured? Britain Before and After 1688,* ed. J. R. Jones (Stanford, 1992), 299–334; R. Webb, "From Toleration to Religious Liberty," ibid., p. 126–98.

23. For a recent treatment of the complex interplay between economic and legal change in eighteenth-century England, see H. Horwitz, "Liberty, Laws and Property 1689–1760," in *Liberty Secured? Before and After 1688,* ed. J. R. Jones (Stanford, 1992), 265–89. For tangled mix and tensions in Scottish literary culture of the eighteenth century, see F. Freeman, *Robert Fergusson and His Scots Humanist Compromise* (Edinburgh, 1984). Again on E. P. Thompson, see John Brewer's review, 14–15. It is not possible to reduce working-class experience to resistance as custom; day-to-day relations between rulers and ruled, bosses and workers, and the propertied and propertyless were entirely too varied and complex. Relations were embedded in a world of tradeoffs and cooperation: just price for provisions, regulation of the grain market, self-regulated work (not clocktime)—these were but a few of the victories "consonant with the interests of the poor."

24. For a valuable discussion of the wider reading public ("middle class") for literature in the eighteenth century, see A. Murdoch and R. Scher, "Learned Culture," in *People and Society in Scotland 1760–1830,* ed. T. Devine and R. Mitchison (Edinburgh, 1988), vol. 1, 127–42. Cf. also F. W. Freeman, 1–23; R. Meek, *Social Science and the Ignoble Savage* (Cambridge, 1976).

25. See Marianne McLean's *The People of Glengary: Highlanders in Transition 1745–1820* (Montreal, 1991), pp. 8–9, for accounts of letters of the tacksmen who served as middlemen between the clansmen and their chief. Concern was evident that migration from the feudal Highlands might result in feuds being transferred from Scotland to Canada. Cf. also J. Bumstead, *People's Clearance: Highland Emigration to North America* (Manitoba, 1982), pp. 68ff. Kenneth Simpson, in his *The Protean Scot: The Crisis of Identity in Eighteenth-Century Scottish Literature* (Aberdeen, 1988), discusses the psychological conflicts evidenced in leading Scottish writers of the period.

26. For citation of the quotation from anonymous author, see *Chronicles of Scotland* (Edinburgh, 1802), Vol. 4, xiv; F. Freeman, pp. 6–7, 53, 186. In considering the shifting semantic range of vocabulary dealing with social arrangements, we might note the alteration in usage of the term "a landed property." Until the mid-eighteenth century, a man's estate was usually his status and "state." His fortune and its display of authority encompassed "social esteem as well as wealth, legal rights, social obligations and measurable acres. . . ." The *Oxford English Dictionary* indicates that before mid-18th century, the term

"landed property" signified possession "of all these things that made estate and lands closely associated terms." See Paul Slack's review of D. Hainsworth's *Stewards, Lords and People, Times Literary Supplement* (5 February 1993), 27.

27. For a discussion of the Man of Feeling, see the classic account of R. S. Crane, "Suggestions Toward a Genealogy of the 'Man of Feeling,'" *English Literary History* 1 (1934), 205–27. The problematics of the existence of individuals in society is evident in the writings of Francis Hutcheson but is absent from those of John Locke. After Hutcheson this became a major theme in literature and moral philosophy; see A. Seligman, *The Idea of Civil Society* (New York, 1992), p. 25. For references to the use of the term "sympathy" in Shaftesbury, Hutcheson, and Butler, see D. D. Raphael, *British Moralists*, pp. 421–22; also Brian Vicars's Introduction to Henry MacKenzie, *The Man of Feeling* (Oxford, 1970), pp. xff.

28. See R. Zeller, "Parliament and the Crises of European Liberty from the Reign of Elizabeth to the English Civil Wars," *Liberty Secured: Before and After 1688*, ed. J. R. Jones (Stanford, 1992), 201–24. See also L. Colley's review of E. Cruickshanks and J. Black, *The Jacobite Challenge, American Historical Review* 95 (1990), 618–19. The Tory party did not support Jacobite plots or the invasion of 1745. Memories of the human cost of the Civil Wars of the seventeenth century (50,000 dead in England, Wales, and Scotland, and more in Ireland) were still vivid and compelling. Colley contends that perhaps what was most striking about English society was not its violence; in fact, when levels are compared with other parts of Europe, as well as with what prevailed in England itself in an earlier time, the decline of violence is evident.

29. On legal changes and constitutionalism, see P. Stein, "Legal Thought in Eighteenth-Century Scotland," *Judicial Review*, n.s. 2 (1957), 1–20; A. Murray, "Administration and the Law," *The Union of 1707: Its Impact on Scotland* (Glasgow, 1974), 40–52; also J. Rendall, p. 74.

30. See Adam Smith, *The Theory of Moral Sentiments*, eds. A. Raphael and A. Macfie (Oxford, 1972), p. 192; also Peter France, *Politics and Its Discontents* (Cambridge, 1992), pp. 106–107; F. Freeman, p. 65; T. Smout, "Towns in the Scottish Highlands from the Eighteenth to the Twentieth Centuries," *Northern Scotland* 5 (1981), 99–121.

31. For the quote from Scott, see J. G. Lockhardt, *The Memoirs of the Life of Walter Scott* (Edinburgh, 1837), Vol. I, pp. 58–59. Scott founded the Bannatyne Club which was the first and best of the many historical associations producing works of scholarship. See M. Lynch, p. 356. The quote from Boswell is placed in context by A. Williamson in his review of B. Levacks's *The Formation of the British State*, in *Journal of British Studies* 29 (1990), 276.

32. For quotes from Scott, see Thomas Crawford, *Walter Scott* (Edinburgh, 1982), pp. 11–12; also C. Withers, *Gaelic Scotland: The Transformation of a Culture Region* (London, 1988). For an assessment of Scott's use of historical evidence to inform his view of the Highlands, see Robert Gordon, "Scott and the Highlanders: The Non-Fictional Evidence," *Yearbook of English Studies* 6 (1976), 120–40; M. Lascelles, *The Story-Teller Retrieves the Past* (Oxford, 1980); C. Parsons, *Witchcraft and Demonology in Scott's Fiction* (Edinburgh, 1964). Scott's early fascination with Jacobitism is disclosed in his comment in a letter: "I became a valiant Jacobite at the age of ten years old." See *The Letters of Sir Walter Scott*, ed. H. Grierson (London, 1932), Vol. 1, p. 343.

33. For literary background, see D. Daiches, *The Paradox of Scottish Culture: The Eighteenth-Century Experience* (London, 1964); Sir Walter Scott, *Waverley* (Oxford, 1982), p. 283. Scott's early fascination with the Stuart Pretender did not blinker him to the futility of the Jacobite revolt of 1745: "A handful of men were disturbing the tranquility of a peaceful people who were demanding no changes of their condition." See *Miscellaneous Prose Works* (Edinburgh, 1836), Vol. 5, p. 345.

34. P. France, pp. 209ff. See the remarkable Scott short story, "The Two Drovers," perhaps the most powerful and tragic narrative of the confrontation between two cultures at different stages of legal and social development with opposed views of justice. Cf. S. Cooney, "Scott and Cultural Relativism: *The Two Drovers*," *Studies in Short Fiction* 15

(1978), 1–9; K. Robb, "Scott's *The Two Drovers:* The Judge's Charge," *Studies in Scottish Literature* 7 (1969–70), 155–64.

35. Sir Walter Scott, *Redgauntlet* (Oxford, 1985), pp. xx, 47; cf. also P. Sosnoski, "Reading *Red Gauntlet*," *Scottish Literary Journal* 7 (1980), 145–54; D. Daiches, "Scott's *Red Gauntlet*," *From Jane Austen to Joseph Conrad*, ed. R. Rathburn (Minneapolis, 1958), 46–59.

36. See D. Winch, *Adam Smith's Politics: An Essay in Historiographical Revision* (Cambridge, 1978) and his "Liberalism as Ideology: The Appleby Version," *Economic History Review*, 2nd ser., 38 (1985), 287–97.

37. G. McMaster, *Scott and Society* (Cambridge, 1981), pp. 156–57. This is a premier study to which I am much indebted for researches into Scott's economic and social thought. Extremely influential on his historical views were the first three chapters of Adam Smith's *Wealth of Nations;* Scott paraphrases a most trenchant passage from this classic work:

> There was . . . the influence which many plebeians possessed as creditors over these needy nobles whom they had supplied with money, while another portion of the same class rose into wealth and consideration at the expense of the more opulent patricians who were ruining themselves. Paris had increased to an enormous extent and her citizens had risen to a corresponding degree of consideration; and while they profited by the luxury and dissipation both of the court and courtiers, had become rich in proportion as the government and privileged classes grew poor. Thus the Third Estate seemed to increase in extent, number and strength like a waxing inundation, threatening with every increasing wave to overwhelm the ancient and decayed barriers of exclusions and immunities behind which the privileged ranks still fortified themselves.

A reviewer in the *Westminster* (1829) asserted that Scott's views had been much influenced by Hume's *History* "frequently in his hands of late." See G. McMaster, pp. 61, 69–70.

38. For the avoidance of determinism in the thought of Adam Smith and others and a discussion of the tension between commerce and virtue, see H. Horwitz, 292–97.

39. S. Rashid, "The Scottish Enlightenment," *Pre-Classical and Economic Thought*, ed. S. Lowry (Boston, 1987), 262–69. See George Watson's excellent introduction to Maria Edgeworth's *Castle Rackrent*. This is the first regional novel in English and possibly in any European language. Her friend, Walter Scott, immediately recognized that the regional novel could serve as an open door to the larger world of the historical novel in which entire societies might be represented. Ample in his praise of Edgeworth, he extolled her "Irish portraits" over and against the novelist Smollett's grotesque types—what Scott referred to as "Teagues" and "dear joys." Edgeworth's informed interest in whole societies and class relations was shared by Scott. For the Ashton case, see G. McMaster, pp. 167–78 and *The Bride of Lammermoor*, passim. Scott recognized the legal benefits achieved for Scotland by the Union with England (1707): "The high and unbiased character of the English judicial proceedings was then little known in Scotland; and the extension of them to that country was one of the most valuable advantages which it gained by the Union. . . ." (*The Bride of Lammermoor*, ch. 15)

40. For entries in the lighthouse-diary, see J. G. Lockhart, *The Memoirs of the Life of Walter Scott* (Edinburgh, 1837), Vol. 3, pp. 153, 206; cf. also T. Crawford, pp. 46, 110.

41. For background on the political treatment of the Highlanders, see R. Mitchison, "The Government and the Highlands, 1707–1745," *Scotland in the Age of Improvement*, ed. N. Phillipson and R. Mitchison (Edinburgh, 1970), 27–34. Cf. also B. Lenman, *The Jacobite Rising in Britain, 1689–1746* (London, 1980). For the response of Scottish novelists to these historical changes, see J. MacQueen, *The Rise of the Historical Novel: The Enlightenment and Scottish Literature* (Edinburgh, 1989), pp. 67ff.

42. For the most recent interpretation of change in basic Highland structures of everyday life, see R. Dodgshon, "'Pretense of Blude' and 'Place of their Dwelling': The Nature of Highland Clans, 1500–1745," *Scottish Society 1500–1800*, eds. R. Houston and I. Whyte

(Cambridge, 1989), 169–98. B. Lenman, in his *Integration, Enlightenment and Industrialization: Scotland 1746–1832* (London, 1981), pp. 28–55, provides an excellent summary of economic developments. On the Jacobites, see J. Gibson, *Playing the Scottish Card: The Franco-Jacobite Invastion of 1708* (Edinburgh, 1988); F. McLynn, *The Jacobites* (London, 1985) and his *France and the Jacobite Rising of 1745* (Edinburgh, 1981). For details concerning the government's treatment of Jacobites and their property, see A. Smith, *Jacobite Estates of Forty-five* (Edinburgh, 1982). For a general discussion of the Scottish novel, see F. Hart, *The Scottish Novel* (Cambridge, Mass., 1978); D. Daiches, *Sir Walter Scott and His World* (Edinburgh, 1971). Especially valuable for background are the studies edited by David Daiches, *A Hotbed of Genius. The Scottish Enlightenment, 1730–1790* (Edinburgh, 1986). For an up-to-date survey of Scottish economic developments with bibliography, see M. Lynch, *Scotland: A New History*, pp. 345–50; also T. C. Smout, "Where Had the Scottish Economy Got to by the Third Quarter of the Eighteenth Century?" in *Wealth and Virtue: The Shaping of the Political Economy in the Scottish Enlightenment*, ed. J. Hont and M. Ignatieff (Cambridge, 1982), 45–72.

43. Sir John Sinclair of Ulbster (1754–1835) was a politician and improving laird. With the assistance of the clergy of the Church of Scotland, he made a survey of agriculture in Scotland, publishing some 21 volumes as well as a digest. See his *Statistical Account of Scotland* (also known as *Old Statistical Account*) (Edinburgh, 1791–99). I have relied on B. Lenman's summary in *Integration, Enlightenment and Industrialization*, pp. 114–28. See also T. C. Smout, "Where Had the Scottish Economy Got to by the Third Quarter of the Eighteenth Century?" in *Wealth and Virtue: The Shaping of Political Economy in the Scottish Enlightenment*, ed. I. Hont and M. Ignatieff (Cambridge, 1982), 45–72. The word "statistics" enters the English language with Sir John Sinclair and his 21-volume *Statistical Account of Scotland* (Edinburgh, 1791–99). Sinclair desired to measure the quantum of human happiness and, in the questionnaires dispatched to the ministers of the parishes (918 responded), he inquired as to the health and well-being of agricultural workers in particular and parishioners in general. This emphasis on using statistics as a base for improving the lot of ordinary folk is, in the judgment of Ian Hacking, *The Taming of Chance* (Cambridge, 1990), pp. 26–28, nothing short of revolutionary.

44. For a discussion of Adam Smith's intentions and the problem of the "invisible hand," see J. Cropsey, pp. 88–101; also J. Rendall, pp. 120ff. For further details on Scottish population, see the studies edited by M. Flynn, *Scottish Population History* (Cambridge, 1977); I. Whyte, "Population Mobility in Early Modern Scotland," *Scottish Society 1500–1800*, 37–58.

45. David Hume, *Political Essays*, ed. C. Hendell (Indianapolis, 1953), pp. 42, xxxvii; quotations from Hamilton, pp. lx, lix. See also N. Phillipson, *Hume* (London, 1989).

46. For the quotation from Hamilton, see David Hume, p. lix. Cf. also S. Wertz, "Hume, History and Human Nature," *Journal of the History of Ideas* 36 (1975), 481–96.

47. See D. Forbes's introduction to Hume's *The History of Great Britain: The Reigns of James I and Charles I* (Pelican Classics, 1970) for a thoughtful discussion of the Scottish philosopher's contribution to historiography; also p. 215. M. Butler's *Jane Austen and the War of Ideas* (Oxford, 1975), esp. first chapter, offers excellent background on historical discourse in the last part of the eighteenth century. See also F. Manuel, "Edward Gibbon: Historian-Philosopher," *Dedaleus* (Summer, 1976), 231–46; John Kenyon's review of D. Wormersley's *The Transformation of the Decline and Fall of the Roman Empire, Times Literary Supplement* (3 December 1989), 1329–30. Hugh Blair's sermons were first published in 1777 and have been marked as the best-selling work, next to Addison's *Spectator*, of all the eighteenth-century writings vended in Scotland. James Boswell praised them for their "comfortable answers" and this they did indeed provide for a wide-reading public. See M. Lynch, p. 349.

48. P. France, pp. 57–73. On John Bruce and Walter Scott, see G. McMaster, pp. 52–57, 72, 77. See also A. MacIntyre, *After Virtue* (South Bend, 1984), pp. 39ff. The author ob-

serves that morality became the name for "that particular sphere in which rules of conduct which are neither theological, nor legal, nor esthetic are allowed a cultural space of their own." Only in the late seventeenth and early eighteenth centuries when distinctions were made among the moral, the theological, the legal, and the esthetic was it to become a "received doctrine" that the project of an "independent rational justification of morality became not only the concern of independent thinkers, but central to Northern European culture." F. L. van Holthoon, in "Natural Jurisprudence and Republicanism," *La Revue Tocqueville* 13 (1992), 43–60, suggests that J. G. A. Pocock's magisterial analysis of neo-classical republicanism has caused the debate on the definition of republican virtue to take a wrong turn. The contention that civic virtue can be defined narrowly as the sacrifice by the individual of his private interest for the sake of public good may be misguided. Republicans accepted the generating of virtue as the common aim of their political community; however, they had a new conception of virtue. It was not classical virtue—that is, prudence, justice, fortitude, and temperance; nor was it the Christian virtue of benevolence. The American John Adams, staunch republican, defined the virtuous person as being neither avaricious nor ambitious. But his idea of "live and let live," while it did not condone the pursuit of self-interest, did in fact *presuppose* it.

49. Peter Stein's "Law and Society in Scottish Thought," 148–68, esp. 150–57 is extremely incisive on Lord Kames's writings and career. See also Lord Kames's *Historical Law Tracts* (Edinburgh, 1758), v, lx–x. W. F. Tyler, *Memoirs of the Life and Writings of Lord Kames* (Edinburgh, 1814), 2nd ed., Vol. I, publishes Hume's letter to Adam Smith, p. 318. Hume was among the very first to appreciate *De l'esprit des lois;* he read this work of Montesquieu's in Italy in 1748 because the author sent him a copy after having read Hume's *Essays Moral and Political.* Upon his return to Edinburgh, Hume saw a translation of part of this work through the press. For consideration of the influence of Montesquieu's "philosophical history" on Hume's *History of England,* Voltaire's *Essai sur les moeurs,* Robertson's *Charles V and the History of America,* and of course Gibbon's *Decline and Fall of the Roman Empire,* see Hugh Trevor-Roper's "The Historical Philosophy of the Enlightenment," *Studies on Voltaire and the Eighteenth Century* 27 (1963), 1667–87. For Adam Smith's debt to Montesquieu, see F. T. Fletcher, *Montesquieu and English Politics* (London, 1939), pp. 45–66. Against the advice of friends who had seen his manuscript *De l'esprit des lois,* Montesquieu published it at Geveva (1748) and it was placed on the Index. However, nothing deterred its sales and this despite the length of over 1,000 pages: it went through 22 editions in two years. See M. Cranston, *Philosophers and Pamphleteers: Political Theorists of the Enlightenment* (Oxford, 1986), pp. 10–11.

50. M. Becker, *Civility and Society,* pp. 143–51; epilogue, "The Fragile Construct." See also J. Dwyer, *Virtuous Discourse: Sensibility and Community in Late Eighteenth-Century Scotland* (Edinburgh, 1981), pp. 10–37, 141–67; M. Goldie, "The Scottish Catholic Enlightenment," *Journal of British Studies* 30 (1991), 20–62. Most valuable is R. Chartier's *The Cultural Uses of Print in Early Modern France,* trans. L. Cochrane (Princeton, 1987), pp. 71–109.

51. Adam Ferguson, *An Essay on the History of Civil Society* (New Brunswick, N.J., 1988), p. 225; also J. Small, "Biographical Sketch of Adam Ferguson," *Transactions of the Royal Society of Edinburgh* 23 (1964), 599–665. For Adam Smith, see N. Phillipson, "Adam Smith as a Civic Moralist," *Wealth and Virtue,* 179–203.

52. J. Millar, *An Historical View of English Government* (London, 1812), Vol. II, pp. 429–30; also W. Lehmann, *John Millar of Glasgow, 1735–1801* (Cambridge, 1960), and his "Some Observations on the Law Lectures of Professor Millar," *Judicial Review* 15 (1970), 56–77; D. Forbes, "Scientific Whigism: Adam Smith and John Millar," *Cambridge Journal* 7 (1954), 643–70.

53. Samuel Johnson's *Journey to the Western Islands,* ed. R. Chapman (Oxford, 1930), was published in 1773, and the citations in the text are to be found in Chapman's edition, pp. 82–83. When Doctor Johnson and Boswell arrived on the Island of Skye in 1772, they were

in quest of a primitive patriarchal society. Instead they discovered that rents paid to lairds were principally paid by bills that tenants had received from drovers who came armed with credit to the Highlands to buy black cattle. B. Lenman, p. 23. Cf. also P. France, pp. 52–53, 207ff.

54. Adam Smith, *An Inquiry into the Nature and Cause of the Wealth of Nations*, ed. W. Todd (Oxford, 1976), 3: iii,12; 3: iv,1, 4; 3: iv,15; 3: iv,17. See also H. Horwitz, p. 294.

55. On plebeian protests, see R. Porter, pp. 348ff. and his review of I. Gilmour's *Riot, Rising and Revolution, Times Literary Supplement* (10 April 1992), p. 21. L. Colley, in her review "Not Many Dead," *London Review of Books* (10 September 1992), p. 15, observes that with the riot of 1715, a Draconian measure was passed by the triumphant Whigs permitting the army to defend civil authority against Tory and Jacobite mobs. Such attempts at "social control" were accorded little prospect of success. A close friend of Walpole's, Lord Hervey, wrote: "When . . . two or three hundred men are ordered by their officers to go against two or three thousand rioters, if they refuse to go it is mutiny, and they will be condemne'd by a court martial and shot, if they go and do not fire, they will probably be knocked on the head, if they fire and kill anybody, they will be tried by jury and hanged. Such are the absurdities of our laws at present." Cf. also L. Colley, *Britons*, pp. 22–23. In Adam Smith's view, the standing army made the government more secure against the threat of violence from the lower orders, thereby reducing the necessity of authority "to suppress and punish every murmer and complaint against it." See his *Lectures on Jurisprudence*, ed. R. Meek (Oxford, 1978), A, 5: 5.

56. Difficulties in modifying traditional patterns of work practice are illustrated by the problems posed when the Earl of Sandwich, first Lord of the Admiralty, initiated his program over the decade of the 1770s in the naval dockyard. He was faced with gigantic problems when he attempted to improve productivity by introducing piecework. See J. Hass, "The Introduction of Task Work into the Royal Dockyards," *Journal of British Studies* 8 (1968), 58; J. Rule, *The Experience of Labour in Eighteenth-Century English Industry* (London, 1981), pp. 124–46. Modernization and monetarization in the local economy was slow, especially in border areas. Furthermore, it was only in the 1770s that traditional fixed wages gave way to market wages. "Putter outers" continued to give spinners and weavers credit for food. Sinclair's *Statistical Account of Scotland* provides much evidence that payment in kind was still common in the late eighteenth century. It was difficult for landlords to know what their real costs were since patterns of work changed during different times of the year. Meanwhile, only recently had efforts been abandoned in the cities to block entry of merchants and craftsmen not matriculated in guilds or merchant companies. Cf. T. C. Smout, 60–68; R. Mitchison, *Lordship to Patronage: Scotland 1603–1745* (London, 1984), pp. 156–60.

57. Adam Smith, *Wealth of Nations*, 3: iii,12,3; 3: iv,15; 3: iv,17; also his *Theory of Moral Sentiments* (London, 1812), 11th ed., p. 86.

58. Voltaire, *Letter Concerning the English Nation* (London, 1733), p. 34, cited in Richard Brown's *Church and State in Modern Britain* (London, 1990), p. 96. Also the entry in Voltaire's *A Philosophic Dictionary* (London, 1824), under the word "toleration":

What is toleration? It is the appurtenance of humanity. We are all full of weakness and errors; let us mutually pardon each other our follies,—it is the first law of nature.

When, on the exchange of Amsterdam, of London, of Surat, or of Bassora, the Guebre, the Banian, the Jew, the Mahometan, the Chinese Deist, the Brahmin, the Christian of the Greek Church, the Roman Catholic Christian, the Protestant Christian, and the Quaker Christian, traffic together, they do not lift the poniard against each other, in order to gain souls for their religion. Why then have we been cutting one another's throats almost without interruption since the first council of Nice? [Nicea]

59. On elections, see Frank O'Gorman, *Voters, Patrons and Parties: The Unreformed Electoral System of Hanoverian England* (Oxford, 1989).

60. Contemporary evidence is abundant that hygiene and housing conditions were better under George III than under his predecessors. Also an improvement in diet has been noted. See P. Langford, p. 458. On the rise of consumption of goods, see N. McKendrick et al., *The Birth of Consumer Society: The Commercialization of Eighteenth-Century England* (Bloomington, Indiana, 1982); R. Porter, pp. 201–26; P. Langford, pp. 59–122. A fall in real wages for artisans of approximately 10 percent begins around the mid-eighteenth century with the sharpest drop occurring between the 1770s and 80s. There appears to be improvement of real wages in manufacturing districts of the North but stagnation or decline sets in in the South during the third quarter of the eighteenth century. Again, the 1780s may likely be a turning point for agricultural laborers as well.

61. See Alan Bewell's recent *Wordsworth and the Enlightenment: Nature, Man and Society in the Experimental Poetry* (New Haven, 1989), pp. 225ff. for a general discussion of the historical context of literary endeavor.

62. On gleaning, see H. Horwitz, p. 284. For a discussion of the ambiguities prevailing between customary rights of workers and the law, see J. Styles, "Embezzlement, Industry and the Law in England 1500–1800," *Manufactures in Town and Country Before the Factory*, ed. M. Berg (Cambridge, 1983). We observe that domestic servants depended on "vails" (tips); tailors had their "cabbage" (stolen remnants); hatters engaged in "bugging" (substituting for beaver inferior materials); tobacco workers engaged in "socking" (pilfering); sailors "knocked off" odds and ends of cargo. Each trade had its particular perquisites or "cheats," depending upon how one views them. See Keith Thomas, "How Britain Made It," *New York Review of Books* (19 November 1992), 35–38. Of course payment in kind continued and in fact certain sectors of agricultural workers were advantaged by payment in grain. The difficulty of making the transition was evidenced in the case of the dayworkers about whom we have already spoken. Giving up their customary rights to waste timber (chips) in return for compensation at naval dockyards was a difficult negotiation. See n. 56.

63. Roy Porter, p. 47. Also see M. McLean, *The People of Glengarry: Highlanders in Transition 1745–1820* (Toronto, 1991) and the review of this work by T. Devine in *Times Literary Supplement* (24 April 1992), 24.

Epilogue

1. Nicholas Boyle, *Goethe: The Poet of the Age*, Vol. I: *The Poet of Desire* (Oxford, 1991), pp. 5–22. Goethe compares the sheer poverty of German history with the British inheritance which falls to the lot of a clever poet. See his *Literary Essays*, trans. J. Spingern (New York, 1921), pp. 280–88. See also H. Emmel, *History of the German Novel*, trans. E. Summerfield (Detroit, 1984), pp. 20–94. James Hardin, in his *Times Literary Supplement* review of Goethe's *Collected Works* (2 March 1990, p. 231) notes the novelist's change of vision from early in his career to the later days when "practicality, specialization and above all, the well-being of society in general are the focal point."

2. The biographer referred to in the text is Nicholas Boyle, mentioned in n. 1. For additional references to Goethe's many knowledgeable comments on Scott and his work, see Eckermann's *Conversations with Goethe*, trans. J. Orenford (London, 1951), pp. 74, 83, 168, 216, 262–64. A Scott letter to Goethe is found on pp. 220–23. On social features of eighteenth- and early nineteenth-century German society, see R. van Dülmen, *The Rise of the Middle Class and Enlightenment Culture in Germany*, trans. A. Williams (Oxford, 1991); also W. Blanning's review in the *Times Literary Supplement* (13 November 1992), p. 22. We can follow the musings of the eponymous hero, Waverley, as he initially (at least temporarily) repudiates the temptation to join the Jacobite rebellion:

Whatever were the original rights of the Stuarts, calm reflection told him that . . . since that period [1688] four monarchs had ruled in peace over Britain, sustaining and exalting the character of the nation abroad, and its liberties at home. Reason asked, was it worthwhile to disturb a government so long settled and established, and to plunge a kingdom into the miseries of a civil war . . . ?

For a general view of Scott's protagonist, see A. Welsh, *The Heroic in the Waverley Novels* (New Haven, 1967).

3. James Kerr, *Fiction Against History: Scott as Storyteller* (Cambridge, 1989), p. 12; also G. Lukás, *The Historical Novel*, trans. H. & S. Mitchell (London, 1962), pp. 37ff. Scott's letter to his younger son urging that he study history almost mimics Adam Ferguson's observations in the first pages of his *An Essay on the History of Civil Society*. Scott writes:

> Man only differs from birds and beasts because he has the means of availing himself of the knowledge which has been acquired by his predecessors. The swallow builds the same nest which its father and mother built and the sparrow does not improve by the experience of its parents. . . . It is not so with the human race. Our ancestors lodged in caves and wigwams where we construct palaces for the rich and comfortable dwellings for the poor. And why is this but because our eye is enabled to look back upon the past to improve on our ancestors improvements and to avoid their errors. This can only be done by studying history and comparing it with passing events.

> *The Letters of Sir Walter Scott,* ed. H. J. C. Grierson, 12 vols. (London, 1932–37), Vol. 7, p. 34.

4. See B. Lenman, *Integration, Enlightenment, and Industrialization: Scotland 1746–1832* (London, 1981), pp. 136ff. for background on the development of historical thought among Edinburgh literati. See also Paul Scott, *Andrew Fletcher and the Treaty of Union* (Edinburgh, 1992), pp. 57–73.

5. D. Forbes, "The Rationalism of Sir Walter Scott," *Cambridge Journal* 7 (1953), 30–35; D. Daiches, "Scott's Achievement as a Novelist," *Literary Essays* (Edinburgh, 1956), pp. 119ff.

6. David Brown, *Walter Scott and the Historical Imagination* (London, 1979), pp. 196–97.

7. For a contemporary description of what Dugald Stewart termed "theoretical or contemporary history," see his "Account of the Life and Writings of Adam Smith," (1793), *Collected Works,* ed. Sir William Hamilton (Edinburgh, 1858), Vol. 10, pp. 34ff.

8. John R. Williams, *Goethe's Faust* (London, 1987), p. 194.

9. See George Steiner's review of Horst Althaus's *Hegel* in *Times Literary Supplement* (8 May 1992), 3–4. The Hegelian dialectic sought to demonstrate that the dynamics of history were generated by the contest between master and slave. This interpretive key was much indebted to Rousseau and had the effect of marginalizing Kant's more benign ideology. Of course it pointed forward to Marx's dialectical view of the struggle between capitalism and the proletariat. Charles Taylor in *Hegel* (Cambridge, 1975) provides a brilliant analysis of the philosopher's thought. John Weightman's "Fatal Attraction," *New York Review of Books* (11 February 1993), 9–12, discusses the continued appeal of Hegelianism to modern French intellectuals.

10. For a discussion of these quotations, see N. Bobbio, *Liberalism and Democracy,* trans. M. Ryle and K. Soper (London, 1990), pp. 17–23.

11. For a discussion and translation of Kant's "Was ist Aufklärung?" see *The Age of Enlightenment,* ed. S. Eliot and B. Stern (East Grinstead, Sussex, England, 1979), Vol. 2, 249–55. See N. Bobbio, p. 17, for a discussion of the quotation from Kant's *Über den Gemeinspruch* (1793).

12. See A. Lovejoy, *Reflections,* pp. 192ff.; also his *Forerunners of Darwin* (Baltimore, 1959), pp. 190ff.; the following quotation from Kant is apropos:

> A craving to inspire in others esteem for ourselves, through good behavior (repression of that which could arouse in them a poor opinion of us), is the real basis of all true sociality, and, moreover, it gave the first hint of the development of man as a moral creature—a small beginning, but an epoch-making one, since it gives man's way of thinking a wholly new direction, and is therefore more important than the

whole series (of which we cannot foresee the end) of extensions of civilization which followed from it. (Lovejoy, *Reflections,* p. 193.)

13. A MacIntyre, *A Short History of Ethics* (New York, 1966), p. 211. S Avineri, *Hegel's Theory of the Modern State* (Cambridge, 1972), provides the intellectual background for the German philosopher's discussion of political economy. I am much indebted to Avineri's monograph and have followed his line of argument.

14. For this and subsequent quotations from G. Hegel's *Philosophy of Right,* trans. with notes by T. M. Knox (Oxford, 1942), see pp. 122–55, 276. For further reflections by Hegel on the themes of state, family, and civil society, see his *Philosophy of Mind* in the *Encyclopedia of Philosophical Sciences,* trans. William Wallace (Oxford, 1894), pp. 119–54.

15. See S. Avineri's discussion "Poverty and the Limits of Civil Society," pp. 147–54; J. Appleby, *Capitalism and a New Social Order: The Republican Vision of the 1790s* (New York, 1984); D. Winch, *Adam Smith's Politics: An Essay in Historiographical Revision* (Cambrige, 1978), and his "Economic Liberalism as Ideology," *Economic History Review,* 2nd ser., 38 (1985), 287–97.

INDEX

MARVIN B. BECKER is Professor of History at the University of Michigan. His previous books include *Florence in Transition* (2 vols.), *Medieval Italy: Constraints and Creativity,* and *Civility and Society in Western Europe, 1300–1600.* He is currently working on a book entitled *Civil Society Under Threat in the Modern World.*